Praise for *Happily Ever ...*

"... uncompromising in calling out the overly romantic, but her sentiments are always laced with kindness. This essential kernel of personal optimism is the heart of the book and its greatest strength, giving heart to readers who may invest too much of their personal happiness in others.... A readable, powerfully worded call for women to get in touch with their inner queens."

—*Kirkus Reviews*

"... a primer that serves as a guidepost, blueprint, and pattern recognition resource that inspires readers on the road to more closely examine not just their lives, but the possibilities of enacting powerful change. Any self-help reader searching for not just answers but strategies to define, locate, and reinforce happiness factors in their lives will find *Happily Ever After ... Right Now* a precious find, indeed."

—*Midwest Book Review*, D.Donovan, Senior Reviewer

"This book of Luann Robinson Hull's is a stunning hit between the eyes. She has complete command of her subject matter, expertly navigating us through waters we probably didn't even know were treacherous. Not once does she lose sight of her destiny using feminine power and finesse to enlighten us of this mysterious abyss called "relationship." Though her target audience may appear to be women, *Happily Ever After ... Right Now* provided me with insight and clarity into something I gave up trying to comprehend long ago. She reminded me not only of what I seek in a partner but helped me set off on the journey of reclaiming the man I have always wanted to be."

—*Branden Blinn, The Branden Blinn Media Group*

"This book is written to support every woman who is wanting to have a fulfilling interdependent relationship with her husband or partner. Luann Hull debunks childhood fairy tales and replaces it with honest insights and proven actions to create real happiness in our lives. She asks some poignant questions to the reader so you can consciously choose your path."

—*Anita Sanchez, PhD*

Happily Every After ... Right Now

Stop Searching for Mr. Right and Start Celebrating YOU

HAPPILY
EVER AFTER ...
Right Now

Stop Searching for Mr. Right and Start Celebrating YOU

LUANN ROBINSON HULL

MSW, LSCSW, D.Min

TOP READS PUBLISHING, LLC

VISTA, CA USA

First Edition

ISBN: 978-1-970107-14-2 (paperback)
ISBN: 978-1-970107-15-9 (ebook)
Library of Congress Control Number: 2019917079

Happily Ever After ... Right Now is published by:
Top Reads Publishing, LLC, 1035 E. Vista Way, Suite 205, Vista, CA 92084 USA
For information please direct emails to: info@topreadspublishing.com
Previously published by HEARN Publishing, January, 2011

Cover artwork: "Father's Garden," acrylic painting made by Birgitta Strobel, 2017 in Oslo, Norway, www.birgittastrobel.com
Cover design, layout and typography: Teri Rider & Associates
Photo credit for images of Luann Robinson Hull: Jedidiah Gabbett, Drifting Owl Studio

Grateful acknowledgement is made for permission to reprint the following:

Excerpt(s) from *A Woman's Worth* by Marianne Williamson, copyright © 1993 by Marianne Williamson. Used by permission of Random House, an imprint and division of Penguin Random House LLC. All rights reserved.

Excerpt(s) from *A Return to Love* by Marianne Williamson. Copyright (c) 1992 by Marianne Williamson. Portions reprinted from *A COURSE IN MIRACLES*. Copyright (c) 1975 by Foundation for Inner Peace, Inc. Used by permission of HarperCollins Publishers.

Excerpt(s) from *A Return to Love* by Marianne Williamson. Copyright (c) 1992 by Marianne Williamson. Portions reprinted from *A COURSE IN MIRACLES*. Copyright (c) 1975 by Foundation for Inner Peace, Inc. Print rights for UK, Australia and New Zealand used by permission of HarperCollins Publishers Ltd.

"The Guest House" by Jalāl ad-Dīn Muhammad Rūmi from *The Essential Rumi*, translated by Coleman Barks. Copyright© 2004 by HarperOne. Used by permission of Coleman Barks.

Every reasonable effort has been made to trace the owners of copyright materials in this book, but in some instances this has proven impossible. The author and publisher will be glad to receive information leading to more complete acknowledgement in subsequent pritings of the book, and in the meantime extend their apologies for any omissions.

Printed in the United States of America

DEDICATION

For "Mimi"

CONTENTS

Prologue... xi

ONE | Entitlement—Let Go of the Longing for the Prince 1

TWO | Magnificence—Choose to be Queen 21

THREE | Majesty—Lose the Slave Girl............................34

FOUR | Sovereignty—Stop Looking for Answers Outside Yourself 53

FIVE | Power—Give up Your Addiction to Love 70

SIX | Alchemy—Take Back Your Projections....................90

SEVEN | Regality—Be Attached to Nothing......................112

EIGHT | Passion—Fully Express Your Gifts to the World 131

NINE | Preeminence—Live Like a Queen Every Day...............153

TEN | Partnership—Revamp Your Relationship with Men.........177

ELEVEN | Legacy—For our Sons and Daughters....................198

TWELVE | Ascendancy—Take Your Queenliness to New Levels for as
Long as You Live.......................................221

Recap, Reflections, and Reminders 242

Epilogue...247

Addendum..251

Acknowledgments 253

Bibliography 255

About the Author 261

PROLOGUE

THE DREAM

In the spring of 1999, I had a dream—a really important dream. I couldn't have known it at the time, but that prophetic dream marked a pivotal turning point in my life. Just before it happened, I had believed my life to be over. And while that was true in a sense, it was the life *as I had known it* that was ending. There would be a new life, and the dream was a foretelling of the future, replete with all of the joys, surprises, and challenges that I was destined to discover in the world to come.

Prior to the dream, I had been trapped in the perpetual drama of what now seems like an endless novel with me as the desperate heroine. It was about darkness and deceit, mystery and madness, depression and despair—piercing headaches and heartaches, and of course, the desperate longing for someone or something to "save" me, which was the unrelenting force that kept me bound and chained to it all. It was a predictable cycle of doom that my patterns and attachments had perpetuated.

I had settled, and settled, and settled again—settled for being a slave to my man, the men who had preceded him, my children, clients, and even my house, yard, and dog. I just wanted to be good. I wanted to be good so that people would stay. Therefore, I would be needed, hopefully invaluable, and less likely to be replaced or abandoned. And regardless of the benevolence I believed myself to be offering, people kept leaving anyway.

I felt powerless over the dreary continuum of loving and losing that I had come to expect in my life. Two days prior to the dream, my partner of ten years created a scene, which was impossible for me to ignore. I will spare you the details here. Suffice it to say that what happened made me take a long, hard look—maybe my first look—at all of the compromises I had been making to ensure what I thought was the "rescue plan" from suffering. It was time to shift, and from some Power that seemed larger than me, I was given the courage to excuse him from my life—and *mean* it. He did take his leave—a permanent one—and the grief from his absence opened the door to some unprecedented challenges. As it turns out, that period of deep, deep sorrow was one of the most growth-enhancing times of my life, and it launched for me a new love—the journey of writing this book. Happily, it is through this work that I am continuing to discover the *real* truth on how to end suffering—altogether.

As I revisit the scenario that put final closure to a relationship that should have ended before it began, I am amazed at the *level* of compromise I was willing to allow in order to "keep" this person in my life. Even though it was obvious to me (and everyone else) that he had emotionally checked out well before the debacle that ultimately resulted in his final departure, for months we both blatantly overlooked the obvious. From his perspective I am sure there are several reasons why that was so—particularly in light of how easy I had made his day-to-day life. And as for me—well, I simply felt powerless under the spell of this man that I had pegged as my "love-object/savior," repeatedly ignoring his froglike ways, which I had originally mistaken for princely charm.

Even though I *knew* my need to cling to this human was utterly absurd, the destructive pattern of codependency and love addiction (see chapter 5) had spread into every aspect of our relationship like an uncontrollable malignancy. No matter how hard I tried to use my knowledge regarding the myth of the "Prince Charming Syndrome," I repeatedly failed. What I eventually began to see is that I had been ignoring the most important ingredient for healing—self-love. And if I was ever going to emancipate myself from the suffering drama, I would need to fully commit to a full-on focus of loving myself.

"Man [woman] is a phenomenon far greater than any other mechanism. If only he [she] had the patience and perseverance to explore him [her] self."

—*Hazrat Inayat*

Like many of you, my cultural and personal conditioning has been strongly rooted in a fear-based paradigm, which hardly allows much space for loving the self. And of course, it is difficult—sometimes seemingly impossible, to get beyond the influences of our conditioned behaviors. Nonetheless, I have come to understand that if I am to make any spiritual progress at all, my conditioning and the false beliefs it perpetuates must be addressed so that there can be a space in my soul for the real truth to emerge.

And what must happen in order to create such a space? For me, it means being willing to expose the raw and vulnerable feelings that I so desperately want to lock down, whenever I am triggered or have a charge around something or someone that feels painful and causes suffering. When the sacred wounds are exposed, I need to pay attention with my *full awareness*, having faith that if I do, the sacred medicine for healing will be revealed.

I have spent much of my life keeping a pretty tight lid available, ready to fasten and affix whenever a trigger or charge would arise. While operating in that mode, I didn't realize that I was like a pressure cooker ready to blast off at any moment. Predictably, there was an explosion of sorts and like any other sudden eruption—it wasn't pretty. Even so, while I was completely caught up in the volcanic magnitude of the thing, in some odd way, it seemed as though I was an observer rather than a participant. The whole disaster actually felt almost too surreal to actually be happening. I doubt I will ever forget the feelings that accompanied this incident or the man who played the part of "perpetrator" in the disastrous debacle. Never before (and not since) have I experienced such an extreme combination of emotions. I felt a sort of exhilarating liberation (while in the "observer" mode) and then almost at the same time, a sense of unprecedented trauma and heart-break (when I was in the "participant" mode). Two nights later, I had ...

The Dream

From the many glorious visions of hope and optimism that were gifted to me in that amazing dream, I remember the last vignette in particular. While taking a leisurely midday stroll, my eyes feasted on a magnificent bright blue sky decorated with clouds that looked like spaceships spun into cotton. The rays of the golden sun merged with gentle, balmy breezes almost dancing with me as I made my way toward a sparkling body of water. Beautiful pyramid-mountains peaked in the distance and glowed like amethysts in the sunlight. It was as though they were stately cathedrals standing watch over the large, natural pool below. As I made my way toward the water's edge, I passed simple, pristine dwellings that were inviting, elegant, and unpretentious—just the way I like things.

The most compelling part of the dream was this: *I was the sole character.* There were no other people, animals, or even insects, around—*it was just me.* And regardless of the absence of any company whatsoever—I felt happy, safe, free, and unconditionally loved. I had no needs, wants, desires, or worries. There was a sense of freedom and wholeness the likes of which I had nothing to compare in waking life. Any feelings of longing for another—for comfort—for respite from suffering and despair, with which I had felt ceaselessly burdened throughout my existence, had totally disappeared and were replaced by an unprecedented sense of serenity and well-being.

Even though I was alone, I felt the enduring presence of peace penetrating every particle of my being. As I continued to move toward the water, I did so without agenda. Some Force was tenderly nudging me in that direction. There was no plan to sun myself on the beach, ride the lapping waves, or fly a kite. I was just going where I was going because I simply knew that was the next right thing to do. It seemed as if I was floating while feeling fully grounded at the same time. In gliding along, I could almost taste the hint of jasmine as its delicate fragrance tickled my senses. The sweet, gentle wind felt like satin stroking my skin—and all the while my eyes were like cameras taking snapshots of the magnificent scenes unfolding before me—so that I would always have a reference for remembering this day. For the first time *ever* I actually felt myself being totally, completely me— and my spirit was entirely, unequivocally *free*.

Having this dream has been one of the most extraordinary gifts of my life. For regardless of how deeply I may have plunged into the depths of despair following that magical night, I have always found my way back to the feelings of near incomprehensible joy I experienced then. Since that time, the lasting memory of those feelings has been ever-present and enduring—even though this experience happened well over a decade ago.

The best way I know how to describe what I felt in *The Dream* is with a word from the ancient language of Sanskrit—*bodhichitta*. *Chitta* means "heart", and *bohdi* means "awake" —or a heart awakened. I know now, just as I did then on some level, that what I experienced in that dream was something similar to the state of bodhichitta. I had fully opened the front door of my heart to offer and receive in kind, unending love and support that the Divine had been patiently awaiting my permission to allow. Simultaneously the back door of this heart of mine had flung wide open, inviting unconditional love to penetrate deeply into my soul and spirit.

A significant shift in my consciousness had taken place. I was no longer identified with my mortal personality. The notion of a separate self, fearful and alone, constantly looking for a source of comfort and salvation had completely vanished. There was a feeling of connection with every living creature, however minute, and a realization that all things imbued with the Life-Force are in some way related and interdependent. Therefore every thought, craving, need, or desire for dependency or attachment had completely fallen away. There was no memory of lack, insufficiency, or craving of any kind. Instead, my entire being had been endowed with a sense of freedom that to this day defies description. Jesus simply calls it "... The peace that passes all understanding."

When I woke up from that dream, I felt like I had been unwillingly slammed back into my skin. My first thought was, "Oh my God! I am awake—it was only a dream!" Though on some level, I really knew that I had had my realities confused. *The Dream* was the *true* reality— the one where I was fully awake or enlightened. The world into which I believed myself to have just returned—was the illusion. And even the vaguest notion of this odd juxtaposition marked a pivotal point in my spiritual pilgrimage. Try as I might to put the whole thing into perspective, I knew what had happened to me that night was more than just having a pleasant dream—it was a rare opportunity to actually *feel* what it was like to have a shift in consciousness.

I have come to realize that in order to have had the experience of such a shift, dream or no dream, I must somehow carry the blueprint for "a new brain" in my DNA (right along with everyone else that is living and breathing on planet Earth). And as the gifted recipient of this awareness, I have been passionate to further investigate the possibilities of how such a shift can happen, where like in the dream, peace, joy, and love prevail—overriding any thoughts of insufficiency, need, dependency, and *all worries and fear*. In this state, nothing external is required for happiness because happiness is the over-lighting influence—no need for fireworks, parades, banquets, or balloons. And of course the idea of a Prince Charming to whisk me off to some beautiful ballroom in a golden coach, promising happily ever after—is completely unnecessary, because I am already living *my happily ever after ... right now*.

Oh, and did I mention that in my dream, there were no Whole Foods, Nordstrom department stores, Four Seasons hotels, or restaurants for fine dining anywhere in sight? And that regardless of the absence of this fancy material version of happiness *nothing* seemed to be missing from the scene? The state of happiness and unconditional love was *normal*. Therefore, I had no concerns for attaining happiness in the future, sustaining a feeling of happiness in the present, or retrieving it from the past because happiness was a given—like breath and a beating heart. No effort whatsoever was necessary to "have it." Happiness was simply present in the everlasting now.

A Pilgrimage for Transformation

I believe I began my journey into *awakening* or *enlightenment* somewhere around the age of eleven. Of course at that tender time, I didn't fully understand my unending curiosity about the purpose of life, or my insatiable desire to unravel the riddle of suffering. Back then I thought that challenge would be resolved by finding and subsequently marrying Prince Charming (as I had been repeatedly promised would happen in most of my favorite childhood fairy tales). Could there be another way out of the pain that seemed to define my existence as a scrawny, scared little girl other than finding *him*?

I couldn't have known how long it was going to take, or how many challenges I would endure, before I would come to realize that *he* was not the answer to my salvation after all. Instead, the key to unlocking the secret garden of my heart had always been accessible in another form. And in order to discover the sacred secrets in my soul, all I really had to do was relax and be available so that I could hear their silent whisperings. The true answer—hidden under the layers of fear and doubt that shrouded my view—had been there all along.

What did I discover when I finally unlocked the gate to that secret garden of mine? There, inside, was a fortress of passion just aching to be discovered. Uncovering that passion (and I don't mean the day-dreaming kind about Prince Charming) is what continues to open my heart to true and lasting joy. Why? Because this passion is *what you and I came here to experience.* Imagine Bono's thrill (lead singer of Irish rock band, U2) when he belts out the song, *Pride (In The Name Of Love).* How gratifying must *that* be? You, too, are destined for delight, as you discover and follow *your* passions. It is my belief that every human being drawing breath on this planet—regardless of past mistakes or misfortunes—not only deserves to feel their version of the "Bono bliss," but actually can—if they so choose.

I readily admit that I have had more than a few tribulations in letting go of the Prince-will-save-you themes. (Keep in mind that Cinderella has always been my favorite fairy tale.) I had years of psychotherapy, became a psychotherapist myself, remained firmly committed to my spiritual path, experienced many beautiful healers and teachers, spent six years in a postgraduate program earning a Doctorate in Ministry, went on retreats, attended countless workshops, and more. And yet with all of this support for releasing the stubborn and defeating patterns that have repeatedly nagged at my heart and soul—it has definitely been a challenge to change.

Through it all, this is what I have come to know: If we once and for all decide that it's time to jump off this gerbil wheel of looking for the answers outside of ourselves, we will be dizzy, and we will be disoriented. We may be tempted to climb back on many, many times, and indeed, sometimes we will keep spinning until we finally see that the vicious circle is just not going anywhere. On some level, we *do* know this, and we *are* ready to transform, yet, we refuse to leave behind the behaviors that we have come to know so well—repeatedly gravitating toward the familiar. Therefore, we have to be willing to experience the unknown, trusting that on some level we are going to be taken care of every step of the way—until at last the idea actually begins to sink in. Our anxious thoughts and imaginations are unnecessary. Fortunately, while on the way to locking in new thought-forms based on faith instead of fear—we have been told that it only requires as little as a "mustard seed" of trust.

> *"I tell you the truth, if you have faith as small as a mustard seed, you can say to this mountain, move from here to there and it will move. Nothing will be impossible to you."*
>
> —King James Bible, Matthew 17:20

I have been fueled by faith for quite some time now, and though it has never failed me, many circumstances have unfolded differently than I had planned or even envisioned—exponentially better to be sure, just not the version of "better" that I had had in mind when I started this journey so many years ago. You see, when I set out to find "the real truth" on how to eliminate suffering, I was still operating out of my deeply conditioned patterns of saving others, and ultimately being saved myself. And so, I first had to undergo an intense de-programming regimen before I could even *begin* to make headway.

Despite my firm belief that I was in the recovery phase of love addiction while in the process, there were still the subtle nuances that kept me stuck in the spin. Try as I might, the patterns persisted. What was I doing wrong? How long would this misery last? How much was I going to have to meditate, study, retreat, isolate, and so on, in order for transformation to happen? I would make progress, though all too often I would repeat the two-steps-forward-three-steps-backward-dance.

Naturally, what I kept realizing with *exhausting* frequency was that in continuing to look for love (or whatever else I thought it was that was going to make me happy), the longing would become exaggerated and stubbornly persistent, creating additional heartache and despair. The more I continued to seek salvation, the more my heart would be wounded from the self-sabotaging behavior that had become my very own prodding iron. In such a state, I couldn't remember that *I already was the love* I had been seeking in other places (a point which will be repeatedly emphasized in the following twelve chapters). And therefore, my longstanding belief that there was actually such a thing as a "love/lose" cycle—was *impossible*.

The elusive Prince (representing all of the cravings that keep us stuck in the spin of external desires) is forever going to be just a little out of reach. He (She or "It") is *never* going to meet our expectations for salvation. Appearing many, many times in a myriad of shapes, sizes, personalities, and patterns, often disguised as the "perfect answer," he will *always* fail us (once again, the idea of "love/lose" is emphasized when we expect *him* to be the source of our salvation). Why? Because we want him to do the impossible. We expect him to deliver something that *he doesn't have*. Instead, it is we ourselves who hold the key *for the final resolve* of this longing of ours. How do I know? Because I have *finally* made this discovery for myself, and know many others who continue to have similar epiphanies.

Does this mean that those of us who have had such awakenings are completely enlightened? And if so, have we experienced full deliverance from the longing dilemma forever? Well, not exactly. What it does mean, however, is that we realize what is *required* of us so that our eventual deliverance from this condition *will* ultimately be permanent. As we continue to support each other in fully engaging the practices that will eliminate the negative patterns of our past, suffering will disappear and eventually melt away. We will then be able to fully embody the glorious state of joy and happiness in which we were all meant to live.

Who knows how many eons we have been in this longing mode of ours. To change requires patience. We didn't learn to walk as soon as we emerged from the womb. It took some time and practice. Each segment of our development supported our taking that first step and we were all motivated from something inside that kept telling us to *go for it*.

Such is the case in our expanding consciousness and ultimate transformation as a species. When we did learn to walk, most of us had nurturing environments in which to practice. As we transcend the outdated patterns that no longer serve our growth and development, we must learn to access the appropriate support and encouragement that will continually guide us to the grace necessary for transformation. Through our combined enthusiasm, we are *certain* to create the momentum for monumental change.

It's Time to Soar

Many believe that the "codes" on how to energize and activate our ability to shine have always been available to us. Even so, I suppose it goes without saying that our human lens can be a bit foggy at times, particularly when smudged and smeared with our dramas, negativity, and despair. And such gloom can certainly cast a shadow on things, definitely distorting the true picture.

Consider one of those paintings popular in the nineties— peppered with endless dots. Hidden within, there is a detailed design rarely obvious at first glance. Your friends and family begin to see it. You notice yourself becoming edgy and mildly perplexed since you haven't a clue what they're talking about. And then, some kind soul in the group gives you a hint at how to best observe what's there. *Relax.* When you stop forcing the issue, your eyes loosen up, and presto! What comes into focus is the Statue of Liberty or something—way cool. Of course, it has been there all along but the only time you could actually bring it into focus is when you quit trying so hard. You let go of your fears about how you weren't "smart enough" to detect what seemed obvious to everyone else, and just allowed what was there to appear. Doesn't it make you sort of wonder if that simple approach might be effective across other areas of our lives?

The God Code

In his book *The God Code,* Greg Braden, scientist and philosopher, shares his research that the basic elements of DNA—hydrogen, nitrogen, oxygen, and carbon—directly convert to the Hebrew letters YHVG. Those letters translate to one of the original names of God, suggesting that the signature of God is carried in every cell of our being. If Braden is on the right track (and he has certainly been in both the scientific and spiritual spotlight with his findings), perhaps then the codes for shifting our individual and collective consciousness into enlightenment (the end of suffering) are encrypted in our cellular memory and DNA. If so, isn't it time to crack those codes so that we can once and for all live in the states of happiness and freedom that each and every one of us is meant to enjoy?

So how can we unlock the mysteries that lie deep within our individual and collective psyche? What if just like in the case of the picture with the dots, we allow ourselves to relax a little, soften our focus, and quit trying so hard? Maybe then the formula will come into view through our awakening hearts and rising wisdom. If we actually do already carry the blueprints for a shift in consciousness, perhaps our human potential will begin to emerge when we get out of our own way and allow who we *really* are to appear.

And how is my own process coming along? Well, I can now actually *experience* the shifts that are stirring in my inner world. What this phenomenon means to me in simple terms is to have an ability to accept what is happening—to actually permit myself to *experience* what is going on without an immediate need to change or fix things. Now this may sound pretty basic. For me, such an approach to life has been transformational. To be able to *allow* my fears, frustrations, emotional upsets, anger, insecurities, and *pain* (including the migraines) just to be there without resistance has been *huge*. Maybe, there is actually some valuable information underneath what appears to be the trigger for discomfort. And if I can let go of the urge to cut and run—it might be possible to neutralize the initial trigger just *by paying attention*.

What I have learned is that my mind will attempt *anything* in order to keep me from having the experience of what is going on right now, no matter whether I perceive that experience to be "good" or "bad." If what is happening is "good," I will want to maintain and hold onto it, worrying that when it disappears, things will deteriorate. On the other hand, when something is perceived as "bad," and I am operating out of fear, my fear-based conditioning might advise me to vigorously resist the situation by shaking it off like a hot coal. The conditioned mind wants you to believe that you need to go over there, behind you, or in front of you, but never *here*. "It" thinks that the only relief from suffering is to exit the scene and take off for somewhere else. And if a bleep of happiness should come across your radar— hang on.

Rather than trying to flee or cling, if I can just *observe* what the mind is doing, instead of identifying with it, I am less likely to be influenced by triggers from the past or fears about the future. If I can avoid getting caught up in the drama or the story about what

I think is going on, then I will ultimately see that underneath the sorrow and the sadness and the despair and the longing—is actually *joy*. Whenever I allow what is there to actually *happen* without trying to fix or change it, the joy *will* emerge—in every moment. It has to, because ultimately, whether I recognize it or not, *joy is all there is.*

Kahlil Gibran in his magnificent book, *The Prophet,* provides a beautiful illustration with the following quote:

> *Your joy is your sorrow unmasked. And the selfsame well from which your laughter arises was oftentimes filled with your tears. And how else can it be? The deeper the sorrow carves into your being, the more joy you can contain. Is not the cup that holds your wine the very cup that was burned in the potter's oven? And is not the lute that soothes your spirit, [carved from] the very wood that was hollowed by knives? When you are joyous, look deep into your heart and you shall find it is only that which has given you sorrow that is giving you joy. When you are sorrowful look again in your heart, and you shall see that in truth you are weeping for that which has been your own delight.*

The Emerging Queen

This might be a good time to mention (even though it may not be what you want to hear) that there has been no Prince Charming involved in my own developing awareness on how to really experience joy. Don't misunderstand. I have finally come to a place where I am open to having a *co-creative relationship* and so recently have been enjoying the exploration process *immensely*. It's just that when I initially made the choice to lose the Cinderella-sweeping-off-the-cinders-syndrome, I decided to go cold turkey (no dates/no men). This decision, of course, was subsequent to attempting every *other* solution under the sun (including many dates/many men) to avoid what had once appeared to be an unfathomable option. Turns out I have *had* to be single for a while in order to really discover how *not* to be single. I simply couldn't concentrate on connecting with my own heart and soul without having a personal love affair—with *me,* first. And in order for that to happen, I didn't need any distractions. I had to find out how to really immerse myself in self-care/love before I could ever expect real love, care, and admiration from someone else.

In reviewing a relationship history fraught with some pretty significant pain, I can see that the choices I made were the perfect reflection of my own self–doubt and in some cases, self-loathing. And the people who served as my mirrors, God love them all, probably had similar issues to mine. None of us was "wrong" or "bad." We were simply wounded, and rather than helping each other heal, we just kept reflecting our injuries back and forth. A significant wake-up-call came when that reflection looked back at me like a maddened monster. It was then that I realized I either had to leave this planet, or find a more peaceful way to live here. Fortunately, I chose the latter.

Now not everyone has to go through immense personal drama to make positive changes. Nor do you need to live a life in solitary confinement in order to develop a true and lasting connection with your own heart and soul. Nonetheless, what I do believe is necessary for such a connection, is that you have the willingness to launch yourself into a deep process of personal inquiry on what is *true for you* (if you haven't already). You have to get really honest here. Where are you stuck? What patterns do you keep repeating that are no longer working for you? Have you tried unsuccessfully to stop these behaviors before? What went right? Obviously *something* must have inspired you to keep digging, otherwise you wouldn't be curious about the topics under discussion here.

As I move more fully into the paradigm of passion and purpose (the concepts for true and everlasting happiness upon which the foundation of this material is based), I can see the evil spell of the "looking for salvation trance" slowly melting away like the wicked witch in the *Wizard of Oz*. If you are familiar with the fairy tale, you may recall that the witch was totally busted when Dorothy finally had the gumption to call her on her stuff. With a single bucket of water, Dorothy drenched the witch, causing the immediate demise of her perceived enemy. When assimilating the valued messages about bravery, brains, and heart from the Lion, Scarecrow, and Tin Man, everything pretty much fell into place. She was able to take a step back and reflect on things while remembering to strengthen her courage and compassion. It was then that her search for the right path home ended—realizing she had been there all along. All she had to do was remember that the true home can only exist in an awakened heart—where there is no need to search anymore.

In following Dorothy's example by dropping into *your* heart, you can feel unending love *aching* to connect with the wisdom that is the true representation of who you are. And as you continue to focus on this union you will experience the undying strength and support that lives inside of you. This link is the lighthouse that is the constant in your life, forever and always guiding you back to safety from the perceived dark waters of the night.

As I look back on my life, I feel overwhelming gratitude for everything that has brought me to this very moment. Now, I can't say that I have *completely* surrendered to the inevitable mystery and impermanence that accompanies a life lived fully in the now (the one where sorrow always turns to joy earlier described by Kahlil Gibran). Even so, I do feel myself edging into a deeper intimacy with Presence, moment to moment, which I find utterly miraculous. It is though I am a budding flower finally opening to the sunlight after several decades of being tightly bound. And I must say it feels exceptionally grand to stretch and expand as the blooming process continues to unfold.

"It is at the edge of a petal that love waits."

—*William Carlos Williams*

Radical Slow Movement

Two years following *The Dream*, I decided to walk away from familiarity in both my personal and professional life. I wanted to launch a full-time pursuit on how to *really* stop the suffering. To the dismay of family, friends, clients, and colleagues, many radical changes resulted from that decision. Operating with simultaneous feelings of exhilaration and terror at the thought of what might lie ahead, I started this strange and exotic pilgrimage, leaving any idea of safety and security behind.

I took this action *not* because I was unusually brave or even reckless as some most definitely believed—but because I continued to receive consistent "pricks of consciousness" that this journey *had* to be initiated. There was no "should do it," just *do it*. Often, when one's life is about to transform, there is a tap on the shoulder (some of you have felt this gentle pat). And sooner or later, what will inevitably occur if you choose to ignore this little nudge is that you might get a whack over the head. Sometimes this blow will be literal, though as many of us have discovered, it can show up in any form. Now if you're smart, you won't be like me and wait for the whopper.

If you *should* choose to leave your idea of safety and security behind (whatever that may be for you), it may be quite uncomfortable from time to time. Though more than likely you are much farther along in your awareness regarding what is *really* safe and secure than you think.

And before you know it, you will become quite adept at assuaging the pesky, persistent fears, which will inevitably try to taunt and terrify you as you proceed on your way to transformation. Realize that these fears are a signal from your zillion-year-old brain, the messages from which you are powerless to control since their existence precedes your lifetime by roughly four-and-a-half billion years.

And so here is the trick—to use this primal pal (primitive brain) to your advantage rather than allowing it to drag you back into the dredges of doubt and despondency. As the monster of fear approaches, let the beast be a reminder of what is really true. *You cannot be abandoned.* Why? Because you are physical extensions of the non-physical—Prime Source, God, the Divine, or your version of what has created you. And since this Non-Physical Prime Source Creator is the *essence* of who you are, being alone and "loveless" is impossible, despite any deeply-entrenched illusions you may have to the contrary. Should you forget about your *essence* in a moment of fear or doubt, just flip on the "love light switch." When you do, you will see that the monster you thought was lurking in the shadows will disappear, just like Dorothy's perceived "wicked witch," when she remembered to use her courage, brains, and heart.

Awakening and the Brain

My ongoing odyssey, which I expect will continue as long as I am drawing breath, has taken me to strange and unfamiliar places. I have been to the depths and soared to the heights while occasionally experiencing some balance in between. After many years of study, school, research, and personal commitment, I have finally begun to make some sense of why we do what we do (even when we *know* it doesn't work) and have learned how to transcend some of the patterns that no longer serve our individual and collective growth. I am thrilled and delighted as I am continually shown the limitless possibilities that magically unfold when I engage with and actually *commit* to making the permanent changes in myself necessary for peace and enlightenment. Perhaps you feel the same way. And as we go forward together, etching new footprints in the soil of our individual and collective journeys, who knows? Maybe we can help pave the way for all of humanity to be happy ... right now.

I have been fascinated for most of my professional life with human behavior, the evolution of emotions, and the possibility that our current brains are already wired for a state of permanent happiness and ultimate enlightenment—particularly following *the dream*. This fascination has led me to many studies on the development of consciousness, one of which was performed by Richard Davidson, Founder & Director for The Center for Healthy Minds at the University of Wisconsin–Madison. Dr. Davidson has unearthed some significant findings regarding how the emotion of happiness can be tracked in the brain. Davidson collaborated with His Holiness the Dalai Lama to study monks, who are experienced practitioners in meditation, with ten thousand hours or more. These monks live in states of peace, compassion, gratitude, happiness, and well-being—making them perfect candidates for Davidson's studies on "The Biology of Joy," as reported by *Time Magazine* in 2005. What the professor discovered in studying the brains of these monks during meditation is that the electrical activity in the left prefrontal lobe of his subjects showed significant increases, while the activity in the parietal lobes (chronically overactive in most people), exacerbating feelings of separation, insufficiency and despair, was reduced.

Davidson has since published his findings from these studies in the *Proceedings of the National Academy of Sciences*. It is interesting to note that Davidson also included novice practitioners of meditation in his studies—those interested in meditation, whom had not previously practiced and were given a "crash course." While some showed minimal changes in the brain, these were not significant.

And so, for the most part, in the absence of mental training, the beginning practitioners' brains remained unchanged. On the other hand, using EEG and follow-up fMRI scans (functional magnetic resonance imaging) on the meditating monks, Davidson and his colleagues were able to demonstrate that mental training can create permanent brain characteristics that support states of happiness and well-being.

Dr. Geshi Lobsang Negi, senior lecturer at Emory University's department of religion, is committed to advancing Emory's ongoing scientific and spiritual collaborations. Dr. Negi was originally sent to Atlanta at the request of His Holiness the Dalai Lama to study Western Science while establishing a Buddhist center. What has evolved as a result of Dr. Negi's commitment is *The Emory-Tibet Science Initiative*, which is successfully bridging the gap between ancient traditions of Buddhist meditation practices and modern science. Included in the Initiative are scientific research efforts to support the efficacy of various meditation practices in ameliorating such conditions as anxiety and depression.

Dr. Negi is currently cultivating the development of three programs, including a pair of pilot studies, which will evaluate the effects of meditation on children in foster care, as well as introducing meditation practices in schools to help with stress. In addition, Dr. Negi is collaborating with Dr. Charles Raison, assistant professor of psychiatry at Emory, to study the effects of compassion meditation on inflammatory responses and stress. Initial studies, published in *Psychoneuroendocroniolgy* in 2009, showed a strong relationship between time spent practicing meditation and reductions in physiological and emotional stress.

Andrew Newberg, professor of nuclear medicine at the University of Pennsylvania, is considered to be one of the world's leading experts on the brain and higher states of consciousness. He has been attempting to combine science and spirituality by observing the brains of long-term meditating Tibetan Buddhist practitioners with SPECT Scans. His studies show similar findings to Davidson—that the left prefrontal cortex becomes more active during deep meditation, while the activity in the parietal lobes is diminished. When the parietal lobe activity reduces beyond a certain threshold, the sense of a separate self dissolves, and there is the natural realization of 'oneness,' which Newberg calls the experience of Absolute Unitary Being. Also consistent with Davidson's findings, Newberg believes the increased activity in the left prefrontal cortex is associated with a sense of well-being that cannot be explained through any outer cause.

The discoveries of Professors Davidson and Dr. Newberg concur: People who exhibit states of oneness, or a shift in consciousness (enlightenment or the absence of suffering) have a strengthening of the frontal lobes (specifically the left prefrontal cortex). Concurrently, the influence of both the parietal lobes and reptilian brain is reduced. And, that mental training (meditation) can help to support this condition.

A Little Human History

In a 2007 lecture on evolution, the late Dr. Henry Lodge shared some research from his bestselling book, *Younger Next Year*, indicating that humans evolved from single-celled organisms more than four-billion-years ago. It took another three-and-a-half billion years before the first multiple-celled organisms appeared. So, for three-quarters of our evolution on this planet, we were single-celled creatures focused purely on survival. There was no love, no caring, no connecting on any level.

The advent of the chemical oxytocin (the "love hormone"), introduced by mammals with the bonding of mother and cub, occurred only 160 million years ago. Until then we were driven solely by the "budgets of energy" (food) that we could absorb to survive in the wild. Makes you sort of wonder what kept our primal ancestors from throwing in the towel. Some call it instincts. I like to think of it as the "God spark"—regardless of how primitive things might have been.

Lodge suggests that Homo Sapiens are a mixture of single and multiple-celled organisms, as well as vertebras and mammals. Miraculously, we are *only one percent human* and ninety-nine percent "yeast, worms, bacteria, and crocodiles." As a conglomerate of all the primates that have ever existed, our unconscious mind operates out of an ancient species-stew, meaning the emotions currently swimming around in our skulls have a roughly four-billion-year head-start on the rest of our brains.

Lodge suggests that the foundation of human brain mapping has been influenced by non-human primates wired for non-human experiences, which are primarily survival based. All human impulses first alert the reptilian brain before moving through the emotional centers in our mid-brains and landing in the neo cortex, or reasoning brain. That means we could be making decisions in "micro-second circuitry" that are not human-specific. If we're not conscious of this reality, we may behave like animals fighting for our lives—as in war, or road rage—until we become aware of the impulse and decide to act from a higher level of consciousness.

Say you have just been stung by a bee on your thumb. The impulse from your reptilian brain will immediately fire a signal of *danger*. Your fight or flight (animal) response triggers a release of cortisol, producing *fear*. By the time all of the data being collected finally reaches your cerebral cortex, you have already experienced a profound adrenaline rush, which is flashing neon signs of "danger," "pain," and so on. Now, it is up to your higher powers of reasoning to help you understand that *you are not going to die*. Even though *you know this*, your throbbing thumb is influential in getting your attention. So for those of us who have not been meditating for ten thousand hours, or using other forms of mental and emotional training that might increase the chances of lighting up that left prefrontal lobe of ours, chances are the freak-out-reptile is going to win the argument on what messages take priority.

Is Change Possible?

As will be discussed in chapter one, some psychologists believe that our *current* brains were being formed during a time of unconscionable catastrophe on this planet during the Pleistocene era, which is the geological period that lasted from about two million to 11,700 years ago. We cannot possibly comprehend the kind of horror that existed during that phase of our evolutionary development—the ferocious flooding, saber-toothed tigers, earthquakes, tsunamis, hurricanes of unfathomable magnitude, and God only knows what else. *Every waking moment was literally about being scared senseless.*

And so, isn't it feasible that we hold the memory of these calamitous events somewhere in the catacombs of atoms, DNA, and subatomic particles that breathe life into our very being? Combine this prospect with the idea that we are ninety-nine percent primate and one percent human. Now then, is it any wonder that we worry about being left, put out in the cold, getting eaten by a monster, or starving to death? Isn't it possible that we are carrying around some pretty significant trauma from our collective past, which has been etched into our cellular memory? If so, what will it take for us to transcend all of this drama and make use of the "God codes," which heretofore may have been hidden by the shroud of our earthly past? Isn't it time that we move fully into our most optimal state of happiness and joy?

The Shift Point—Homo Sapiens to Homo Luminous—The Age of Enlightenment

According to the British biologist Rupert Sheldrake, a quantum leap in evolution can take place whenever a critical mass within a species has learned a new behavior or moved to another level of consciousness. He calls this "morphic resonance." Sheldrake hypothesizes that a group's thoughts, actions, and insights create an energy pattern (resonance), which makes it more likely that people otherwise unaware of the thoughts or occurrences will experience similar insights, etc. If all of this seems difficult to absorb, consider television, radio, and microwave transmissions. Their signals send out energy patterns, which broadcast information. Even though these signals cannot be seen, they translate into sounds and images, which when picked up by the appropriate receiver, can be interpreted.

Carl Gustav Jung, Swiss psychiatrist, believed that intrinsic, intuitive characteristics ingrained in the human psyche influence major themes in the collective unconscious. He termed these characteristics "archetypes." Consistent with the famed theories of Jung, Sheldrake also believes that to the degree of similarity people agree upon information gathered and shared in a "story," the chances are greater that the "story" will catch on. Implicit in the principle of this phenomenon is that individuals will actually make an "energetic imprint," or energy pattern by perpetuating a thought in the masses. He labeled this process "morphic resonance." As subsequent collections of people concur, the "imprints" created by their combined agreement will gain momentum (with more and more energy). At some point, the thoughts produced by that "imprint" will create a story that changes the culture and shifts the collective consciousness into new thought forms—such as when the Civil Rights Movement eventually was able to make the point with people like Rosa Parks.

Malcolm Gladwell has popularized Sheldrake's and Jung's theories in his bestselling book, *The Tipping Point*, by demonstrating how shifts of consciousness begin when small numbers of influential people start behaving differently. Gladwell states that when a behavior continues to gain momentum through an increased, favorable, and shared response, at some point, a critical mass "tips" the behavior into being accepted by large groups. According to Gladwell, the characteristics of this phenomenon replicate what happens when heat spontaneously combusts into flame, which can then proliferate into rapid spreading fire.

The famous "Hundredth Monkey" miracle further illustrates the point. In 1952, on the island of Koshima, Japan, scientists decided to see what a colony of monkeys would do with sweet potatoes dropped in sand. In the beginning, only one innovative monkey found the sand unpalatable and took the time to rinse off her potato. Intrigued, her mother made note and subsequently repeated the exercise. Before long, other monkeys caught on. At one point, let's say when the number of monkeys washing their potatoes reached one-hundred, the behavior began to transfer to monkeys on different islands where potato-washing had never been observed. Nonetheless, like a light switch going off in their heads, the other monkeys just knew what to do. This well-known phenomenon demonstrates what Gladwell is saying—that when a critical number (of people, animals, organisms, etc....) adopt or take on a certain belief or behavior, either or both is strengthened to the degree that it can be transferred from mind to mind without direct physical interaction. And when a critical mass is reached, the awareness of *some* then becomes the conscious property of *all*. Therefore, isn't it possible that the entire human race could upgrade if enough of us light up our prefrontal cortex and tip the consciousness in the right direction?

Transformation

Whether or not you believe we started from a sea squirt a few billion years ago, Adam and Eve, or something else, you cannot deny that we are marvelously complex beings who have come together at a most incredible time in human development. Some of us feel that we have an unprecedented opportunity to change our outdated ways of behaving in the world. And as we do, we will continue to morph into magnificence —beyond our most favorable imaginings. I could not be speaking to you about this possibility without having had the privilege of transcending some of my own wearisome ways of managing in the world. Happily, I have actually begun to experience longer and longer periods of spontaneous happiness and joy, which I felt in *The Dream*. And that evasive "formula for change" mentioned at the beginning of this prologue, which initially seemed like a riddle that couldn't be resolved—is finally being exposed. Now, every time I see a "space-ship-cloud" or view the mountain landscape just outside my window, I am reminded of *The Dream* and the possibility that I am indeed stepping into the "awakened heart," which I felt so fully on that mystical night over a decade ago.

Oh yes, I have spent a number of hours meditating (or whatever my version of that is). However, I doubt I will ever make it to the impressive ten thousand hour mark that some of the esteemed monks in Professor Davidson's studies have achieved. And, since I was a single, working mother of two in the midst of this spiritual journey of mine, it wasn't exactly practical for me to take extended excursions with the guru of my choice. So, I am most fortunate to have serendipitously "stumbled" across many tools, techniques, and teachings, which have supported and jump-started my own journey into *Happily Ever After ... Right Now*. And it is my honor and privilege to share some of my "aha moments" with you, as they continue to be revealed in new and magical ways, every minute, every day.

At this writing, there is no doubt in my mind that something dramatic has changed in me—though I cannot say with complete certainty that this shift has happened because of any one thing or another. Rather, I believe it to have resulted from a collection of all of the synchronistic events divinely orchestrated on my behalf. I believe that those of us who are making note of how to diminish the effects of the parietal lobes and reptilian brain—are probably onto something. From my own personal experiences and as a practicing psychotherapist, I have seen how difficult it is for people to change even an *inch* of their addictions, co-dependencies, depression, anxiety, and so forth. I have also watched some pretty intolerable side effects from the psychotropic medications prescribed to help ameliorate these conditions. And, having been a patient myself at one time, I have my own horror stories to tell about the effects of these drugs. Medication is appropriate in some cases, though seeing the mental health world through the lenses of a practitioner and a patient, I must continue to emphasize the importance of people being open to new and innovative ways for restoring mental, emotional, physical, and spiritual well-being.

Based on everything I am continuing to learn, the idea of neurobiological shifts in the brain and creating the environment for peace and happiness makes perfect sense. Further, it has now been proven that this neurobiology can be strengthened by stimuli (energy) or focus (meditation). It is interesting to note that a successful experimental treatment for depression aired on CNN in 2006. Dr. Ali Rezai, neurosurgeon at the Cleveland Clinic, used a probe to stimulate *electrical impulses (energy) in the brain, successfully relieving the condition of depression* in an impressive number of subjects, who had suffered chronically from the disease and had had no prior success in other interventions, including medication and psychotherapy.

The Time is Now

From everything I can gather, it definitely appears that this is an extraordinary time for opening to our most optimal human potential. And I am deeply honored to share the ongoing journey that continues to support my own spiritual awakening. You may be meditating frequently to the mantra of your choice, or simply staring up at the bright blue sky to find your own version of those space-ships-clouds I saw in my dream. Whatever the case, it is up to you to decide how serious you are about change in your life. How pressing is your desire to shift things more favorably in the direction of awakening and enlightenment where suffering ceases to exist? How will you continue to allow your own inner brilliance to shine through the illusory mist of your fears and insecurities?

My utmost desire is to support you in having a foundation for cracking your very own personal code to unravel the patterns, habits, and cycles that have held you captive and kept you from reaching *your* full and most optimal potential—your very best destiny in this life form.

The material in this book can provide an opportunity for connecting some basic scientific and philosophical knowledge while motivating a depth of spiritual inquiry. It has a three-part focus: *Education*—to offer a fundamental historical and scientific perspective on why you repeat certain behavioral patterns, even if they don't serve you or your growth. *Awareness*—to support you in being *aware* of what you are doing, so that you can strengthen the behaviors of your choosing, and *Transformation*—to offer tools for completely transcending your outdated ways of operating while moving fully into your *happily ever after ... right now.*

I believe in serendipity. You have picked up this book. To me, that means you are ready to move fully into your most optimal potential for joy, love, freedom and growth—*now.* And with all of my heart, I support you in the process.

Love,

Luann Robinson Hull

ONE

ENTITLEMENT—
LET GO OF THE LONGING
FOR THE PRINCE

Jewel: Jasper for Protection, Grounding, and Letting
Go of the Past

"What are you waiting for?"

This is a cosmic love story, viewed through the magical mirror of
our souls—yet many parts of the narrative are unknown because the
yarn is spinning as it is being written. And even though the outcome
can seem mysterious, there is a subtle understanding that all is well,
replete with a happy ending. We know, and we don't know. So, it is
just about listening and remembering, one minute, one person, one
partnership at a time. This is no ordinary tale—for its purpose is to
provide a new foundation for living your life from a place of freedom
and peace—while learning to be comfortable with uncertainty as you
break through the generational spells that have kept you endlessly
bound in fear and longing. It is time to celebrate the Entitlement of

royalty—as we wake up and recognize how to access our only real security from a place of conscious, compassionate awareness. As we step into our powerful Queenly nature (our true Essence)—we will effortlessly accept or change whatever is in front of us with impeccable discernment—thereby eliminating suffering from our lives altogether.

And whether you realize it or not, you have decided to bring forward and empower the inner wisdom that can quiet and eventually dispel your needless fears and haunting imaginations. Now is the time to create a new love story on Planet Earth, and you are playing a significant role in how that story will unfold. Well done.

The Longing

Every woman knows the longing that seems to keep happiness just out of reach. It flutters like a butterfly at the periphery of our consciousness when we listen, as children, to fairy tales and family stories about meeting Prince Charming and living happily ever after. It's the subtle backbeat of our teen years that drives our aching desire to be asked to the homecoming dance or prom. Will I be popular or pretty enough to snag a date—to be chosen by someone—anyone?

We have scanned for the Prince since we were old enough to download some of the messages in the Cinderella story (my personal favorite). Who will meet my gaze as I come cascading down that magical aisle? Will he be able to fulfill my heart's desires? Will I measure up to his expectations? The longing whispers in the shadows of our soul as each guy shows up (is he the one?), and it screams in our faces on dateless Saturday nights when he hasn't called back. We have waited untold hours for the phone to ring, suffering ceaseless heartbreak when the deafening silence stubbornly persists.

Cloaking ourselves in sophisticated suits to match the role of successful professionals, we have raised and sometimes shattered the stubborn glass ceiling in the work place. We have learned to juggle career, home, and family—while still somehow finding time to get to the gym. We have mastered the art of independent living, championing the cause for strength and courage as we confidently announce, "I can do it all!" Even so, isn't there something that hasn't quite resolved in the collective female psyche? What is it that can bring us to our knees—right smack dab in the middle of our proudly acquired brains, and bravado?

In many of us, lurking just beneath the radar of our "I have it all together" facades, is that pesky, persistent longing. This unfortunate condition can be triggered on the most inconvenient occasions—typically when our hearts are vulnerable and raw. It is then that we are ruthlessly reminded that something is missing from the picture of wholeness that we so desperately want to complete. Without warning—often at the moments when we most need to focus—while negotiating a deal, hammering home a point in the boardroom, teaching a class of first-graders, trying to keep an order straight from a demanding customer, or attempting to meet the impossible demands of our boss—we are suddenly distracted. "When is *he* going to call? Does *he* love me? Am I important to *him*? Is *he* gonna stay? And if *he* doesn't, will I ever find someone who will— someone who *really* cares?" *He* is ever-lurking in the corners of our consciousness, playing havoc with our hearts, while interrupting even our most disciplined attempts at concentration.

When the Prince does appear and we agree to a partnership—for a while it can all seem fairy-tale-perfect. And then, out of nowhere, things begin to deteriorate—life isn't completely happy-ever-after, and we return once again to the longing. We know the longing better than we know the Prince or anyone else—even better than we know ourselves.

With each disappointment, we begin again. The longing can drive us to mutate and mold ourselves, hoping to be good enough for long enough to attract and keep the Prince. We diet, work out, and change our bodies with starvation, surgery, or both. We set aside our passions and redouble our efforts, concentrating our powerful energy on either finding the perfect relationship or holding onto the one that's there—regardless of any glaring dysfunction. We become "bitches," play "games," or follow outdated "rules" and worry that "he is just not that into us." In our desperation, we can become people-pleasers, conforming to however the culture defines beauty and desirability at the moment. We smile and laugh when we don't feel like smiling and laughing, keep quiet instead of speaking up, and shave off the edges of our soul in our quest to be chosen. Of course it doesn't work. We can't find him, or else when we do he lets us down.

With some exceptions (though none immediately come to mind), most of us have had an innate craving to *find* and *keep* the "perfect" partner since time immemorial. The New Age version of the Prince is called our "soul-mate" or "twin flame"—the one who is "destined" to complete us, when (and if) Providence provides an opportunity for our paths to cross before we croak. If we *are* fortunate enough to meet, the endless longing will cease and yes—we will be happy together—forever.

Now, I have definitely had my own experiences with the perceived soul mate/twin flame types—only to find that in the absence of *conscious awareness*, my impossible expectations of him—soul mate or not —have always produced a predictable result. Alas, what I have repeatedly discovered is that *he cannot and never will* be able to resolve the insatiable longing that aches in my soul. This has been a rather shocking awareness for one who so wanted to believe the fairy tale. What I have finally come to understand is that this need based, find-something-else-to-save-me approach to life is inconsistent with the magical opportunity before us as individuals and as a species—*there is so much more to life* than being engaged in the exhausting, endless search. A closer look at how love got into this need-based-dilemma will help to guide us into a grander, more expansive way of being.

Transcending the Origin of Our Insecurity

Our minds are a morass of thoughts, beliefs, words, nonsense verses, verbal jumble, fantasies, and fear. This fear in us is primal and has its foundation in our earliest origins, which were based on survival. The messages of fear still live inside our heads—literally—in our brain stem, which is also known as the "reptilian brain." Deepak Chopra calls this ancient brain "the animal in us; … it has no heart and cannot love." It is constantly vigilant, scanning for threat and danger, always pessimistic, and completely paranoid. It alerts, eats, breeds, and kills. It sees itself as separate and in need of physical survival. It can be our captor, and when we are in its grip, we live in the illusion that we will never be released.

This part of our brain, when allowed, will rule with a ruthless and clever cunning. It can pull us down into the lower regions of our primitive nature, interrupting our ability to respond in the more expanded states of consciousness from which we are now capable of operating. If, however, like Dorothy in the *Wizard of Oz*, we continue to defy our fears and not let the Wicked Witch inner voice scare us away from finding our true internal home (actually *using* our expanded consciousness instead of letting it lie dormant), we can watch the terror sizzle and burn off as we refuse to allow it to have power over us.

Some of us believe that in order to be a part of the evolving consciousness of the species, we actually volunteer to come into this life form (on Planet Earth), agreeing to leave the world of pure spirit, while taking on a form of spiritual amnesia. Our motivation for doing so is because *we know on some level* that choosing to embody here with this amnesic condition can be an incredible motivator for human evolution. As emissaries for light (enlightenment), we know we must actually *feel* what it is like to be here so that we can be fully empathic with the human condition. And in order to do so, we have to be exposed to some of the emotional toxicity resulting from thoughts rooted in our primal beginnings—based on fear, separation, and ultimate death. When we arrive, we will have forgotten that *transcendence is our mission*. Even so, because of our exposure to suffering, we are highly motivated to be emancipated from its effects. Our Inner Guidance system will always provide the most direct route back home (to our Divinity)—if we can just stay focused on the faith and fortitude required for us to pay attention. Inevitably, there will be a multitude of distractions—most of which will be driven by the desire to survive. If we move in the direction of Spirit, we *will* keep finding reminders, which will prompt our awareness that there is nothing to survive. We are eternal, energetic beings, who just change form. As we find our way back to our *true* heritage, others too may be inclined to remember their Divine roots. And then perhaps at some point, all of us will awaken to who we really are.

Dear Reader, I realize that this theory may seem far-fetched to some, resonate with others, and to a few—may even seem preposterous (or at least outrageously indirect). Nonetheless, we cannot deny that humanities' use of free will has resulted in some pretty interesting debacles for our planet—and that discovering our Internal Divinity—even if it is one heart at a time, is of urgent import if we are to transcend our current dilemma.

If in the midst of discovery, we haven't quite yet seen the light of who we are—the longing to return to our spiritual beginnings will ache in our hearts (even though we may not remember our true origins). How dearly we want to find peace, tranquility, and *happiness*. And when stuck in our state of amnesia (forgetting we are descendants of the Divine) it may appear that the only solution to our salvation is to be rescued by another human. If we stay stalled in this longing mode, we can become entrenched in the victim-perpetrator-rescuer loop—which definitely gained its roots from the primal world.

In a fear-based reality, which is based on insufficiency and need, we see life through the lens of scarcity. We feel separate, alone, and disconnected from the Divine. *Everything*, regardless of whether it is personal, professional, or otherwise, can take enormous energy. It might literally feel like you are dragging yourself around in a pair of lead boots. Operating from such a state, there is a greater tendency to crave relief. (Surely I can find someone to help me yank off this heavy footwear). Of course, what we repeatedly find is that whenever we try to grab for salvation, our desire to cling will ultimately cause the very pulling away of that which we are attempting to grasp.

In such a state of insecurity, we feel cut off from our internal link to love and therefore come to crave connection from other places. We want to love and be loved, overlooking an important truth: *we are already that which love is made of.* We believe that the attachment to the blessed other (thing or substance) will provide the solution to our happiness dilemma. Operating with such a mindset, we often seek the "perfect relationship." We believe this will be the key to unlocking the mysteries of our heart's longing and resolve the insecurity that accompanies the endless, empty search. Surely they will bring us closer to the happiness everlasting that we are so desperate to find.

In this all-too-familiar need-based paradigm, we see ourselves as fragmented, lost and alone—believing that the only solution to our perceived dilemma is some sort of external salvation. We feel hopelessly incomplete, and we can move from mild anxiety to sheer panic if we believe that our saving grace (whatever that may look like) appears to be inconveniently delayed. If what we are awaiting happens to be the Prince, and he doesn't show up on schedule, or the one who does appear turns out to be an imposter, our feelings of desolation and despair can become more exaggerated than ever.

In such a state, we compromise, sacrifice, use sex, splinter our spirits, become drudges, and give up our dreams. Constricted and shut down, we are tempted to settle for a life of mediocrity. Either we choose to compromise and sell out by being with someone who enables the very shrinking of the soul that we came here to expand, or we continue in our desperate search for Mr. Right, forgetting all of the passions and inspirations that are the *true* source of our joy and happiness. If we stay here too long, we can spiral toward chronic self-doubt, depression, dependency, or drugs/food/alcohol—to name a few toxic crutches. Who can save us from this doom? Here's a clue: There is no white horse or shining armor involved. When we can move toward all that will assist us in balancing the heart and mind—our Queen Essence—we will let go of the conditioned fear that binds us to an outdated belief system. Only then do we create the foundation for happiness and ultimate freedom.

Reacting from a fear-based paradigm was understandable as Homo Sapiens evolved during the Pleistocene era mentioned earlier. It was a time of extreme hardship and constant struggle when our very survival was dependent on whether or not we used our instincts effectively. Our current brains were forming during this period of extreme adversity and as a result, became accustomed to looking for what was wrong. Scanning for the catastrophe in every single situation kept us from becoming extinct. This way of behaving was quite effective during the time frame in which survival depended on whether or not we could outwit our enemies. However, solely operating through this primitive lens of perpetual fear is *outdated*. It doesn't work anymore. In the current phase of our evolution as women and as a species, we have the opportunity to open to grander, more expanded versions of ourselves where avoiding death is no longer the most significant issue. We are primed and ready to be in harmony with all that will take us from *Homo Sapiens* to *Homo Luminous*.

When we can love with our minds and think with our hearts, we can individually and collectively put the constant whispers of the internal fight-or-flight "monster" in its proper place. And in the absence of being able to yank the thing out of our skulls, perhaps it would behoove us to notice how this crude and mysterious part of our ancestry *does* serve us and use it only for that purpose. First, we can offer gratitude for its role in contributing to the survival of our ancestors. Without it, we literally would not be here today. Next we can realize that the *current* function of this primal partner is to protect us in certain ways, such as keeping our hand out of the flame, signaling hunger or physical pain, and preventing us from walking off the cliff. That's *it*. That is its *only* role. In a way, it is like a long-time caretaker with a lifetime employment contract who doesn't have enough to do so they keep trying to stir up work. Our job is to balance and avert the clever, manipulative messages from this irrational, bully-beast.

In combining our developing wisdom with a compassionate heart, we *can* come to tame the fiendish ghosts from our individual and collective past. And when our thoughts as a species can synchronize to agree that such a balance is necessary, we lay the foundation for the metamorphosis that will catapult us into the next level of our development, where living *happily ever after ... right now*, is as natural as drawing breath.

Breaking the Spell

It does appear that the state of the world could be at a critical juncture—that we are operating more out of our collective shadow than the light (or en*light*enment). We are challenged in our relationships globally (as in warring nations), with ourselves (as in the inner wars and conflicts that cause us suffering), and with each other—in our most intimate partnerships. The current model of marriage seems to be failing. Divorce rates have declined in the past several years from fifty to forty percent of all marriages, but only half of Americans ages eighteen and older were married in 2017. The second highest cause of death for pregnant women is homicide, and the primary cause of death for women in general is heart disease.

Headline news—whether televised or in print—is frequently about war, catastrophe, or controversy. Even the officials who make up the United States Government (one, which is supposed to be "... of the people, by the people, and for the people ...") appear to be locked down in firm positions and partisan biases. And, what about our right to "... the pursuit of happiness ..." for all? What's *really* going on with the economy, health care, education, military costs, and national debt?

And as far as choosing another location on the planet to reside besides America? Author and researcher Daniel Pinchbeck states: "We easily forget ... that across vast swathes of the Earth, women are still in bondage, treated like serfs, denied their basic freedoms. They are systematically raped during genocidal wars such as the Bosnian conflict. In India, they are burned alive as brides over dowry disputes. In China, female babies are sometimes smothered by parents longing for a male heir. 'In the less developed world, women's contribution is immeasurable, intense work that is never recognized as valid, never rewarded with money and never considered part of the economy,' world hunger activist Lynne Twist writes in *The Soul of Money*. Even in the West, compensation for men and women remains inequitable, with traditionally female areas of employment such as nursing, childcare, and teaching given short shrift in salary terms, compared to work in the military and financial sectors."

Based on the state of things, it would appear that not everyone on this planet is coming from love and light—and that in large part, we humans are still steeped in an anciently driven fear-based paradigm. Recall the description of the reptile earlier discussed—

"it has no heart and cannot love." And so isn't it crucial that we shift from an *archetype of fear (reptilian based) to a paradigm of compassion (heart based)* before we annihilate ourselves? Or is it even reasonable to think that a change in the consciousness of humanity could be accomplished given the apparent chaos currently palpable on the planet? Many believe, myself included, that such a shift starts at an organic level—one person, one relationship, one family, one community at a time. And if enough of us "sign up," we may just gather the momentum to tip the collective human family into the right direction. And so what is our part?

When you choose to let go of the longing and stop "acting like a bitch" so that you can "go from drudge to dream girl," you will become the truly powerful Queen all men crave and all people are drawn to. Rather than being a "dumb fox who's true to herself," become true to yourself for your inherent value. Instead of cutting a man off because "he is not that into you," decide to attract resonant souls into your life. Instead of molding yourself to fit a cultural stereotype, *change the culture*. If enough of us let the inner Queen emerge by loving and honoring ourselves and then reflecting that love and honor to everyone we meet—we *will* transform the world. Emmet Fox, revered spiritual philosopher, puts it this way: "If you wish to make any advance (in shifting your consciousness) ... you must get rid of all sense of resentment and hostility. You must change your own state of mind until you are conscious only of harmony and peace within yourself, and have a sense of positive goodwill towards all."

And how can we know that we are being guided in the direction toward this "goodwill-towards-all" attitude? When our heart's deepest truth nudges us toward the desire to be all of those things, which we seek from another ... when we *get* that there is nothing to *get*. As we consistently go to that place, we can start cracking the code to peace everlasting. To face our individual and collective struggle is axiomatic and fundamental toward awakening our true and happy state. Where do we start? Here's the short answer:

Realize That What You Are Seeking Already Exists Inside of You

The only time we can come to quit longing for happiness is to notice that what we are seeking has *always and forever* been available. In revisiting Dorothy in *The Wizard of Oz* we can see that when she was able to stop, take a beat, and calm down from the frenzy of her search for the wizard—she attracted the Good Witch, who reminded her that she had always been capable of returning home. Upon the Good Witch's instruction (often we *do* need a wisdom teacher, who can give us a few tips on technique), she clicked her heals and found herself immediately back with Aunty Em. Now admittedly, Dorothy was wearing those magical, ruby red slippers. Nonetheless, I would imagine that if you have yourself in the right frame of heart/mind, your Nike Livestrong sneakers will work just fine.

Many of us have repeatedly placed our hopes and dreams in our version of the Wizard only to be disappointed that they are an imposter. And if we are still overcome with yearning and longing, it will be difficult for us to get past the voice of fear, which so urgently wants us to believe that the way of the wizard is the *only* solution. We will just have to calm down and get quiet for a bit, so we can drop into the *real love* (our true internal home), that is the God Essence to which we are intimately connected. It is here that we will always find direction back—and if we need a little nudging from a wise guide— well that's okay, too.

Buddha found enlightenment only when he stopped seeking and allowed himself to wake up. Enlightenment had never evaded him. But his endless search had distracted him from noticing the peace that was ever-present in his heart-mind. All he had to do was awaken to what was already there. Jesus taught that when you bring forth what is within (the *inner* Queen), what emerges will be your saving grace. Through His life and teachings, He taught us how to *save ourselves*. He also warned that if you continue to bury that which is yours to bring forward by seeking salvation outside of your very own Divinely endowed soul, eventually, you will destroy yourself. The universal message is the same: the answer to the longing and to a happy fulfilled life is to stop looking outside and bring forth what's *inside* with all of the discipline and determination you can muster.

Instead of longing for him to do it for you, allow the source of real love and devotion, which you so desperately want him to provide, *to flow from you*. Having the expectation that he is the answer is a set-up for failure. How can you be assured of what he is going to do in the future, when you can't even know your own destiny? It is up to you to notice the presence or absence of happiness and peace in your life, and then take the necessary steps to improve, enjoy, or find contentment in your circumstances.

We each have come to Planet Earth with a divine and blessed purpose—*to be happy*. If you check in with your heart—you absolutely *know* this to be true. And what is your part in bringing your Divine potential for happiness into form? It is to relax and *allow* in all that is *aching* to grow you into your most optimal expansion. If you can just open the door even a little to the prospects that await you—before you know it, magical opportunities are certain to appear beyond your most favorable imaginings. Included in your smorgasbord of choices could just be a partner to share your life, who recognizes, appreciates, and understands what you are about, or the tools to help you and your current partner polish up your relationship—should you find it is less than ideal. When you are able to finally let go of the longing, what will naturally emerge is your authentic, original self—the Essence of who you are. And in operating from this "self," you will find that no games or rules are necessary for you to be happy; only some simple guidelines to keep you on course, which are constantly being directed by Divine, internal messages from your very own heart. How do you know when the Divine is "talking?" The Divine always speaks through the voice of love.

Re-Programming Ourselves

So, if it is our ancient *conditioning* that keeps us stuck, then how can we emancipate ourselves from its grasp? The primal beliefs and thoughts etched into our consciousness can be automatically triggered by an event. Just like the enchantment that caused Sleeping Beauty to fall asleep when she pricked her finger on a spinning wheel at age sixteen, our old fearful spells kick in when we feel rejected or alone. We can dismantle the power of our ancient conditioning (which wants us to believe that we are prey for the lurking monsters) by creating new beliefs and incantations of *Entitlement*.

The point is that we need to be committed to becoming aware of when a response to an event is not in balance or appropriate, given the circumstances (refer to the bee sting incident in the prologue), and then take the necessary measures to bring ourselves back to center, back to sanity, back to wholeness. When we can quickly catch ourselves going into a spin, we have the chance to create a new reality, both inside and out. And then we have an opportunity to pop open the portal to an expanded, magical world. We just have to decide to do it.

But what about the longing? What about the yearning? What about when you are **alone** (*that dreaded, awful feeling*) and everyone else has someone but you? Or, what about the disappointment you feel when you *are* with someone and he doesn't measure up to your expectations? What about when he is a "jerk" and says things to hurt or dishonor you? What about the feelings you experience when he forgets to call? Why doesn't he send you flowers? Why doesn't he do something to make you feel better about who you are, or why can't you find someone who can?

Letting go of the myth of Prince Charming can be an arduous process, burdened by what could be a stubborn reluctance to surrender the dream and finally get a grip on reality. Shifting your consciousness involves a steady, centered commitment toward waking up from our Sleeping Beauty dream state by focusing on the internal, rather than the external world. In negotiating this mysterious journey toward the inner landscape, you must map out what can feel like uncharted territory. Like Hansel and Gretel, who found their way out of the forest by leaving a trail of white stones that glowed in the moonlight, we too have a trail of wisdom to help us untangle from the diabolical twists and turns that are the forests of our minds. But in order to actually see the truth, we have to be *looking*. Then, once we have made our discoveries, we must be willing to engage all of the courage, discipline, detachment, obedience, and surrender that we can muster in order to follow where we are guided on our very own moonlight path. Feelings of discomfort—often intense—will most likely accompany the pilgrimage. Going deeply *into* all that we do not want to feel is part of the process. We cannot keep stuffing away our discomfort. Sooner or later those feelings will emerge in one way or another. We might as well address them now, before they brew, bubble, and finally *explode.*

The only way we can discover *true happiness* is to be *thorough* in our investigation of Self. It is here that we can begin to awaken the sleepy, sluggish dreamer, who may have been operating on autopilot. As we take the wheel into our own hands, we are primed for uncovering the passions inherent in our being that every Queen knows is the secret to *happily ever after … right now.* Of course, a Queen needs a crown of jewels. Whether dormant and disguised or fully operative in their most optimal brilliance, the polishing of these gemstones is what will awaken us to the true callings of the heart.

Crystals have been recognized and valued throughout history for their decorative and healing powers—dating back as far as ancient Egypt around 4500 BCE. Apparently, King Tutankhamun's funerary mask has a lapis lazuli band arranged around his eyes. According to Judy Hall, crystal expert and author of *The Encyclopedia of Crystals*, lapis represented the god, Amun, whose function was to open spiritual insight as beings journeyed to the "other world."

The following are some gems for you to consider collecting either in the form of jewelry or simple stones, which you may decide to place on a sacred altar as you contemplate your queenly nature in the chapters ahead. Most of these crystals should be available either online or in a local shop. Have fun investigating and doing your own research on possibilities for this fascinating resource.

The Queen's Jewels

1. *Entitlement*: Let Go of the Longing for the Prince
   Jewel: Jasper for protection, grounding, and clearing
2. *Magnificence*: Choose to be Queen
   Jewel: Jacinth for wisdom, honor, and riches
3. *Majesty*: Lose the Slave Girl
   Jewel: Chrysolite for manifesting dreams into reality and attracting love
4. *Sovereignty*: Stop Looking for the Answers Outside Yourself
   Jewel: Sapphire for focusing and calming the mind
5. *Power*: Give Up Your Addictions
   Jewel: Amethyst for love and spiritual power
6. *Alchemy*: Take Back Your Projections
   Jewel: Sardonyx for harmony

7. *Regality*: Be Attached to Nothing
   Jewel: Aquamarine for invoking high states of consciousness
8. *Passion:* Fully Express Your Gifts to the World
   Jewel: Beryl for actualizing potential and loving unconditionally
9. *Preeminence*: Live Like a Queen Every Day
   Jewel: Rose Quartz for attracting unconditional love
10. *Partnership*: Revamp Your Relationship with Men
    Jewel: Angelite for courage in speaking your truth and acceptance of others
11. *Legacy:* For Our Daughters and Sons
    Jewel: Emerald for domestic harmony and loving unconditionally
12. *Ascendancy:* Take Your Queenliness to New Levels for as Long as You Live
    Jewel: Diamond for light and illumination

Your ability to reign over your life is a function of the number of these jewels you possess. *We are that which happiness is made of.* Layers and layers of fear and doubt are conditioned in our memories. These ruts in our brains have perpetuated information carried forward throughout the generations that have preceded us. The fear provoked by this conditioning will always stifle the joy rooted at the core of our being. Together, we can uncover and dissolve the miseries of our past and shift into a new way of being. Let us open our hearts and melt into our Divine connectedness.

We are meant to live joyfully in all of the moments of now, not just someday in the future. All that is required is the realization that we *can* create a *happily ever after ... right now*, by changing the patterns and programs that have run our lives. It is time to begin (or continue) expanding ourselves into the unlimited potential that is ours to claim. Some of us are already engaged in the process and realize that it does indeed require commitment. If you are just beginning your "happily" journey, this book will show you the formula for your own happiness everlasting ... right now. If you are already regaining your sense of *Entitlement*, it will guide you and take you to new levels. Your part is to gather these jewels and then wear them in your own unique and glorious way.

Our individual and collective story is unfolding, and those of us who share the desire to awaken to the possibilities of what this amazing life has to offer realize on some level that we *can* be transformed—*now*. As we move toward all that will support us in changing the *archetype of fear* to the *paradigm of compassion*, together we will open the floodgates for fulfillment. Let us join hands as we bring into our lives all that will allow it to happen. The time is now, and YOU are the one to start the momentum. You have answered the call to wake up to your grandest, most glorious self. All happiness, all delight—starts with you.

Famed dancer and choreographer Martha Graham believed our individual life force is unique, artistic, and always accessible. In her own words:

> *There is vitality, a life force, a quickening*
> *That is translated through you into action,*
> *And because there is only one of you in all time,*
> *This expression is unique.*
> *If you block it,*
> *It will never exist through any other medium*
> *And be lost.*
> *The world will not have it.*
> *It is not your business to determine how good it is;*
> *Nor how valuable it is;*

Nor how it compares with other expressions.
It is your business to keep it yours, clearly and directly,
To keep the channel open.

You do not even have to believe in yourself or your work.
You have to keep open and aware directly
To the urges that motivate you.

Keep the channel open.
No artist is pleased.
There is no satisfaction, whatever at any time.
There is only a queer, divine dissatisfaction;
A blessed unrest that keeps us marching and more alive
than the others.

—*In Conversation with Agnes De Mille*

New Stories, New Enchantment

The code for breaking the spells of the past has been shared time and time again, in ways we *can* understand if we just listen. But often we have chosen not to hear. The masters and avatars have spelled it out for us in a language so simple that we can hardly believe it really works, especially if we are operating from our primitive consciousness of "me first, then you" … or "I need to get something from you in order to be okay." Start (or continue) to replace your fearful thoughts with affirmations like:

I am intimately connected with that which created me. I am originally blessed with this Divine Essence. Therefore:

I have the power and the capacity to manifest anything I believe to be possible, because all possibilities exist in me.

What I give to you, I give to me because we are not separate. And what I give to me, I give to the world.

I am committed to making the changes in myself that I wish to see in others.

I live in the eternal now. Therefore I have no fears about the future, or concerns about the past.

All of my past has been purified of error.

All of my experiences up until this very moment provide the perfect foundation for my most expanded joy and fulfillment.

I am complete and satisfied across all areas of my life.

I awaken to the Essence that lives in the core of my being. I listen only to Her/His voice of love for guidance and direction.

❦ EXERCISE ❦

Start a journal for transcendence. Commit to making loving observations of behavioral patterns—whether subtle or significant—that may be keeping you stuck in the victim-perpetrator-rescuer loop. Who are the wisdom guides that are showing up in your life to help you remember your Divinity? Can you discipline yourself to commit to a path of transcendence as you listen to the voice of love and truth?

TWO

MAGNIFICENCE— CHOOSE TO BE QUEEN

Jewel: Jacinth for Wisdom, Honor, and Riches

"All You Need Is Love."

—John Lennon and Paul McCartney

As a psychotherapist, I have listened to hundreds of clients repeat the same story. They are either looking for the perfect relationship, or else they are in a relationship that has turned out to be less than perfect and they want their partner to change. Need I mention that most of these clients are women? In every case, they have set aside their power and forgotten their innate sovereignty. Instead, they are looking outside, to the world or to someone else, to be their saving grace, the answer to their heart's desires, the key to long-term happiness. They have forgotten their value. They have forgotten their worth. They have forgotten that they are Queens.

Merriam Webster's definition of a Queen is "something personified as a woman, who is considered the best or most important of her kind." That *something* is *Magnificence. That's* what's inside of you. *That's who you are*—A powerful woman. A grounded woman. A woman, whose self-esteem radiates from every cell of her being. Begin to think of yourself in these terms. Every single event that has brought you to this moment has laid the foundation for your *Magnificence* to emerge. *Claim it, now.*

Queens We Have Known and Loved

No doubt, you've seen and perhaps even know women who have chosen to live in their *Magnificence.* They exude inner strength and confidence and are respected and admired by others. Mother Teresa, Oprah Winfrey, Katherine Hepburn, Eleanor Roosevelt, Maya Angelou, Audrey Hepburn, and Queen Noor of Jordan come to mind as examples. Consider the saintly qualities of Mary, Queen of the Heavens, and *Magnificent* mother of Jesus—picture Hera, Queen of the gods, who reigned as an equal partner with Zeus. Literary characters can also serve as models. Visualize Ayala in *The Clan of the Cave Bear*, Jean M. Auel's epic work of prehistoric fiction, who embodied the Queen essence even as she was scorned by the less-evolved tribe that adopted her. Many of us will also never forget the African Queen in Alex Haley's *Roots* who kept her regal bearing even when enslaved, naked, and chained.

Imagine yourself as embodying all of the best qualities of those you admire most in the world. You may want to choose a specific woman to emulate. Maybe your grandmother maintained a quiet, stately manner that you admired. Or your favorite aunt had a joyous and powerful partnership with her husband. Perhaps you feel intrigued by your daughter and her friends, who radiate a different level of confidence than you ever experienced at their age. You will also start to catch qualities in *yourself* that you admire and want to expand. Get creative and begin noticing the Queen essence whenever you can.

Catch Yourself Being Queen

Recall the moments when you've stepped fully into your *Magnificence*. It may have been the first time you addressed your parents from a powerful place as an adult, or when you performed beyond your expectations in a leadership role. Maybe it was in attaining some cherished goal or winning an award. Perhaps you are becoming more authentic in your relationships, feeling comfortable identifying and expressing your truth. If you are willing, capture your victories and answer these questions in your journal. Read your responses often.

> *What are your most Magnificent qualities?*
> *Have you ever gone beyond your comfort zone in pursuit*
> *of your passions?*
> *What goals have you accomplished?*
> *In what ways do you deserve praise?*
> *What is it about you that is strikingly grand or impressive—*
> *exceptionally fine?*

Use this process as an entry point to spark the momentum of a life without limits. Notice all the ways you are already *Magnificent*, and expand from there. If your mind starts to argue, saying "you are not," or "you can't," allow the disclaimer to act as a reminder that fear and doubt are not anchored in love. *And only love is real.* Learn to identify and only listen to the voice of love. It speaks gently, with the perfect blend of compassion and truth. There has never been a time when it was not available to you because it is the Essence of who you are—the foundation of your Queenly nature. Declare it *now*.

Be What You Seek in Him

Give up the longing for him to be the answer. *Become all that you want him to be.* For example, if you insist on a partner with financial wealth and independence, then first focus on how to create your own financial freedom. Expecting him to do it for you is part of the myth that can keep you feeling enslaved and helpless. When you make him responsible for your well-being, there is more than likely a part of you that feels "less than." If you are willing, stretch your imagination and begin to recognize the multitude of ways that *you* can create a life of abundance—regardless of your education level or perceived skill sets. *Do not limit yourself with your old beliefs.* We live in a world of endless possibilities. Seize some of these and bring your *Magnificence* into form.

Realize, as well, that your partner can join you in your growth. *You do not have to be a rugged individualist.* The two of you have come together to expand into a greater version of yourselves—though neither of you should expect the other to be the source of his/her fulfillment. Rather, together you are discovering how to *contribute* to each other's expansion. Each of you is already *whole,* and you have connected so that together you have the possibility of becoming a *grander whole unit.*

Is it really true that only men can be rich and powerful? If you want him to be rich, meet him with your own version of wealth (compassion, money, talent, energy, vitality, cheerfulness, or however you see abundance). Then combine your assets and strengths and enjoy the infinite possibilities that emerge as you blend the creativity and genius you each bring to this union.

Queens Love Themselves

You may have already discovered that we attract people who share some of our same attributes and weaknesses, even though these may not appear in the same form. So as we retrieve the parts of ourselves that may have splintered off in search of something else for salvation, we are announcing to the Universe that we are ready to return to our wholeness, and therefore are prepared to attract *whole people* into our lives. And perhaps one of the simplest ways to get started is by beginning to master the art of loving ourselves. Love is the fuel of the Universe. When you deflect it toward others (away from yourself), you are disconnecting from your Life Force. In making a commitment to love yourself, you are strengthening a bond with that Life Force, which will always support you in your desire to step into your full and most optimal *Magnificence.*

In focusing on this *Magnificence,* we can begin to direct the flow of love inward. And when it expands and grows, it will radiate outward. As we emanate love, we become magnets for love. *From our wholeness, we attract wholeness.* In continuing to live our own *Magnificence,* we reflect his to him while he cycles it back to us.

Matthew Fox, legendary philosopher and modern day mystic, offers an interesting viewpoint in his breakthrough book, *Original Blessing.* Fox suggests that rather than being "originally sinful" (as some religious philosophies suggest), instead, each of us is "originally blessed" with Divine consciousness. This God-Essence is inherent in all living creatures, *regardless of their religious beliefs, spiritual traditions, philosophies, or ideologies.* Therefore, we are all direct descendants of Divine love from which it is impossible to be separate. So, the knack for maintaining a happy state is an *inner,* organic process—starting with having a true and lasting love affair with ourselves. The seed from this authentic, self-love is what potentiates the possibility of loving and being loved by others. All of us emerge from the same Unified Field of Love and so, therefore, Love is who we are—though when it is shrouded by our fears and insecurities, we forget. This Love-Essence vibrates life into every cell of our being. As we tune into its frequencies, we *become* the love and eternal joy we have been endlessly seeking. There is nowhere to go. We are already home, nestled in the womb of eternal peace. And, at last, the longing and suffering finally cease.

Like the other avatars that preceded and followed Him, Jesus taught personal responsibility, equality, love, truth, compassion, and mercy. Is it possible that His mission was not to "save" but rather to illustrate how salvation is possible for each of us by choosing the way of life He demonstrated with His presence here among us? In the insightful book, *Love, Truth, and Perception*, Kathy Oddenino illustrates the point:

> *Jesus devoted his life to merging His physical nature with His divine nature, which was His purpose upon Earth. Refusing to accept responsibility for our behavior allows adultery, sexual abuse, dishonesty, robbery, murder, greed, and all criminal acts to be acceptable within the perception of the mind ... The important issue for us to remember ... is that the intention of the Hebrews and Romans was to execute Jesus because they did not believe in His teachings of personal responsibility, equality, love, truth, mercy, and compassion. Jesus knew that He was not the Messiah that had come to save man, because He knew that man would always be responsible for saving himself. Jesus knew that the Messiah is the spirit within us, and He knew that it is our own divine nature that must save us.*

From this perspective, God is not placed on a pedestal, but rather is simply the Source of one's existence. God does not preside over the Heavens but *is* the Heaven in all that exists. And the inner Queen that is you can always be in touch with this Heaven by *loving herself, unconditionally.*

Queens Act like Queens

The idea of *Magnificence* can bring sharply into focus all of the ways you do not feel *Magnificent* in the form of your shortcomings and faults. We are constantly exposed to the emotional toxicity that has accumulated in the world, bombarding us from every angle. We know it well. This negative conditioning (provoked by our "old, rugged brain") can exaggerate fear, confusion, worry, and anxiety, all of which impede growth and disrupt the journey toward love, joy, freedom, and truth. The "hell" created from venomous thoughts, deeds, and actions is a part of our individual and combined story. When we subscribe to this way of operating, we perpetuate hell's grip on us, interrupting our soul's purpose, and losing our innocence. True happiness, which lies at the center of our being, is overshadowed by anguish and suffering. One way to overcome any fear-based negativity is to practice functioning from a loving foundation by learning to love all of the parts of yourself.

> If you are still hoping the Prince will appear and save you, *love that.*
> If he doesn't call, and you are panicking, *love that.*
> If you forget to act like a Queen, *love that.*
> If you feel too fat, too thin, too old, or just generally not okay, love *that.*
> *If you feel gorgeous, sexy, wise, and utterly Magnificent,* love that.

Do you get the idea? You step into your *Magnificence* when you can love in 360 degrees. Most of us have been directing that love outward, toward the idolized other. At our center lies the deepest, purest love, which we can only have the delusion of being without. We are bathed in this love. What connects us fully to the awareness that it exists is the *love and acceptance of ourselves.*

A classic piece of career advice is to dress for the job you want, not the job you have. When you do that, people begin to see you in the more elevated role, and then it becomes natural for you to expand into that position. This is one way to *live large* and into your future.

Similarly, you can *act as if* you're the Queen you want to be. First, you must see yourself as a Queen. Assume a regal demeanor. Now, believe and then *know* that *it is absolutely possible for you to live your Magnificence.*

Think of yourself as two parts: One is already a Queen, and the other is a Queen-in-training. Just as you'd love and encourage a friend or a child, the Queen part of you can love and encourage yourself. If you feel afraid of being alone, comfort yourself. If you feel angry about something he said, soothe yourself. If you feel sad because he has left you, console yourself. And, *when you are excited about your own developing Magnificence, celebrate yourself.*

Oprah and Lisa: Queens We Know and Love

Oprah Winfrey is an icon for *Magnificence.* She is a living example of Queen Essence. Launching her career in broadcasting at the age of nineteen, she was the youngest person and the first African-American woman to anchor the news (at Nashville's WJZ-TV). She went on to become the third woman in the American entertainment industry (following Mary Pickford and Lucille Ball) to own her own studio.

In 1986, the Oprah Winfrey Show was the highest-rated talk show in television history, and remained on the air for twenty-five years. Oprah embodies the spirit of *Magnificence* across every aspect of her life. She uses the spotlight to help others live their lives in ways that make a difference. Her generosity and philanthropy are unparalleled. She has learned to blend determination, discipline, love, and compassion to create a miraculous formula of beneficence for the world. Oprah Winfrey is a Queen. Study her life and know that there are no limits.

Lisa Halaby, an Arab-American from a distinguished family, was one of the first women graduates of Princeton when she received a degree in architecture and urban planning in 1978. Four years later,

King Hussein of Jordan proposed marriage to her. Unlike how other Queen candidates might have responded, Lisa was not immediately taken by the offer, even though at the time King Hussein was considered to be one of the world's most eligible bachelors.

Lisa was well-aware of the tremendous advantages such a union would produce. Nonetheless, she refused to allow herself to be wooed by the absolute fairy-tale-frivolity of becoming a Queen (she already was one). Instead of fantasizing, she got real with herself. Her concerns were practical as she began to ponder the consequences and possibilities of such a marriage. What would the implications be for the country of Jordan—for the United States? Even though she carried an Arabian bloodline, would she be suitable?

Marrying for social advantage was not part of Lisa's Queen consciousness: although she did realize how King Hussein's companionship might come to enormously enhance her already-blossoming, brilliant life. She absolutely got that the guarantee for happiness *did not* depend on her marriage to him.

Lisa was gifted with rare insights that helped her to know how to follow her own passions and dreams. *And look what happened.* Without ever seeking or longing for "him," she ended up not a princess but a *Queen.* She did decide to marry King Hussein and became Noor al Hussein, Queen of Jordan. And the King remained, for all of the years they were privileged to be together, "the light of her life." Was her marriage to the King like a fairy tale? Was it a dream come true? Were her days filled with parties and light-hearted frivolities? Hardly.

Her beloved husband preceded her in death. She watched him suffer a long, painful exit. And she allowed herself the opportunity to experience the profound and agonizing feelings of loss when he finally did go. Reason tells us that we simply cannot have relationships that last forever in this particular life form. Our bodies will eventually decay and die, and even if we *do* experience a long-term relationship with another, sooner or later one of us *will* go. Queen Noor agonized over her own bitter and potent pain, while maintaining her strength through the heartbreak of losing her husband to cancer. Through the struggle, she has demonstrated enormous tenacity and the courage to follow her passion and dream in continuing to carry on their combined legacy. She survived her heartbreak with a stunning dignity and grace.

If Lisa Halaby had been too timid or shy to date a King, she would have denied herself the opportunity to experience "an unexpected life," (as noted in the title of her autobiography). What might happen if you say "no" to taking your first Queenly step because it feels too scary? Things definitely would look different from the floor, should you remain in crawling mode.

Today, Queen Noor comes across as dignified, graceful, gorgeous, and wise. She speaks with impeccable intelligence and insight and yet is able to balance her intellect with a gentle and stunning grace that is truly breathtaking. She had created a life for herself back when she was just Lisa, long before the King entered the picture. Setting aside her own passions, dreams, and values in order to first "catch him" and then "keep him" simply was not part of her reality. Had she not married her dear King, this brilliant woman would have gone on to fulfill her life's purpose in other glorious ways. She would have been happy. Yet she chose another way. Today she is vibrant and alive. She has always known that the true seeds of happiness must be sprouted, watered, and grown from within.

We always have a choice and *can* choose again, and then again, should we decide to maintain responsibility and sovereignty over our lives. Through Queen Noor's example, we can see that even though change and death are inevitable, we need not continue to suffer endlessly when our life takes an unexpected turn. We can go on and make meaning out of the existence that is ours to experience—*now*. Such an attitude is our only hope in accessing the underlying peace that is always available to us. When we do muster up the tenacity and courage to proceed, we will never be denied the comfort, love, and support necessary to move us forward.

Inviting the Queen In and Out

When we take on the mindset of *Magnificence*, we absolutely *can* uncover the mysteries of happiness everlasting. Our powerful inner wisdom guides us to the awareness (whenever we are willing) *that love is in all that exists.* Therefore, it is impossible to be separate from love, our loving nature, and the love that connects us to every living atom on the planet.

Choosing to be a Queen opens the portals of infinite possibility for our lives, and that can feel both exciting and terrifying. We worry about the challenges and changes we will face as we welcome the mysteries of our magnificent nature. What if it doesn't work out? What if it is too hard? What if it is dark and difficult? We can make ourselves crazy with the "what ifs." If we can just *stay still* long enough to actually experience the intense vulnerability (rather than running away from our frightful feelings), something magical happens. *Our most creative nature can crack open and emerge.* If you have ever watched a baby chicken hatch, this glorious miracle provides the perfect metaphor. As they finally emerge, the scrawny, skinny newborns sprawl with exhaustion. Nonetheless, right beside them are their sisters and brothers, hatched a few hours earlier, already fluffy and frolicking from their awakened sense of freedom. It goes without saying that persistence, tenacity, and will are the keys here. The momentum for that little critter to peck its way out of the shell came from the creative life force that pulses within each and every one of us.

> "... *The shell must be cracked open*
> *If what is inside is to come out.*
> *If you want the kernel,*

You must break the shell.
We must learn to break through things
If we are to grasp God in them."
—*Meister Eckhart*

None of this makes sense when we are awaiting the Prince (or anything else) for salvation. It is often difficult, and may even seem impossible, to believe that true love and happiness start from within. We struggle to imagine or comprehend the idea of having a relationship with our own Higher Consciousness (Self) *first*. And yet, *we must believe we are Magnificent* before we can reign in another world. Be a Queen. Be sovereign over your life.

New Stories, New Enchantments

Use these affirmations as a guide to begin (or continue) bringing forward your *Magnificence*. Then, add to the list or create your own.

I radiate love. I attract love. I deserve love. Others deserve love from me. The past is purified. The present is eternal. The future is the possibility. I am living a life beyond limits.

"The self that God created needs nothing. It is forever complete, safe, loved and loving. It seeks to share rather than to get; to extend rather than project. It has no needs and wants to join with others out of their mutual awareness of abundance"

—*A Course in Miracles*

I have confidence, self-worth, and personal integrity. My challenges are the foundation for my growth and ultimate freedom. My victories provide momentum for expansion. I have access to infinite possibilities. I am the possibility.

I am extending my talents and gifts outward, moment to moment. There is a profoundly deep calm at the core of my being that is unmoved by any external turbulence. The truth comes to me effortlessly and spontaneously. I am at peace. I am peace.

The Ultimate Ground of my being is the only reality, the only Source of all that exists. It is being played out inside of me. I bring it forward to share with the world.

There are infinite possibilities for me to express my Magnificence. I imagine that the entire universe can be healed from my very intention that it is so.

I now affirm and know that my successful results appear, effortlessly.

❧ EXERCISE ❧

If you are willing, write this statement in your transcendence journal: *I am Magnificent.* Good. Now re-read it for seventeen seconds. Time yourself. See if you can be committed to doing this daily until you actually start to believe it. Take note of the subtle and even profound changes that begin to occur—in your favor.

THREE

MAJESTY—
LOSE THE SLAVE GIRL

Jewel: Chrysolite for Manifesting Dreams into Reality and
Attracting Real Love

*"At every moment a woman makes a choice: between the state
of the queen and the state of the slave-girl. In our natural state,
we are glorious beings. In the world of illusion, we are lost and
imprisoned, slaves to our appetites and our will to false power.
Our jailer is a three-headed monster: one head our past, one
our insecurity, and one our popular culture."*

—*Marianne Williamson*

It's one thing to choose to be Queen. It's quite another to give up
our slave-girl identity. We can be making Queenly gestures, but if
our hearts, minds, and bodies are still immersed in the master/slave
paradigm (and we are the slave), we will never create an enchanted life.
We've all managed Queenly moments, which we may even sustain,
but most of us are still strongly attached to being a victim in one or
more areas of life. Often we are not even aware of the subtle patterns
of behavior that perpetuate our enslavement. Perhaps without

knowing it, we allow our partner, parents, boss, or our children to be the masters of our lives. Wherever that slave-girl lurks, it's time to let her go.

According to Webster, the word "slave" derives from the enslavement of Slavs in central Europe. Each of its definitions holds a valuable message for those of us who are ready to roust out any remnants of the slave-girl

1: a person held in servitude as the chattel of another
> Are you feeling possessed or do you at times even want to be possessed by a man?

2: one that is completely subservient to a dominating influence
> Do you let your partner or our culture's messages dominate you?

3: a device (such as the printer of a computer) that is directly responsive to another
> Do you typically respond, rather than initiate?

As women we are often inclined to over-function and frequently put the needs of others ahead of our own. In fact, we have been conditioned to this modus operandi. The Queen responds differently. She first checks in with herself and then creates a natural pulsing back and forth between her own needs and those of others—a circular rhythm, rather than a one-way flow of giving.

Webster defines the word "slavish" as "copying obsequiously or without originality." It's what we do when we deny our innate, unique individuality to emerge. We fall into line with the culture's definitions of what is desirable, beautiful, and admirable.

Queens individuate from the whole. They are originals. Television's *Desperate Housewives* were women rebelling to an outdated societal script that bound them to monotonous mediocrity—especially in relationships. They refused to forfeit their creativity by settling for less than who they were. They defied old models of women as subservient, compliant, resigned, and submissive—cowering, cringing, fawning, and obedient—like dogs.

Victims are Volunteers

We always have a choice about how we view the world and how we live our lives—whether we see ourselves as victims or as Queens. Choose to see yourself as a powerful part of the cultural shift that will transmute the old story. Usher in a new way of being and help balance the current patriarchy, which seems to favor masters and slaves. In his brilliant book *The Last Hours of Ancient Sunlight*, Thom Hartman points out that every patriarchal culture in human history has failed. The past has shown us that too much testosterone (masculine) combined with a lid on love and compassion (feminine) is a lethal formula that will eventuate in destruction *every single time*. And if we observe what is happening in the world today both individually and globally, what is the mix? Are the masculine and feminine energies equally yoked? *Hardly*. Isn't it time, then, that we wash away the madness of the master/slave model by calling forward our feminine, Queenly nature? Let us begin by letting go of any remnants of our victim identity. Don't be a slave. *Be a Queen*. Bring balance to your life and to the world.

Victims, Villains, Rescuers

Some of the most powerful stories that continue to play out in our world today are those of victim, villain, and rescuer. Read the front page of any newspaper, which will likely emphasize the point. Often we are tempted to cast others as villains or rescuers and ourselves as victims. It does not matter whether we observe the smallest of interactions between individuals or centuries-long feuds among nations because all the players seem to use the same script. We tend to make our perceived enemy wrong, often holding ourselves in sanctimonious righteousness.

When things fall apart and you feel betrayed, you have forgotten that there can be *no victims or villains*, because in truth, *there is only one of us*. We have all come from the same Ultimate Ground and are therefore united in our shared, Divine origin. One of Mother Teresa's most famous quotes is "One, One, One." When we inflict injury on others, we inflict it on ourselves as well, even though it might not be obvious to us at that moment.

Still, even though we are all connected, there is likely no one who sees the world exactly as you do. *Individuation*, or the healthy emergence from the whole, *is a key element to growth*. As we bring forward our strengths and talents, we have the opportunity for interdependence with others. We can then weave the threads of our combined existence into a masterful tapestry, replete with the different textures and tints that can serve to represent a collective masterpiece, one that we certainly could not have created alone. And yet our contribution added just the right color and hue to perfectly accent the others.

As we reflect on human history, we can observe that combining our strengths to enhance the whole has not always been the tendency. Rather, we have been inclined to focus on grievances, righteousness, and individuality (implying a singular, separate Self). Identifying with our disparities instead of the common ground that can bring us together has caused human atrocities and provoked wars. Isn't it time that we seek to harmonize our diversity? Why else would we have signed up to come here?

What will it take for us to finally comprehend that *inflicting blame or harm only inhibits growth and progress?* Be aware of an important truth. *What you resist in the other is a reflection of what you are resisting to notice in yourself.* I know. It isn't pretty. We don't want to look at our shadow nature. And yet, if we are going to extinguish suffering, both individually and collectively, we *must* be willing to delve deeply into those aspects of ourselves and others that we are reluctant to face. It is only when you are open to looking at all possible parts of the scenario that you will learn the lesson and avoid repeating the tedium of the "instruction" yet one more time.

If you attracted someone significant into your life and it didn't work out, you cannot erase the experience. It is indeed an important encounter. And while you are hurting, you may notice a strong desire to make him wrong. It helps you to feel better if he can be the villain. Then, losing him is easier. *There is a price to pay with such an attitude.* Some of us know it by heart. If we don't learn now from this valuable experience, we are going to push the replay button, only next time the volume will be louder and the drama more pronounced. Therefore, rather than concentrate on his mistakes and shortcomings, move as quickly as possible to a place where you can honestly ask yourself:

> *What's up for healing here?*
>
> *Why am I responding with such intensity?*
>
> *Can I see a pattern of behavior played out in this scenario?*
>
> *Has this happened to me before?*

Remember, what you want is to *extinguish the pattern* of behavior that is no longer serving your growth and most expanded potential. To attempt to make him (or anyone else) know how right you are and how wrong he is only inhibits and weakens you. You have missed the point, and you will keep re-creating the situation until you finally get that *this is about you, not him.*

Be aware that you must not snuff out or stuff away your pain. If you deny it, it will come back to haunt you, eventually causing more suffering and despair. Feel, and feel deeply, all that you are experiencing. Your primal fears will scream at you to run. Do not listen. Instead, use their message as a signal to move at full velocity *toward* all that you are most terrified to face. It is here that you will discover the kernel of truth that you thought had always evaded you or was just out of reach. Your healing has now begun. As your true inner heart is aroused, you start to notice a mounting enormity of love swelling inside. So profound is this love that it awakens you to possibilities you could not have imagined in your state of peril and confusion. As you stay focused on this Loving Essence, you will begin to release all of those maladaptive methods for salvation that have never worked for you before. The late spiritual teacher Henri Nouwen said that the Loving Essence will "permanently fulfill your deepest need." All you have to do to activate that Essence is to allow yourself to be available to it. In his beautiful book *The Inner Voice of Love*, Nouwen adds: "Make your pain available for God's healing... God does not want your loneliness; God wants to touch you in a way that permanently fulfills your deepest need."

The Payoff

How did we get to be such drudges—such slaves? Cultural stories steadily seep into our psyche like a leaky faucet that never gets fixed. Then, our conditioning ensconces them into our skulls. One story goes like this: "There is a payoff for playing the part of the pitiful and pathetic." We are taunted and tormented by the twisted part of ourselves that would prefer to be right instead of happy. And, when we identify with the victim, we don't have to be responsible for our lives. Instead, we can blame someone else when things fall apart. Mired in the murk of our drudgery, we don't have to face the fear of expanding into larger lives than we've ever experienced before.

Over time, patterns of thought and behavior become rigid. They form fixed physical connections in the brain. So, even as much as we can visualize a life of peace and happiness, actually taking responsibility for making it happen can seem to be a formidable challenge. Our old beliefs continue to haunt us. Many of us have spent most of our lives believing that the Prince is out there (rather than in here), and so we must be gentle with ourselves if we continue to cling to the daydream. As we become more alert to the old, outdated beliefs, we can use them as a signal. They can serve to trigger our thinking in another direction—noticing all the ways we can move more fully into our *Majesty*.

In our firm resolve to become the Queen and let go of the drudge, we must live our lives by using insight, instead of instinct. Insight is about listening to the soul. Instinct is the reactive part of our nature, directly linked to all of our primal conditioning, which provokes the perpetuation of the dull, dissatisfied drudge. When we listen to our intuition, or insight, our fears and ego may continue to bring on strong and challenging arguments. In fact, as we make changes in ourselves, deeper and deeper layers of conditioning and fear rise to the surface for healing. It takes courage to change. No problem. You are that which courage is made of. Your valor is always available to you, because it sleeps in your substance. When you are willing to call forth your warrior spirit, nothing can stop you. You will hear the still voice inside—guiding you through your doubt and quieting the subtle fears, which sneak in to stunt your progress and growth.

Catch Those Slave-Girl Thoughts

In his classic book *The Power of Now*, Eckhart Tolle wisely points out that we must choose between "... resistance or surrender ... bondage or inner freedom ... suffering or inner peace." How? By monitoring your thoughts, words, perspective, and actions with constant vigilance.

There are physiological studies to provide scientific evidence demonstrating that patterns and conditioning can be extinguished. Dr. Candace Pert, best known for the findings discussed in her book *Molecules of Emotions,* was featured in the popular documentary film *What the ?!&* Do We Know.* Dr. Pert demonstrates that when thoughts and beliefs are no longer supported, the neuro-nets and pathways in the brain that have strengthened them literally fall away. This research explains how it is possible to undo our conditioned responses and reactions. We *can* retrain our minds. We just have to decide to do so. Practice letting go of your negative thoughts by having a positive response ready to replace them. Then, keep affirming the positive thoughts, repeatedly, so that they become locked in to substitute the old beliefs. Try it and begin to notice the magical shifts you are creating in yourself.

Another incredible study, performed by the late Dr. Masaru Emoto of Japan, further emphasizes the power and influence of thoughts, images, and events. He proved empirically that water (of which humans are seventy percent) has the ability to copy and memorize information. Dr. Emoto found a way to study water molecules, first by freezing them and then by observing how they change when paired with certain events. For example, when exposed to the words *love and gratitude,* the frozen water crystals take on the appearance of perfectly formed snowflakes. Playing Mozart or Vivaldi creates a similar effect. If exposed to "heavy metal" music or phrases like, "you fool," or, "you are stupid," the crystals seem to go into chaos and lose their shape. The pictures in Dr. Emoto's book *The True Power of Water* offer a remarkable demonstration of the living quantum world and the power that thoughts and events have over water (and us).

Your words have the energy and power to create your world. Queens choose their words and thoughts carefully. Drop the word "victim" from your vocabulary as well as phrases like:

"You made me feel ..." (It's a choice.) Instead say, "When this happened, I felt ..."

"I couldn't help it." (You can.) Instead say, "I take responsibility for my part, and what happened was really disturbing to me."

"It's your fault." (It isn't. You both created this experience.) Instead say, "No one is to blame. We both contributed. How can we learn to communicate more effectively?"

"You made me do it." (He didn't.) Instead say, "Because of what happened, I felt very vulnerable. My vulnerability influenced my behavior. And, I take responsibility."

Beyond a Victim Identity

"Miracles are healing because they supply a lack; they are performed by those who temporarily have more for those who temporarily have less."

—A Course in Miracles

When the Dalai Lama interviewed a Tibetan monk who had been tortured for eighteen years in a Chinese prison, he asked the monk to describe his most critical danger while in captivity. He responded by saying, "I feared losing compassion for the Chinese." The monk had the impeccable vision to see beyond the unconscionable behavior of his torturers and constantly strove to be "temporarily more" for those who took on the appearance of being "temporarily less." Perhaps he can serve as a powerful reminder. Few of us are in prison, unless we have created one. So, we don't have to stick around and continue being beaten, battered, or bruised either literally or figuratively. We are free to go at any time. If we do stay under less than desirable circumstances, we must conclude that we are our own captors.

Beyond a Victim Identity with Men

> Have you ever found yourself saying or thinking something like this?
>
> "He treats me like a tramp." *Why do you let him?*
>
> "He is the same as all the others." *What are you re-creating each time?*
>
> "There are no decent men." *Where are you looking? What are you being? Why are you not attracting decent men? How are you seeing yourself?*
>
> "I don't do relationships very well." *Learn. There are tools everywhere.*
>
> "All the good ones are taken." *This translates into, "I am not good enough." Be good enough. Now.*

Our pain comes from our interpretations. Decide to change your point of view about yourself, and your world will transform today. Old, outdated conditioned responses will fall away. *It will not even occur to you* to use victim statements because you won't be identifying with that role anymore. You won't stick around if he treats you disrespectfully and refuses to change. And, when you consider new relationships, you will learn to have impeccable insight as you follow your Queenly nature.

He will give you hints about who he is in the first few minutes of your time together. If you learn to listen to these clues without dismissing them, you will always know whether or not it is wise for you to proceed. You will not agree to "blind dates" because you won't be tempted to go into any more encounters with your eyes closed.

If someone else is setting you up with that "perfect someone," and it sounds too good to be true, *it is*. If you do decide to go, however, arrange to casually meet him for coffee so as not to waste your time in case you don't hit it off. You will know. You do know. You are now attracting only resonate souls who can meet you in your wholeness.

Rooting Out Victim Behavior

As we grow and evolve, we must agree to extinguish any personal behavior that does not represent the true soul-self. As each of us makes the commitment to let go of old patterns, which we KNOW do not work for us, we will all eventually take the higher road, avoiding the urge to give way to our primal nature. Instead, we will ask the conscious self to choose for us. Here are some simple questions we can ask ourselves to help in turning up the voice of the soul:

> *Am I loving with my mind and thinking with my heart?*
> *Does this action, word, or deed produce peace and love or*
> *doubt and fear?*
> *Does this behavior serve progress and growth, or does it*
> *produce constriction and regression?*

Queen or Drudge? Which One Do You Choose?

You may not be able to change your perspective and thoughts overnight, but you can catch yourself behaving like a slave or a drudge. Begin with the outer behavior, and the inner changes will follow. Here are some guidelines:

> *Drudges wait by the phone. Queens rarely give out their*
> *phone number. If he wants to find you (or you him),*
> *it will happen. No waiting. No worrying.*

Drudges expect others to read their minds. Queens speak their minds.

Drudges wait for the Prince. Queens wait for no one and only accept Kings.

Drudges want to be desired. Queens are desire.

Drudges react. Queens respond.

Drudges make excuses. Queens tell the truth and take responsibility.

Drudges focus on the man. Queens focus on their passions.

Drudges need a man to be happy. Queens know they must fully embody the spirit of happiness to attract the right man. And the happiness is the focus. Not the man.

The Magic of Majesty

As you diminish your victim thoughts, words, and actions, you will begin to tap into the magic of the Queen. Like the heroines in fairy tales who had to accomplish some seemingly impossible task, you will be able to set aside apparent "real" limits and move steadily to your goals coming from the inspirations of your heart. The Grimm's (fairy tale) girls invariably did what they needed to do—they got a good night's sleep—and allowed the guidance of their inner wisdom to handle the rest. The internal womb of stillness will always point us to peace. Our only task is to listen and then follow where the insights direct us.

You are not a victim and you are not alone. Your inner happiness is *always* available to you. When your partner appears (or is already there), you see him as someone who can help to enhance your already-happy state. You do not depend on him; rather, together you learn the art of interdependence. Your commitment is to growth, authenticity, truth, love, joy, and a foundation of compassionate, honest communication. Each of you knows that there are no guarantees for "ever after." If, at any time, your peace is interrupted, you are willing to share and negotiate. And when there can be no resolve because he refuses to negotiate with you, or you with him, you know what to do. *Move on.*

King or Frog? Key Questions to Ask Yourself

Whether in the first flush of attraction or long-time partnered, you may find it helpful to ask yourself some discerning questions as you develop your Queenly instincts.

Can I talk to him about my passions, hopes, and dreams and feel supported?

When I watch his body language, do I notice affirmative gestures or does he seem bored, anxious, or not in touch?

Do we have similar values and ideals?

How does he treat others, especially his mother?

Does he rage on the road or make snide, cruel remarks out of the blue?

Is he quick to judge or blame or does he see the thread of connection between all beings?

Can I be authentic with this man?

Can I express myself freely and be heard, or do I feel railroaded and controlled by doing things his way?

Do I feel so authentic in his presence that I can be completely myself, almost as if I were alone? (I can throw up, belch, have a bad hair day or stay in my pajamas, not brush my teeth or comb my hair and never give it another thought. This one may seem a bit odd, but pay attention. It is important.)

Does my body feel natural with him?

Do I get stomachaches or yummy yearnings while in his presence?

Do I think I have to sacrifice or splinter myself in any way in order to be with him?

Do I feel like a Queen in his presence, or more like a drudge?

Make your own list or add to this one. You do know when you are resonating with another, and you do know when it is time to go, even if part of you wants to clutch and cling. And, if he's the one who wants to exit first, release him, even if every fiber of your being is screaming, "no!" Ya gotta let him go. No villains. No victims. His truth is your truth. Your hanging on will only make the agony worse for both of you. When you do set him (and yourself) free, the eventual outcome will be transformational. You will create more freedom for both of you across all areas of your lives. You will remember that happiness is always underneath, despite the painful challenges that the illusion of separation might present. You emerge. You survive. You are the Queen.

Cinderella: Slave, Drudge, or Queen?

Cinderella has been the quintessential Prince Charming story for many of us. In viewing Cinderella from the she-needed-to-be-rescued model, she could be perceived as a misplaced, unappreciated girl who had been destined to a difficult life. With such a mindset, the Prince would be her only hope for salvation and happiness. Iona and Peter

Opie, however, make an interesting point in *The Classic Fairy Tales*:

> Cinderella is not an ordinary girl being scrubbed clean, dressed sumptuously, and endowed with virtues before being conveyed to a gathering of her social superiors. Her story is not one of rags to riches, or of dreams come true, but of reality made evident. Despite her menial position in the opening scene—a position she accepts with dignity and good humor—Cinderella is a woman of "unparalleled goodness," who accepts her lot with dignity and grace...no fairy godmother was required to make her beautiful. Her clothes only, not her features, are transformed by the magic wand; her feet do not become large after midnight; and the courtier who comes from the palace searching for the unidentified guest recognizes her beauty despite the shabbiness of her attire, and urges she should be allowed to try on the glass slipper...The magic in this tale lies in creatures being shown to be what they really are."

In viewing our heroine from the lens of "unparalleled goodness" and accepting her "lot with dignity and grace," we can expand the story to better serve our emerging Queen consciousness. Cinderella continually brought forward the love from the core of her being to stabilize the circumstances of her external existence. Her loving nature had already provided salvation long before the Prince ever got there. It would not be necessary for her to go elsewhere to obtain love, for she was aware of never having been separate from love in the first place. It might be argued that she was actually quite content with her life and had few, if any, complaints or expectations for the future.

Cinderella took responsibility for her life and did not pollute her own personal glory with any sense of negativity. She made a decision to stay anchored in authenticity, avoiding the resistance to conditions she did not believe herself capable of changing. She accepted her circumstances with a quiet dignity. The chaos of her surface world did not disturb the internal glow of happiness, which she effortlessly maintained. Not unlike the Tibetan monk who thought the most critical danger he faced was losing compassion for his Chinese torturers, Cinderella sustained a constant state of forgiveness and pardon for her unconscious stepfamily. And from the radiant gift of love that she so lavishly shared without any expectation of what she might receive in return, Cinderella attracted glorious abundance beyond her most expanded imaginings. It all came to her because of her authentic, loving nature, which could not be disguised by her ragged attire or the menial position of cleaning cinders.

Queen Cinderella and a New Relationship Paradigm

In a relationship model where happiness (*not to be confused with immediate gratification or pleasure*) is the primary value, the Prince could be seen as a gift that Cinderella had not expected. Had he not shown up, she would have gone on to live her life contentedly. (Naturally, the same would be true for the Prince). He was a partner with whom she could experience an even grander version of herself. Their combined love and devotion would provide a new opportunity for growth, individually as well as a couple. They would come to know that their relationship was just one of a multitude of choices for developing their personal and collective talents and treasures.

Cinderella and Prince Charming would have a chance to open to more glorious versions of themselves moment to moment, both as individuals and as partners, by contributing to each other's strengths. "Happily ever after," however, *is not guaranteed* in this new version of the story, where freedom is the foundation of the relationship. In such a paradigm, happiness *moment to moment* (Happily Ever After …

Right Now) is the key. Their love and growth would be a daily process of choice, compassion, truth, and *free will*, where they would be replicating the divine example as described by spiritual author Neale Donald Walsch, "In loving you, I want your will for you." They might see themselves on a common journey toward growth and expansion in *this* moment, but later would belong to the mysterious unknown.

Most everyone resists the idea of being alone, which can trigger our primal fears related to abandonment. Yet if Prince Charming and Cinderella could sustain a degree of conscious awareness, they would know on some level that ultimate separation through death or dissolution would be inevitable. If Cinderella happened to be the one alone again, she would likely go through some periods of normal grief and bereavement. And yet, assuming she maintained her autonomy and individuation in the relationship, her transition into becoming "single" could actually be seamless. She doesn't have to create dramas or go into self-pity and blame, but instead can look upon all that has happened as a foundation for her ongoing growth and continued contributions to the world. As she moves through challenges and changes, she has the opportunity to be directed by new passions and inspirations to which she may have been awakened as a result of this recent experience. She can keep opening her heart and then melt into grander and more glorious ways of being, involving new projects and people. The possibilities are endless.

We Can Be Our Own Fairy Godmothers

You don't need to wait for a fairy godmother to bestow surprising and wonderful gifts on you. Instead, become one yourself. How? Show up. Bring balance to the masculine and feminine aspects of your nature. Have faith and charity of heart. Follow your insights. Bring forward your passions. Become that which you seek from another. Emanate love and happiness from the core of your being. *Herein lies the basic view from which all successful relationships can develop: I do not need you, but rather I choose you, so that I can contribute to your growth, and you to mine.* From this lens comes the most stunning opportunity for magical *Majesty* to unfold in your world. You will continue to discover that the Universe loves you, serves you, and wants you to experience abundance. Unburden yourself. There is enough. Enough men, enough women, enough money, *enough of everything.* Would God want that which S/He created to lose? The *only* interruption toward the awakening of your full glory is your own *belief* that it cannot be so.

New Stories, New Enchantments

As we become more and more willing to be completely transparent in *all* of our relationships, the more freedom we will have for unlimited growth. And, in our willingness to be totally open and honest, we provide the space for others to choose clarity and integrity for themselves. When speaking and living the truth without being concerned about others leaving when we do, the more people are inclined to stick around. They are attracted to our authenticity and openness. It is fresh and alive. It works. When we stand tall to face the stark, screeching terror of abandonment, we create an opening to remember that divine love can provide the only rescue. It is from this reality that we can connect and harmonize with the essential security that is always available. I am safe. I am home. *I am free.*

One way to practice overcoming fear is to offer Tonglen (sending and receiving prayer), which Buddhist nun Pema Chodron details in her book, *When Things Fall Apart.* The purpose of this activity is to awaken and open your heart, noticing when you are feeling pain or beginning to suffer. Instead of breathing out your pain and trying to get rid of it like a hot potato, you first acknowledge all others in the world, who feel distress right along with you. You realize that you are connected to these others. Now you ask and give thanks not only for your own transformation, but for everyone else who suffers, as well. As you *breathe out* healing, love, and light to all, watch the steady transformation in yourself and in your surroundings.

Claim your Majesty. Be the Queen.

❧ EXERCISE ❧

Start a gratitude list in your journal for transcendence. Use phrases such as "I am grateful for my senses, for my eyes, ears, and taste." Extend the list as long as you are willing. Add to it each day—especially whenever you are tempted to feel like a victim, villain, or rescuer. See yourself instead as the powerful Queen you are—grateful, capable, loving, and free.

FOUR

SOVEREIGNTY—
STOP LOOKING FOR ANSWERS
OUTSIDE YOURSELF

Jewel: Sapphire for Focusing and Calming the Mind

"Beware of mirages. Do not run or fly away in order to get free; rather dig in the narrow place within you; you will find God there and everything; God does not float on your horizon, [S/ He] sleeps in your substance. Vanity runs, love digs. If you fly away from yourself, your prison will run with you and will close in because of the wind of your flight; if you go deep into yourself you will disappear in paradise."

—Gustave Thibon

How is it that we have often come to be fixated on a love object rather than concentrating on the development of our own *Sovereign*, loving nature? What will it take for us to embrace the true spirit of love in a way that causes us to be free, powerful, compassionate, joyful beings? In amplifying the love within our own hearts, it will eventually overflow and attract resonate souls. As we let go of the need to get something from someone or somewhere else, we realize how much we already have. And the others in our lives can contribute to our growth and expansion as we simultaneously contribute to theirs. This is real love. This is how to operate from the heart. Any preoccupation with first seeking love *outside* before growing it within ourselves is actually *anti*-love and *anti*-growth.

A Course in Miracles offers an exquisite explanation of some important aspects of *true* love: "... it does not seek power because it is power. It does not search for freedom because it is already free." Instead of embracing the laws of freedom and growth inherent in love, we sometimes define love as the feeling that "inspires" us to become fiercely attached to one another. This kind of "love" wants to receive rather than to extend. It wants to accept rather than to give. It feeds dependency rather than interdependence, and it fosters immaturity rather than growth. It operates out of fear by attempting to constrict and limit, rather than offering more, freedom and liberation. It seeks to focus only on sustaining the sparks of pleasure and passion in the initial stages of affection, which will inevitably fade and fizzle (how dearly many of us have paid to learn this powerful lesson).

True love has nothing to do with the hit of ecstasy and bliss common to the beginning phases of romance. Nonetheless, this idealistic period offers the possibility for a deepening connection that does have the *potential* to evolve into love. But unless this romance is tended and developed from a place of desired growth and care for each individual involved (What can I give? What will you give to help us grow, individually and as partners/a couple?), it is only a temporary solution to an eternal quest. The late Scott Peck, in his legendary book *The Road Less Traveled*, defines love as "... the will to extend one's self for the purpose of nurturing one's own [and] or another's spiritual growth ... and we are incapable of loving another unless *we love ourselves*, unless we are nurturing our own spiritual growth."

When we limit the possibilities for love and expansion, we are like the creatures who swim the seas and believe the world is confined by their water-home. Similarly, when operating from our fear-based egos, we perpetuate the illusion that our physical bodies are restricted to an earthbound existence. Limited by human scripts and shortsighted beliefs, we feel compelled to solve the riddle of longing that continues to tug at our souls by attempting to focus on a love object, rather than being our own objective to love. What we eventually come to learn from our repeated failures at forcing false solutions is that the powerful passions that churn in our souls and long to be born cannot be developed unless we are willing to chip away at the hardened layers of dread and doubt that drive our need-based behaviors and keep us stuck in patterns that do not work. Once we can excavate these passions by getting out of our own way, we then can allow our true, creative nature to emerge and *become* the way.

So, what are the characteristics of this creative, passionate woman? How will I recognize her when she appears? Here are some guidelines:

> *She is the stability in me who lives in a state of potent, peaceful awareness.*
>
> *She embraces the mystery and allows the flow of life to carry her.*
>
> *She does not use effort or force to bring about results.*
>
> *She embodies a state of peace, regardless of what goes on in her external world. She does not listen to the voice of fear.*
>
> *She lives moment to moment fully awake and present with whatever is happening now.*

What will cause this woman in me to steadily make her *Sovereign* presence fully known? As we lift the veil that has separated her from our awareness for centuries upon centuries, let us do so with patience and persistence, for our fear-based habits have an extremely long and powerful history. We know she is there. We have felt her. She is not far away. So let us review some of the barriers that have prevented her from fully revealing herself through the ages and gain a more practical understanding of why we are tempted to look outside of ourselves for the answers while keeping our true spirit submerged.

The Brute and the Babe

Our ancestors, who we will call the Brute and the Babe, evolved during a time of hardship and turmoil. They were constantly stalked by scary creatures and faced long freezes and ferocious flooding. Living lives of near intolerable adversity for thousands upon thousands of years conditioned the human brain to expect catastrophe and disaster. The Brute and the Babe were completely reliant on each other. They started the whole dependency dance based on an instinctive drive to survive. Their entire existence revolved around how to connect with what would keep them alive. The Babe needed the Brute for providing food and shelter and to protect her from the dangers of the rugged, ancient world. The Brute, on the other hand, needed the Babe to keep the campfires going, satiate his sexual urges, and to procreate. Often, women would mate with numerous Brutes, multiplying the chance for survival, both for themselves and for their children.

The Babe was focused on how to avoid perishing *all of the time*. She was absolutely dependent on the Brute to make it through the daily hazards of her wicked, untamed environment. *He* was the only element that stood between her and the big, bad saber-toothed tigers that were going to eat her alive. Therefore, her best bet for avoiding certain demise was to seek out the strongest and most virile chap of the lot. Why in heaven's name wouldn't she want to hook up with her ancient version of Prince Charming? Can you see where our desire to snag the Prince and our tendency toward negativity and pessimism originates?

The dance of the Brute and the Babe has maintained a powerful rhythm throughout the eons. In fact, this dance continues into the present. We are still largely operating from a need-based, fear-oriented perspective. Of course, we are significantly more sophisticated than our ancient ancestors, but the remnants of our instinct to stay alive and the fears that emerge around the issue of survival continue to have strong influence over our thoughts, words, actions, and behaviors.

The Illusion of Separation

When influenced by ancient history, our worldly perspective can be skewed and single focused. The catastrophic brain *did* work in the ancient world. However, we don't need it in the same way that we used to. So, it is time that we come into balance with our expanding consciousness. This awakened consciousness is the only tool that *will* serve to guide us in the right direction. When we view ourselves as separate, disconnected, and incomplete beings, we are seeing through the lens of the old, rugged brain, which can overrule our awareness of the Divine roots that we all share. In this state of amnesia, we are tempted to seek external solutions for situations we may view as potentially disastrous. When we believe we have finally found the answer, often in another person, place, or thing, we want to cling. Our catastrophic brain kicks in to remind us of the possibility of pending calamity and tries to trick us into attaching ourselves to someone or something for salvation. Ah, but somewhere in our heart we know this method will never satisfy the deepest longing in our soul. Most of us have already learned that the cycle of seeking to be saved and then finding and attempting to snag the savior will always result in the emptiness that we are so desperately attempting to avoid. When we listen to the lingering messages of the Brute and the Babe, we severely restrict our chances for true happiness and peace.

The Salvation Story

The outward search has been reinforced by the fall/redemption paradigm, which has a foundation in religious theology. In this story, the only means for salvation exists in a savior who will rescue you from your originally sinful nature. He is eternally good. And you are eternally bad, unless He liberates you from your evil ways, which were inherited from your fallen ancestors, who made choices over which you had no control. The message in this myth is rooted in the interpretation of religious doctrine, and, according to Eckhart Tolle, this dogma has shrouded the true spiritual messages of the masters with superfluous material that is likely based in a different agenda than the avatars originally intended.

For example, Jesus Christ was not a theologian or a businessman. He was an enlightened soul who volunteered to be a human servant and model for us a way to live our lives without limitation. He brilliantly shared the formula for freedom and joy by showing us how to take responsibility for ourselves, while remembering that we are not separate from our brothers and sisters. He was a living demonstration of how to operate from a place of compassion, love, and justice while teaching that, as we emanate love, the natural result will be love's bountiful return from all directions. This is the simple and profound prescription for peace and happiness with which He so generously endowed humanity.

Did Jesus die for the purpose of taking on the collective karma of "evil" for the entire human race? Or did He "die" to be a living demonstration of eternal life so that we, too, would understand the powerful nature of love and compassion? When Christ asked God to forgive the unconscionable crimes ("sins") that were committed against Him, He paved the way for a new age. He laid the foundation for the future that we are living right now. Those of us who see the possibility for Heaven on earth must carry the torch for Him and the others who gave their lives for a similar cause. And as we do, one by one we will alchemize the centuries of darkness and separation into the dawning of the golden age of love.

Philosopher Matthew Fox has devoted his life's work to helping us embrace the teachings of the mystics and masters who shared the inclusive belief that we are all part of God and therefore, opening to our joyful, happy nature is a natural process. And, as mentioned earlier, having a love affair with the self is the impetus from which all loving and balanced relationships emerge.

As we move from a state of fear (operating on instinct) to a state of love (operating on our developing insights), we will be more focused on resurrecting the Godself and letting go of the need to crucify and condemn ourselves and others. If we cannot be separate from the Divine Presence that "sleeps in our substance," then there is nothing from which we need to be saved, after all. *Deliverance is our birthright.* Therefore, accessing happiness is an *internal* process. We are all born from the same Creative Life Force, and thus have the capacity to be with (and in) Divine Communion with that which brought us into being. Therein lies our peace, love, and eternal joy.

Old Stories, Old Behaviors

Is it possible that the *archetype of need* has been conditioned and etched into the trenches of our consciousness from the start of our existence? Even though we live in the twenty-first century, we are still influenced by our primal origins. As noted earlier, renowned psychiatrist Carl Gustav Jung was a powerful pathfinder with his careful examination of the mazes of stories that appear to run our lives. He believed that archetypes—those energetically imprinted ideas etched into our individual and collective consciousness—have a direct impact on our day-to-day lives. Beginning in the deepest archives of our ancestry, they continue to unfold as we gather stories and ideas about who we think we are and what it is that we believe we are supposed to be doing while traveling this adventuresome journey together on Planet Earth. These become imprints (as tagged by Sheldrake), generally known as myths. One myth that has endured since the time of the Brute and the Babe is this: *A woman should spend her time seeking and finding the perfect Prince Charming to protect and take care of her. When (and only when) she does, and succeeds according to those rules, everything will be okay.*

Could it be that, despite our advances over time, the predominant female prototype is based on insufficiency and dependency—on women needing to partner in order to survive? If so, no wonder we are traveling in unknown territory when we attempt to individuate from these outdated thought forms. This is what we are up against: powerful ancient beliefs that lurk in the shadows of our minds, like trolls or monsters. They are as dangerous as any wicked witch, cruel stepmother, or disgruntled fairy. It's time to diminish their hold over us and invite new and more powerful ideas to inspire and guide us.

Our Popular Culture

The fear and insecurity provoked by primal messages organically embedded in our DNA is still screaming to be heard. These tendencies are grimly played out in defensive struggles and wars between couples, families, communities, and nations.

Change is challenging, particularly considering the overpowering pressure from our culture, which continually besieges us with strict standards and stories of acceptable, preferred behavior. It would appear that we are all under one huge spell that influences us to choose the comfortable status quo of societal scripts rather than move into the mysterious, where the only *true* comfort exists.

Has there ever been a time in your life when you have yearned for refuge in the mystical unknown? If you have even had the slightest inclination toward such a desire, congratulate yourself. (If not, be open to simply entertaining the idea.) In following the unfamiliar, you will definitely be on the cutting edge of a much needed and long overdue change in consciousness for yourself (not to mention the entire human race). As we make friends with the mystery of possibilities that extend beyond our most favorable imagination, we begin to understand that the comfort we seek does not exist in a world constricted by our mind-based fears. True eternal safety is ever available to us if we are willing to open the door to the expanded potential that awaits us (while having the courage to dive into the dark abyss of the bountiful unknown). It is here that the opportunities for our illumination and expansion are birthed. And, when we are ready to open the magical portal to the unfamiliar, our fears will be alchemized into the true gold that creates the foundation for eternal bliss and joy, where any illusion of scarcity will forever fade away.

Popular culture teaches us to place limitations on how we become connected to others, whether it is to a partner, a friend, or a family member. It tells us that we need to be right, to have it our way, and *on our terms*. Society also tells us that we need *control* because the use of *power over* something or someone is our method for assuring safety and ultimate survival. When we operate from this mindset, we want to be attached, and we want the attachment to last *forever*. We don't want to let go, because we are *afraid of being alone*. We don't want to be in the dark for a single minute (such an attitude definitely prevents us from diving down into the mystery—too dim—too scary). And so we continue to fiercely seek whatever it is that we think we might be able to find in order to avoid the dark and lonely times. In such a state, we forget that the opposite of a peaceful state means giving in to the grinding drive for a permanent safety zone. If we are continually seeking that which we think will make us secure, we can never relax into the comfort and safety that is already a sure thing: the Essence that is our true Ultimate Ground from which we have never been separated.

Changing Our Minds

We now have the opportunity to expand from the constrictions of a need-based, primitive paradigm and move full throttle ahead into our *thriving* mode. Don't we get that it is no longer necessary to live with pessimism and vigilance? Aren't we sick of the internal monster (catastrophic brain) that constantly stalks us and tries to prevent our expansion and growth? We absolutely *can* recognize the difference between operating out of *love* (we are passionate, safe, secure, happy, compassionate, and connected) and operating out of *fear and lack* (we are separate from love and we must seek to find salvation elsewhere while being constantly vigilant for threat and danger). In opening to our natural state of love, we can easily harness our passions and strengths for guidance and support. When we allow our panic and fear to shroud that love, we can't remember how to do that.

Transforming our old belief systems starts with a decision, one person, one relationship, at a time. The human spirit has repeatedly proven its unlimited capacity for growth and change. If you doubt such a possibility, imagine yourself having a conversation with Mahatma Gandhi, Oprah Winfrey, Martin Luther King, Helen Keller, Mother Teresa, or Abraham Lincoln. Take Gandhi, for example. He was an ordinary man, who as a child was considered extraordinarily shy. Nonetheless, his spirit and sensibility guided him to follow the wisdom of his heart in an unprecedented search for truth and integrity. By allowing himself to be guided from the inspirations, which continued to spark his unfailing spirit, he facilitated freedom from foreign subjection for a fifth of the human race. Gandhi did not listen to the voice of fear.

We must continue to use all means known to us (and keep discovering new ones) for overcoming the powerful messages from our past that continue to live in us today, in the form of our fears and insecurities. It is time to create a different way of seeing the world, like

Mahatma Gandhi, who restored justice to millions by opening his heart. He was a living demonstration of wisdom, truth, love, honor, and compassion. He responded to violence with nonviolence; hatred with love; defensiveness with non-defensiveness; righteousness with passion; hypocrisy with integrity; and judgment with consideration. He was an ordinary man with an extraordinary vision. Imagine what would happen if the entire human race followed his example.

Isn't it time that we leave behind the thought forms etched in the dark trenches of our primal consciousness that dictate our impulses to fight-flight-fear-struggle-seek-survive? Wouldn't we be so much more peaceful, free, and loving if we could realize that nothing is *required,* other than honest and sincere commitment to change, to obtain the sense of happiness, fulfillment, and well-being that we perceive is always just out of our reach?

We can change our mind about who we really are. In letting go of the myths that no longer serve our growth, not only do we ourselves benefit, but we also help humankind as a whole. For example, just a little over two generations ago, most Americans considered segregation to be a normal fact of life (even if they personally objected). When a few brave souls dared to challenge the accepted cultural view, and their philosophies began to gain momentum and clout, society and the story of segregation took a new turn. Our shared consciousness morphed into a different ideology, which included racial interaction and integration. Those of us who were alive at the time were witness to this immense and monumental change. What will it take for us to quit segregating our happiness from ourselves by continuing to look for it on the outside? How can we individually contribute to changing the collective belief system of what it means to be happy and how that condition is discovered?

Happiness can only evade us if we are searching for it in the wrong places. Once we are willing to dive toward the ever-open branches of our heart, the singing bird will come and show us how to soar.

And when we get quiet enough to listen to her sweet song, we will be effortlessly guided toward all of the mysterious, exotic destinations that will fill our hearts with more joy than we ever thought possible. All we have to do is be willing to embark on the journey to *Always Land*. It has been there all along, inside of us, waiting to be discovered. Let us go there now and leave *Never Land* behind, forever.

What You Are Seeking Already Exists in Your Inner World

When we focus on and trust our insights and inspirations (which are the voices that guide us to fulfilling our passions and dreams), the urgent need to obtain security in the other or outside of us will begin to melt away and eventually disappear. Widows who have learned to become dependent on their husbands, for example, often discover a multitude of inner strength, courage, and wisdom following the death of their spouse. The same is true of women who have broken up with their partners. As they move through the stages of grief, they are frequently astounded by the sense of power and delight that accompanies the process of developing their independence.

Sara made some important discoveries about herself while spending almost an entire year without a significant other. Even though she missed having a boyfriend at times, she realized that there were aspects about being single that brought her absolute joy. Her discoveries included learning about her dining preferences, what movies she liked, and when she wanted to stay home to enjoy a quiet evening alone. A few months into the experience, she began to notice a sense of fulfillment and joy that was unprecedented in her life. During this time frame, her career soared, and several friendships with both women and men flourished. When she started a relationship with Tim, whom she now describes as "the love of her life," she was ready to meet him with her own ideas, strengths, and hopes.

While single, Sara had chosen to create a rich, full life for herself and was then prepared to start a relationship with someone who could complement her discoveries and share the happiness she was already experiencing. She recently commented, "I really unraveled some of my narrow views on what I thought it took to be happy, like thinking that it was impossible without a boyfriend. Eventually, I stopped waiting for someone else to complete me. That is when Tim showed up. Now, I am becoming more whole day-by-day, and even though I love and adore Tim, I know that he is not the answer to my happiness. I am."

Unity Minister Susan Burnett-Hampson tells of a significant break-up she went through before meeting her husband, Stan. "I had strong feelings for this man, and as we were parting, I realized that, *the love is in me. It is mine. It will go with me. And this will attract a similarly high level of love.* It may sound obvious, but the message this time was more profound. I really got it." Susan's connection and subsequent loss helped her to realize that *she* was the source of true love. That love moved within her, wherever she was. Eventually, she took that love with her into a happy and fulfilling marriage to Stan.

In recognizing that the buck stops with us and that there is no one to blame for feelings of despair or credit with our happiness (*except ourselves*), we are creating the true foundation for lasting joy. Instead of focusing on what we can get somewhere else, or who we can blame if it doesn't happen, let us be willing to become immersed in the delight of our own being. When we decide to do so, no longer are we bothered with the fading fears and outdated messages of need and want. Eventually, our Queen Essence will emerge as our only reality, and we will then be emancipated from the prison of lack and insufficiency.

Our Ticket to Happiness, Here, Now

No one else has the capacity to give us what we want. And when we finally hit the tipping point that helps us to make that connection, the quintessential theme of our life will become a burning desire to pursue our unlimited potential through the expression of our emerging gifts and talents. This quest is the fuel that drives us toward the state of enduring happiness. Classic dancer and choreographer Martha Graham called it "a vitality, a life force, a quickening that is translated through you into action." She described its inspiration as "a blessed unrest that keeps us marching and makes us more alive than the others." By accepting the invitation to be "more alive," we are exposing ourselves to cosmic possibilities. And, everything that will assist us as we keep the channel open *will* show up.

We now (and always) have the opportunity to expand from the primal messages and primitive archetypes that have kept us constricted, closed down, and mired in our individual and combined relationship struggles. Whether seen through the lens of couples, families, friends, communities, or nations, we have all been challenged under the current relationship paradigm, which has its foundation in our primordial instincts based on need, want, fear, force, control, and survival.

In recognizing the driving force behind our fears, we can move to take the necessary measures for change. Brother Brute and Sister Babe are old news. Once we become aware of the patterns that they established, we can more carefully begin to notice when we are operating on our conditioned imprints and move beyond our crude, ancient beginnings—creating the possibility for "morphically resonating" into a new way of being.

The Dance of Interdependence

Even though this highly individualized process of gaining our *Sovereignty* starts with the personal, we cannot ignore the reality that we are social beings. Therefore, we must allow ourselves to be *interdependent* with those who will assist us along the way and whom we will help in kind. While in the process, let us make certain that we are keenly aware of the difference between *dependence* (no one takes responsibility) and *interdependence* (everyone takes responsibility). Such an understanding is vital because without it we can't know when we are falling into patterns of attachment or addiction.

We have all emerged into this life-form to *become more fully ourselves*—to discover the Queens that we truly are. That is it. That is all. And as we open to our *Sovereignty,* we begin to learn the skill of partnering with fellow travelers on a similar quest. They serve as our companions and guides. We do not need them for this journey, but they enhance our voyage exponentially.

It is time for us to let go of the stories and myths that keep us stuck in our ancient reality and create a new twist on the "rules of relationships." There need be no games, no worries about if he will call, if he is into you or not, or if there could be a happily ever after with him. For as we continue to realize that *he* is not the thing we really need in order to survive and be happy, we can relax and allow him to join us in our ongoing journey toward uncovering the essence and truth of who we really are. That means no games, and no manipulating for the purpose of getting our own way. We don't have to keep him guessing, so he can have his fun with "the hunt" (like in the days of the Brute) because we realize that we don't want to play that game anymore or enable him to be a part of such a folly. We have lost the inclination to live a faux life. *We are beyond it.* We have chosen to let go of any identification with the Babe and to bring forward our true, royal Queenly nature. Put on your ruby, red slippers, girlfriends. And I don't mean the glass variety. This is *your* ball, baby, and you are the one to create the invitation list. King, Prince, or Brute? Who is the *true* match for your glorious, golden, *Sovereign*-self?

New Stories, New Enchantments

All of life is interdependent, though the attainment of happiness is an organic process that starts inside each one of us. From there, happiness expands in all directions to enrich and benefit the world. It continues to multiply and grow, connecting with other souls, who send it back to us. Once we receive it, we immediately let go and then offer it up again. This abundance of happiness keeps exploding in an ever-infinite circle of delight. There is no end to the peace, joy, and love that starts from within.

As we go forward in the direction of all that aches in our hearts to be shared, we will not be denied. The entire Universe will conspire to help us realize that which we are passionate to birth into the world.

Our Queenly spirits are calling us up. They are telling us that we are meant to fly, and as we connect to our *Sovereignty*, we absolutely know that without any doubt, we do have wings to support us. We were meant to live in a permanent, Heavenly state, here, now. Any thought that does not support such a Divine and blessed destiny must now be extinguished.

❧ EXERCISE ☙

A New Vision

Imagine yourself as a powerful woman in her most Sovereign state. This is the person you want to birth into being. She is living inside of you right now. Bring her forward and watch in amazement as your world shifts dramatically in your favor. You have chosen power instead of force. You are prevailing and in charge. You make the final decisions that affect your life, and you ultimately accept the consequences for the outcome of those choices, regardless of how they might be perceived by others: good, bad, happy or sad, it makes no difference to you. In your wise state of being you know the way. No one else has to be convinced. You will follow the only voice that will guide you toward the truth—no matter what. And underneath it all, you have a profound sense of peace and happiness, right now.

Decide that at this very moment you are being completely released from the inherited collective mind patterns that have kept you stuck in the false illusion of lack and insufficiency. Go deeply toward the Dark Void of inner knowing. Let go of the external chatter and connect to the deep, unshakable peace that lies within.

Visualize a powerful energy emerging from the base of your spine. Imagine it circulating through your heart and mind as it pulses and extends outward from your core in a circular motion. See it filled with love, compassion, and the power to heal the world. As it swells, watch it expand into the Universe. It now influences the entire cosmos with peace, liberation, health, and eternal happiness. Now, imagine that this powerful energy attracts into your life prosperity, health, loving, whole relationships, happiness, and peace beyond your most dazzling expectations.

You are that powerful. You are that grand. You are Sovereign over your life.

FIVE

POWER—
GIVE UP YOUR ADDICTION
TO LOVE

Jewel: Amethyst for Love and Spiritual Power

"Addiction is the number one problem of our civilization. Without it, our human potential is limitless."

—*Deepak Chopra*

In the primal sense, which is still alive and well, man is all about the hunt and the chase. And woman is all about being saved. If her fears take her over the edge and cause *her* to do the hunting, the subject of her chase will most likely choose to retreat. Instinctively, he does not want to be caught, or to be responsible for saving anything. He wants to be free, and actually, so does she. By reverting to primitive methods for attaining that freedom, the idea of insufficiency, need, and dependency is re-enforced, perpetuating the drama of the Brute and Babe (our ancient ancestors).

It is time to end the pain/pleasure cycle that began centuries ago. By moving fully into our internal *Power* we will naturally invoke all that will open us to the grandest version of ourselves, where the need for comfort and security will eventually fall away. We must quit reinforcing the lingering, haunting messages from our prehistoric past. By refusing to give this ancient babble any authority over our lives, eventually these old, outdated thoughts and beliefs will disappear and we will be free to move forward into our most expanded and unlimited potential. At the moment, many of us are only using a very limited amount of this vast reservoir of possibilities.

When you are fully operating from a foundation of *Power*, you are not concerned with chasing or hunting anything. You have a fundamental sense of abundance instead of insufficiency. You have developed an inner awareness that automatically kicks in to remind you that you are safe whenever feelings of fear emerge. You spend your time concentrating on what you can offer and create rather than what you can grab or get. Many of us have caught glimpses of this powerful state. You now have a choice to use all of the tools that will help you sustain that way of being for more than a fleeting moment. You want to create a life that will support your peace, happiness, and well-being, so that you don't have to go looking for it anymore. It *can* be done. But first, you have to be able to notice even the most subtle behaviors that keep you from operating from your own central base of *Power*.

About Addiction

To be addicted means to be driven by a habit over which you have lost control. In other words, the habit now controls your behavior. Addictive behavior is not discriminatory. You can be addicted to a substance, a person, a place, or a thing. You can even be addicted to a habit, an attitude, or a point of view. Anything that controls your life because you have become obsessed with getting it, keeping it, or repeating it is an addiction. Becoming attached and eventually addicted to that which you believe is going to make you feel better (save you) is a substitute for soul-growth. And, there are no stand-ins for growing the soul. So, when you attempt to use one (or more) you will suffer. And, the suffering is a signal for you to stop doing what you are doing. When you don't listen, you will stay stuck in the cycle of pain/pleasure. If, when pain occurs, you automatically jump on the fast track to the "fix"—whatever it is—you know you are hooked. And if you keep repeating this behavior, eventually you will spiral into a nightmare of never-ending misery, where the pleasure part becomes a distant memory, ever out of reach and no longer attainable. *And*, you don't have to go there. *Ever.* Instead, become more intimate with who *you* are—even if it is inch by inch. How? Stop long enough to listen to your heart. It will guide you if you pay attention.

The soul's longing to know itself through its physical, earthly experience (the reason for our existence) is frequently misunderstood. When we are influenced by ancient conditioning, our fears and insecurities will take over and deceive us into believing that the longing we frequently experience is about finding salvation and happiness through people and things that exist in our local, external reality. When these outside circumstances and events bring temporary relief from the longing, we can convince ourselves that we have found the formula for freedom, happiness, salvation, and lasting contentment. We feel good now, and we want to continue feeling good. So we keep attempting to sustain the euphoria by attaching ourselves to the person, the place, the circumstance, or the event that we think is the source of our salvation. And, if we keep tying our happiness to these externalities, we become attached and eventually addicted.

It is irrelevant whether we think it is a drug, a romance, or something else that will satisfy the tug at our souls. What is important to note is that these surrogate solutions for liberation are *always temporary*. Eventually, the ever-lurking low will jump out, grab us, and rob us of our bliss. And, of course, this dreaded event is what we most fear and thus want to avoid at any cost. So we keep knocking on the same door again and again. And, who is the repeated respondent? The sticky seduction that sucks us back into the cycle of chasing after the external pleasure/s that will briefly numb our discontent. This pattern is what addiction is all about.

There is no stand-in for the true path to peace. It is a journey toward a non-local, ever-present field of infinite possibilities, more expansive than we can imagine. Ironically, peace can only come to us through our willingness to detach ourselves from all that we believe we have to possess in order to obtain it. How exquisitely we design the human architecture that keeps us "safe" from an emotional meltdown/ explosion. We build skyscrapers around our hearts, closing off the true entry point to peace. We believe these stubborn structures will reduce the risk of loss or pain, and so we continue our external search for what we *think* will make us safe while keeping the true answer to the longing under lock and key. Fully engaged in our desperate search, we skim over the "hidden" source of happiness. Only it is not really hiding. We are.

In attempting to save or be saved by focusing on the outside, we have severely limited our chances for connecting to that which actually *will* offer genuine redemption. Ultimately, the true initiation into becoming fully powerful is to have the courage to admit the possibility of powerlessness (letting go of the need to control) and opening ourselves to real intimacy (the willingness to be completely vulnerable by letting go of the need to be attached). By allowing ourselves to go toward the deep abyss of darkness, we infinitely expand our chances for seeing the light. When we can finally quit being so white-knuckled and begin to loosen our grip, the Life Force within will be free to circulate again. As the blood returns to our veins, we wake up and realize that the Source of true strength is ever available to us. Now we are ready for the marathon.

We know we will be out of breath. We know we have the potential to fall. We know we will feel like quitting. We know there will come a time when we absolutely believe that we cannot take another step. Still, we must proceed. We approach and finally cross the finish line. Suddenly we forget all of the trials. The triumph is what matters. We see what we are made of when we just allow ourselves to extend a little over the edge of what we think is possible. *And so the secret to answering the heart's longing can only be accessed by going just a bit beyond what we know to be safe and secure.* By continuing to choose the "I think I can" attitude like in the classic childhood story of the *Little Engine That Could*, we create a natural opening for transformation. I know, it feels strange, and yet, dear hearts, unless we are at least willing to stick our toes into the pool of possibilities that await us, we will remain stuck in the proverbial cement on the edge—confined to mediocrity at best and downright disaster at worst. So, let us welcome the peculiar, even when we are petrified. In doing so, we exponentially enhance our chances of moving into *happily ever after ... right now*, where addictions and attachments will no longer be necessary to see us through.

The immediate gratification driven by pleasure-seeking, which is really the act of avoiding power and intimacy, will never bring us the happiness for which we so desperately desire. Once we finally begin to realize that we may never attain true salvation by pursuing it in the old, familiar way, we will open the portal to end our suffering for good. And if we can begin to quiet our minds long enough to pause in the nanoseconds between our spinning thoughts, we will actually begin to experience the silent voice that calls us to the inspirations guiding our soul's purpose here on this planet. It is in this gap that the seeds of our passions patiently wait to be tended, grown, and developed, and where the answer to all of the internal questions that have been churning in our hearts are resolved.

Peace and freedom begin when we actually become aware that what we long for can only be accessed by creatively discovering what is ours to bring forward in the world. We just have to be still long enough to "hear" all that patiently awaits our willingness to listen. *You know this.* You have had glimmers of awakening that tell you it is so. Catch these flutters (fleeting as they may be), discipline yourself to notice what they feel like, and go with them. For it is these moments that have the pure potential to take you to the only thing that is real in your life: the essence from the one field of ultimate potential that lives in you and lives in all of us.

For many, an addiction to drugs, alcohol, or "love" has become a crutch believed to bring happiness. We can be tempted to sell out by substituting something else for a truly joyful life. It is only in developing the potent power within that we will find true freedom. And yet we struggle with our fear-based conditioning, which screams at us to scatter when things get tricky and uncomfortable. We want an easy, quick way out. We don't want to endure the perceived grit and grind of going toward the true self by chiseling away at the layers of conditioning that have kept us locked in fear and limitation. So, we unconsciously sabotage progress by adhering to old patterns which, of course, only means that we create more despair and desolation. And, the longer we remain stuck in our old ways, the more likely we are to favor helplessness and dependency over helpfulness and interdependency. We have forgotten where our true safety lies, but why? Why do we make it so hard to claim the happiness that is our birthright? At this point, it may be useful to continue looking at what has influenced us to keep ourselves from sticking our toe in the proverbial water, let alone actually jumping in.

The precedent set by the Brute and the Babe is not the only force that lures us into favoring our instincts (body) over our insights (soul). Consider our neighbors in the animal kingdom, whose behaviors are based purely on instinct. Their conduct is driven by a constant fear of getting killed or running out of food and water. They are territorial, completely resistant to change, and almost never choose to go beyond their conditioned behavior. They do not consider themselves free *or* constricted. Rather, they are preoccupied with the confines of a relentless hierarchy of power, a natural selection, which keeps them ever vigilant and constantly suspicious, negative, and ready to defend. Remaining intimate with the familiarity of their surroundings is their only hope for survival. In their natural habitat, wild animals are more likely to sense the threat of a perpetrator, and then have a better chance for outwitting their enemies. So, their entire existence is completely focused on the external threats to which they are constantly exposed.

Like our brothers and sisters in the wild, we don't want to walk into the lion's den. We, too, have a will to survive. And yet there are significant differences between us and these creatures. We have the gift of *awareness* that there is something beyond natural selection. It is this aspect of our being that we must find the courage to develop by making choices which take us forward, even if we sense the lion lurking (in whatever form it appears). If we don't choose now to follow the *true* voice that will guide us beyond danger, we will miss the point of our lives. It is time to jump in and swim.

Learned Helplessness

Operating out of the learned helplessness that originates from a fear-based reality is one example of missing the point. This type of dependency in its most extreme form can be observed in the predictable cycle of abuse that occurs in the relationships of "battered" women. Typically, in the developing phases of the connection, there is what appears to be a romantic period. The two "lovers" are inseparable (a dangerous sign). It is "love" at first sight (another dangerous sign). As the relationship progresses, the couple will inevitably show their individual and combined weaknesses. Instead of using this time to deepen the relationship, which is how real love begins, she becomes needy and dependent. He starts to squirm, wanting more freedom. She resists. He rages. And she becomes the target of his fury.

Eventually, he is remorseful and they experience a brief "honeymoon" period. She now believes that the abuse is over for good. It surely will never happen again. However, the underlying issues (fear and abandonment), which are pervasive in both, have not even been addressed, let alone resolved. Since neither of them wants to risk being left, which they believe will surely happen once they start examining what went wrong, they enjoy whatever time of deceptive bliss they can steal before the whole cycle of abuse starts all over again. Eventually, she has to go to a shelter for safety, he is arrested for domestic violence, or both.

Love Addicted, Love Avoidant

"Love addicts" dance to an unending drive for finding pleasure and safety. The illustration of the battered woman is a sobering example. Why would she stay in a relationship that is so damaging to her body, mind, and spirit? And yet, we may also be engaging in relationships that slam at our souls and hammer at our hearts. We just don't want to experience what we would have to go through to admit it. In her book *Facing Love Addiction*, love-addiction expert Pia Mellody indicates that "love addicts" appear to demonstrate predictable patterns of behavior which they act out in order to avoid abandonment. They seek a lover to "save" them from feeling lonely and therefore focus on this lover to provide pleasure and ultimate happiness.

Oddly, what the "love seeker" most often attracts is an "avoidance addict," or "distancer," who appears to be her polar opposite, though plagued with similar fears of abandonment. The "distancer" may seem extraordinarily attentive during the "romantic phase," but once they sense the pursuer's deepening connection, they begin to pull away. Alas, the "love addict" will do almost anything to keep the "beloved" and, in her attempts to restore the relationship, will further produce the disconnection they are hoping to avoid. Sooner or later, one or the other will take no more of the anguish and will choose to leave the relationship. Often it is the "love addict" who exits first, but only because they hope to find a "better" and "more fulfilling" relationship (or already has one lined up). Spending some time alone to look a little deeper at what might be going on is rarely a consideration. Can you see the ancient patterns of the hunter/chase/savior themes so alive and well here?

In the love/avoidance paradigm, both the "love seeker" and the "love distancer" are terrified of abandonment (their primal conditioning is screaming at them to avoid being left at all costs), yet on the surface, they act out their fears in very different ways. Nonetheless, each is attempting to keep from being left, and sadly, they almost always create a set-up for that to happen.

A "Love-Addict" Self-test

Mainstream "love" addiction is not as easy to spot, probably because it is so prevalent. It can be subtle and sneaky. Here are some frequent warning signs:

1. *You spend much of your time attempting to please your boyfriend, partner, or husband.* You worry more about what he wants than what you want. Often you don't even know what you want because you are always focused on him. Or you are constantly thinking about how to find a boyfriend, husband, or lover.

2. *You don't speak up because you worry about the consequences.* He wants to go and visit his parents for

two weeks, and this trip will serve as your summer vacation. His folks live in Gary, Indiana. You do not particularly enjoy his parents and Gary, Indiana, is the last place on the planet that you would ever *choose* to visit. However, instead of risking his disappointment and possible wrath, you go along with the program and secretly feel enormously resentful.

3. *You accept behavior from him that you would not extend.* This one is critically important. Here is a subtle, seemingly benign example: When it is your "together time," he sits in front of the TV for hours watching what *he* wants to see, never asking you for *your* preferences. Furthermore, he is constantly changing the channels, which drives you nuts, and he takes control of the changer, refusing to relinquish it. *You could never imagine yourself behaving this way, and yet, you don't speak up. Why?*

4. *You manipulate him to get what you want by using sex or other tantalizers.* Ask yourself what it is that stops you from being direct. What are you afraid of? What prevents you from speaking openly and honestly here?

5. *You manipulate him with guilt.* This is *major* projection, girlfriends. When you can't get your way by any other means except to try to make him feel guilty, you are setting yourself up to get it all blasted back in *your* face. Trying to somehow induce his guilt serves no purpose and will only perpetuate your misery. If you are dumping digs on him, there is most definitely something that you have not uncov-

ered in yourself that is bothering you. *Look deeply into your heart, find it, forgive it, and let it go.* If you don't, you will keep trying to make him wrong, so you don't have to look at your own stuff. *Take back your power, own what is yours, correct it, and go forward.*

6. *You play the part of martyr.* I am certain we would all agree that Joan of Arc served an important role in history by willingly sacrificing herself. However, it is not necessary for you to replicate her behavior in order to obtain the results you desire. *Lose the drama.* Simply learn to identify what is true for you and find ways to say it. It isn't that hard. *You can do it.* And, if you feel as if you are going to be burned at the stake for sharing what is in your heart, you better try to determine why in heaven's name you are still in this relationship.

7. *You don't want to be without a partner. You do not want to be alone. You will do anything to keep your boyfriend. You will do anything to find a boyfriend.* Please be aware of even the slightest thoughts you may entertain related to any part of the above. Remember, when we are not completely conscious of our actions and thoughts, the overpowering influences of our cultural and primal conditioning can take over. Start identifying unhealthy patterns that limit your choices and begin *now* to stop them. *You are ready. Go.*

If you can identify with any of the behaviors described in the self-test, it is time to take a look at how to re-program yourself. *Now.*

Reprogramming Ourselves—Planting a Healthy Seed

Letting go of lifelong habits involves introducing new thought forms to replace the old ones and learning how to make them stick. We all have the potential to begin our relationships from a healthy seed, but when it is neglected and left to rot, it cannot germinate and grow into its full and lasting potential. The endless cycle of "love"/loss repeats itself until or unless the participants individually and collectively become conscious of what is causing the decay.

Our addictions cannot be released until we recognize them as such—until we can admit to ourselves that what we are doing is a sure recipe for disaster. That is the first step. The next step is to change. Naturally, we will resist. *Any* transition can seem formidable (not to mention the idea of giving up an addiction), and yet the more dangerous position is to remain stuck in what does not serve our growth and expansion. Recognizing the self-defeating tendencies that result in misery and suffering is the task at hand. We *can* transcend these patterns. Let us die to these outdated, constricted ways of being, so that we can truly *live* the lives we are destined to enjoy. We owe it to ourselves and to our children to offer a new legacy of love.

When we expect someone or something to be "the answer" to all our needs, we overlook the fact that our authentic self can only emerge and be actualized through Divine access. No "thing," person, place, or event in the external world can provide a link to our unique, heavenly umbilical cord, which is the only connection to true and lasting happiness. This is an internal and blessed lifeline from which we have never been disconnected in the first place. We simply *have* to remember that when we are operating out of separation, we are forgetting our *raison d'être*: we were given the gift of life so that we could imagine ourselves into our unique *Magnificence*. We stand on the threshold of possibilities. We came here to create and bring forward something that humanity has not yet experienced. It can only happen through the vehicle that is *you*. Therefore, it is the responsibility of those of us who are willing to wake up, one by one, from our individual dream states and deliver what we came here to share. And the awakening into truly loving and being loved starts from within.

When you are having a bad dream and believe yourself to be chased by monsters, what is the quickest solution to your plight? One way is to stop, turn and face the monster, then watch as it melts away—like when the Wicked Witch of the West disintegrated in *The Wizard of Oz* as Dorothy faced her fears. Maybe a simpler approach is to just wake up and find yourself snuggled safely in your own bed. What will it take for us to jolt ourselves out of what we perceive to be the nightmare of our lives? We must begin by letting go of our tendencies to attach and cling, particularly to situations that are burdened with adversity and pain. Even so, it does take enormous courage to change the behaviors that have become so familiar to us. Somehow, we have convinced ourselves that the unfamiliar is more formidable than the formidable familiar.

Observing the behavior of children who are wards of the state because of abuse and/or neglect by their parents or primary caretakers provides a remarkable example of resistance to change. Frequently, if given a choice, these children would prefer to stay in environments of intolerable suffering rather than agree to be placed in a potentially loving, secure foster homes. The children's desire to choose abuse and neglect rather than to alter their environments shows how fear of the unknown influences our decisions and choices, especially when we feel threatened. (Recall that wild animals will also do anything to keep from having to change.) We are often more freaked out by the unknown than almost anything else, including predictable patterns of abuse and neglect. Even though it seems absurd that we would prefer cruelty and mistreatment (such as in the case of "battered women") to liberation and freedom, the fact is, we often do. These patterns are deeply conditioned in us. *And, we have the power to move beyond* the paradigm of fear-based behavior.

Examining Your Fear and Waking into Your Life

When your entire identity is invested in shielding and protecting yourself from the indeterminate future, you remain behind the curve of your life. What would it take to drop everything that keeps you bound to the story of fear? Is it possible that, if you let go of all that you think you need to protect yourself from harm's way, you might eventually emancipate yourself from your non-existent demons? When you pay attention, your *Powerful, Sovereign* nature comes to the fore, and you emerge to claim the full, radiant being that you are. Granted, it takes concentration and practice to shut off our individual and collective schizophrenia—to quiet the voices that are not our own. They are fierce, and they are loud. Nonetheless, when we claim our *Power*, no pathology can have *any* influence over us whatsoever. As we continue to identify with the one authentic voice that answers the call of our heart's true longing, the devils of fear and defeat retreat into the shadows and eventually evaporate.

The alternative to addiction, then, is to turn and face the monsters that stalk us, realize that they are frauds, and eventually watch them melt away for good. As we continue the practice of moving toward the things that scare us rather than retreating or running the other way, we will be released from the bondage of fear *forever*. And when we create these kinds of changes in ourselves, we are not only making our individual contribution—we are endowing all of humanity. The willingness to go courageously *into* the eye of the storm (our panic) when everything seems scary, strange, and unfamiliar—takes incredible courage. Nonetheless, the result is *transformational*. When we are willing to actually stand in the proverbial fire, the patterns that have kept us stuck and immobilized will continue to burn off and fade away until they eventually have no further influence over our lives. And then, like the phoenix, we will rise up from the ashes fully renovated and ready to take flight.

Radical Simplification

The Divine equipment for creating such a personal and collective renaissance resides within each one of us. How can you know if you are a part of this reawakening? If you are truly living and expanding your life, then there is nowhere else you want to be or need to go—other than here. When we are living someone else's dreams (as in "stand by" or "glom onto your man") while abandoning ourselves, we chase the tale of endless longing until we become dizzy and dumb, sell out, and stop short of tapping into our own unlimited potential. If we can move beyond this lightheaded, shaky state—just even a little by giving ourselves permission to go steadily forward in the direction of what *appears* to be the dark, dangerous waters that call us—then we are destined to uncover the glorious refuge that lurks in the mist. In moving toward our own Essence (from which we have only had the *illusion* of being separate), it will sparkle and shine us into the true fullness of who we really are.

Yes, we are young as a species, but perhaps we are ready to move out of our adolescence. This manic-depressive, bipolar way of being is a roller coaster ride. While we love the thrill of it, we also hate the jitters and jolts we experience along the way. Aren't we ready for a little more of what will stabilize this turbulence? Haven't we had one too many whip lashes? If so, we must be fiercely dedicated to whatever spiritual practice or path keeps us grounded to and aligned with truth and integrity. Again, this kind of commitment takes discipline, detachment, obedience, and surrender. Yet the journey doesn't have to be difficult. If we can muster the courage to claim our authenticity by noticing what no longer works, we will have taken the first step in diminishing the hold that our attachments and addictions appear to have over us. And then we have positioned ourselves to catapult into a more expanded, evolved state, not only contributing to our own well-being, but to the welfare of the entire planet. When we remember our Divine birthright, we can easily recognize that paradise is not some distant heaven up in the sky. It is here, now. All we have to do is be open to receiving it.

Some tools for launching the process are:

1. *Begin by knowing that it will take discipline and commitment to change. Then, commit yourself to change.*

2. *Find or continue the ability to obediently engage in the practices—meditation, affirmations, yoga, exercise, nutritional support and/or any other processes for conscious, awake living that you can muster.*

3. *If you believe you may have a tendency to be addicted to love, join or create a loving support group that concentrates on conscious awareness, or seek some counseling from a supportive, well-trained professional who specializes in issues related to growth, health, and wholeness. Then, be accountable to the group and/or your professional—but most of all to yourself.*

4. *Be willing to face your fears. Surrender the outcome to the One who permanently resides within you and who knows the way. Remember that you are never alone. You have a multitude of cheerleaders from both the seen and unseen world. Ask for help with a grateful heart, and then be willing to receive that support.*

5. *Realize that love (which is always birthed from within and has nothing to do with attaching to someone else) is the most potent form of power available to you. Remember these straightforward equations: true love = freedom and anti-love = attachment.*

6. *Be authentic. Be willing to claim and state your truth, secure in the significant loving presence that is YOU. Let go of your need to be in control. Become all powerful so that control is no longer necessary. Realize that when you break the cycle of addiction, you have launched yourself out of the suffering drama. You won't have a desire to relive the suffering story any longer. You will be more concerned with creativity and passion, letting go of what does not serve you, and releasing any need to make the past and all the players (including you) right or wrong. Just go forward and glean from your experiences what you can to make more meaning out of your life. Who you are will continue to enhance the lives of others. And of course, the gifts that you offer the world will repeatedly come back to you in infinite supply.*

Giving Up Control

As we become more and more willing to be completely transparent with who we are in *all* our relationships, the more freedom we have for unlimited growth. When speaking and living authentically without concern that someone is going to leave as soon as we reveal the truth, the more people are inclined to stick around. They are attracted to our courage. It is fresh and alive. It works. As we stand tall to face the stark terror that our conditioned fears of abandonment produce, we create an opening to remember that the love within our own hearts is the only certain rescue. It is from such a foundation that we can move to harmonize with the *essential* security of our lives. I am safe. I am home. I am here, now. I am enough.

Living the Questions

The progression of awakening to new and *powerful* ways of being is a process. There is no definitive entrance to the path, but rather a gradual opening accompanied by some occasional backslides and forward momentum. Any preoccupation with making strenuous efforts toward completion will often result in going off road, which can easily be recognized by the jumps and jolts experienced along the way. Getting back to a smooth, flat surface takes practice, but it can be done. Begin.

New Stories, New Enchantments

You are now invited to seat yourself at an imaginary round table. There will be five other individuals joining you.

1. *The first person is someone you are attracted to, they fascinate you. You feel compelled to get to know them better. Yet in your state of admiration there is something mysterious that makes you feel slightly unsafe, or, worse still, you feel "less than" in their presence at times. They sit beside you on your right. You feel a rush of enthusiasm or excitement, while at the same time experiencing some discomfort.*

2. *The second person to join you is someone who repels you. You can't stand this individual. Everything about*

them makes your skin crawl. You want them to leave or go away. This person sits to your left.

3. *Number three is someone with whom you feel a certain level of comfort and a sense of enjoyment. You like this person, but you are not compelled to constantly seek out their companionship. Your conversations are stimulating and the time that you share together is always enjoyable. You feel a balance and even a sense of peace in the relationship. You complement one another, and yet you don't have to be with this person to feel okay or happy. They sit beside person #1.*

4. *Number four is invisible. You don't really see this individual, recognize them, or even know who they are, and frankly, it doesn't really interest you to find out. They are seated beside person #2.*

5. *The last person to join you at the imaginary round table is of some interest to you, but you have little in common. They have a career in computer science, which you respect and admire, and live in NYC. You are an artist, living in Taos, New Mexico, and you really dislike even being exposed to a computer or to the East Coast. They sit beside person #4.*

All of the five individuals who make up this group have something in common. They are seated at your table. They have come into your life, and so they may be mirroring some aspect of who you are, or your behavior, which you now have the opportunity to see.

❧ EXERCISE ❧

Here are some questions you may want to ask them, or ask yourself:

Who are you? What have you come to teach me?

What can I do with this chance to look further into myself, my patterns, and the people who show up in my life? What does it feel like to have the person I am attracted to right next to me? And what is it like to have someone who repels me at my left? How will I maintain my integrity in the presence of threat— in the presence of someone who triggers certain responses/reactions/emotions in me and whom I vigorously resist? How will I stay centered when I am wooed by someone whom I know may not be good for me? What will help me to notice if I am tempted to become attached? What will I do when the invisible face comes forward and wants to chat? When I see them, how do I feel? Why were they invisible to me? Was there something that I didn't want to see?

Realize that everyone who is seated at your imaginary table might actually be with you in some form or aspect of your life, right now. And, you have the power to create the most positive outcome from your interactions with them from this moment forward. You know what to do. Proceed.

SIX

ALCHEMY—
TAKE BACK YOUR PROJECTIONS

Jewel: Sardonyx for Harmony

"There is always the potential to create an environment of blame or one which is conducive to loving kindness."

— *Pema Chodron*

Many of us still live and breathe our childhood fairy tales. We know these stories by heart. The Prince will come and be the saving grace. He may be disguised as a frog, but when we kiss him, he will alchemize into the charming, handsome man we have always dreamed about. Of course, the story frequently, if not always, happens in reverse. We kiss the charming, handsome guy, and he then transmutes into a toad. As we start to commit ourselves to the relationship, he begins to ease away. His charms fade and eventually disappear, and we become more aware than ever that he wasn't the savior after all.

Like Sleeping Beauty, we go under the spell of our ancient heritage. We don't see our part, and our projections flourish like the aggressive vines that kept the Prince and her separate for so long. We feel deceived and tricked. How desperately we want to project our anger and feelings of betrayal by blaming him and trying to make him wrong. And yet, when we are willing to get real with ourselves, we have to dig a little deeper. The Prince and Princess archetypes are still alive and well in our collective culture. Nonetheless, we have to get beyond cultural stereotypes if we are going to move out of suffering and into *happily ever after...right now.* Prince Charming is a myth. His personality profile was created from a flipping fairy tale based on *fantasy.* Girlfriends, it is time to get over it.

When our partner chooses to act out in less than acceptable ways, it is appropriate to make him accountable, while at the same time taking note of what we might have contributed to the perceived demise of our dream-come-true. If we focus our attention on him with anger and blame, we will miss the hidden treasure in this tricky scenario. Our challenge is to find a way to turn the perceived poison into the very potion that will induce our healing and growth. One way to do this is to muster a little humility by taking a long hard look at ourselves. In turning our gaze inward, it just might be possible to get a glimpse of our own dysfunctional patterns of behavior. And then we can take the necessary steps to correct whatever is out of whack. In making such a choice, we have opened ourselves to the possibility of unearthing the buried treasure—the hidden gift of this perceived drama.

And so how do you do this? You can start by taking responsibility for what is going on in *your* life. When you do, you create the foundation for taking back your *Power.* You remember that you are not some helpless Princess waiting to be saved. You are a Queen. And Queens expect to be accountable for their lives requiring their partners (Kings) to do the same. So, as you notice what you want to correct in yourself, be clear with your partner about how you expect to do that. Then share from your heart-mind what you notice about his behavior that does not work for you *without blaming him.* Just state the facts. "I notice that when you don't call me for three days, it bothers me. I know I need to speak up when I am upset, and I intend to do that now." Rather than, "You Jerk! You haven't called me for three days! Who do you think you are?"

Determine your boundaries in the situation, state what you are willing to deliver, and then negotiate from a place of loving compassion, first for yourself, and then for him. Be willing to listen to what he has to say while remembering all the while that you are *utterly Magnificent*. Be strong. You will *not* receive behavior from him that you wouldn't dole out. And you don't want to dole out behavior that you wouldn't want to receive. If he has treated you less than honorably, speak up. And, if *you* have acted less than honorably, take responsibility, make the necessary corrections in yourself, and move on. (Lose the guilt. It doesn't work.) He will either negotiate with you and then deliver what he agreed to or he won't. And, you, in your Queenly state, will not hesitate to go forward with your life, no matter what. If he is a match for you, he will follow through. If not, well ...

When things begin to fall apart, we can get caught in the dizzy drama of anticipating abandonment. If we can learn to catch ourselves before the story turns into a full-blown tragedy, we can use our developing education to help us remember what is really going on here. Something from our primal past has gotten triggered. The ancient reptile in us is starting to raise its rugged head and tell us that, if we don't get our act together, we are going to be left and that will definitely *not* be good. If we can *watch* our spinning minds and distance ourselves from them, even just a little (rather than getting trapped in our deteriorating thoughts), we actually have a chance to turn things around before they get out of control.

Whatever is happening has triggered fear and worry, evoking your deepest drives for survival on some level. You want to lash out to save yourself (the response of *fight* is probably more likely than *flight* here). Don't. *This tactic will not help you.* Going for the kill *is not* the most optimal solution. Something at a deep level has evoked your discomfort. How desperately you want to return to peace, but in the absence of peaceful intentions, words, and deeds, it is impossible to reach a peaceful solution.

It is time to clarify your goals. What do you really want from the relationship? What is the relationship for? Is it for your growth? For his? Would it serve you (and him) if it continued? If so, be clear on what you want and how you see both of you going forward with integrity. Own your mistakes and celebrate your contributions. *Don't fight.* Cite or pinpoint what is happening, starting with yourself, and then decide to summon whatever it takes to resolve the situation. Treat him only as you would want to be treated. Before you engage in any discussion, picture the two of you happy and harmonious whatever the outcome. Be empathic and understanding, yet firm in your self-advocacy. Intend that all of your actions, words, and deeds from this moment forward will contribute to peace and balance between you.

Attempting to slay the dragon single handedly is clearly not the most optimal solution—particularly when he has more physical muscle and might than you do. If you find yourself up against an unfriendly foe, who is blasting his hot, fiery breath at you, stop yourself before you react. Wouldn't it be better to use your wit and sensibility to diffuse and disarm the beast rather than to defend yourself against him? By walking away from a fight before engaging in a full-blown assault, you can avoid a potentially disastrous, irreversible situation. If things are going sour, it may be time to reflect and ask yourself some personal questions. For example, is it at all possible that you could have created a set-up for disappointment based on your expectations of how he ought to behave in the relationship? Have you gotten any clues or hints along the way about his character, personality style, and whether or not he is really a good fit for you? Have you ever hoped he would be someone he actually can never become? Did you permit him to treat you in ways that diminish your self-worth?

It requires incredible courage to actually strip down and stare at the raw truth. When we *do* get real with ourselves, we have to face our tender, vulnerable hearts. Alas, the longing, which we had so hoped his presence would resolve—has returned. Though, if we are truly being honest, we would probably have to admit that this longing was always there, even if it had been dormant for a while. Good news. If we are just *willing* to shine the light on that "monster longing," we might possibly see it in an entirely different form. Maybe we can learn from the past. In your childhood, if you were ever brave enough to turn the lights on and look under the bed when you were scared out of your wits that the giant was going to reach out and grab you, you probably discovered that the only thing hiding was your fuzzy slippers.

In our willingness to shine the light on the "longing monster," we will likely discover that the freaky Frankenstein is an illusion created by our catastrophic brain. "He" is just about as harmful as the warm, fuzzy slippers under our childhood bed. And once we have exposed the truth about his identity, maybe then we can go on about the business of lighting up the inspirations that nudge at our souls by answering the true callings of the heart. In recognizing that the "longing monster" isn't real, we don't have to be concerned about being rescued anymore. Letting go of our anxiety about how we are going to be saved allows for much more time and energy to focus on our purpose and passions. Can you begin to feel the joy of actually creating the dream that *you* want? Isn't that ever so much more rewarding than concentrating on what "your Prince" may or may not be doing?

"Longing has no goal, but it has a source. Look deep into your heart. Listen to the still voice within. And remember. Life is fulfilled only through longings. Never through ambitions."

—*Osho*

Projections Are Reflections

The term "projection" has its origins in Freudian psychoanalysis. Simply put, what happens when we project is that we concentrate our attention on what someone else is doing, rather than noticing our own participation in an event or interaction. The most common form of projection is blame, or making a strong case that the other person is wrong to elevate our own righteousness. Witness this behavior in warring nations and their unmovable positions against the perceived foes. Projecting is an instinctive response, with its origins in survival. It is a behavior that is deeply conditioned in us from our instinct to stay alive—and has nothing to do with love, growth, or insight.

We blame our boyfriend for the discomfort we experience when we don't believe he is attentive enough. We blame our boss for our unhappiness because we don't like our job. We blame our parents for left-over anger and feelings of betrayal from our childhood. We blame other drivers for close calls on the highway, TV for the decline of our youth, the government for high taxes, and the weatherman for ruining our weekends. We even project on whole cultures and classes of people—blaming illegal immigrants for taking away our jobs, certain interest groups for controlling the global economy, and terrorists for creating an uncertain world. But the people we are inclined to blame the most are the ones closest to us—especially the Prince (our partner, or our boyfriend).

Alchemizing Our Interactions

Webster defines alchemy as:

> 1: a medieval chemical science and speculative philosophy aiming to achieve the transmutation of the base metals into gold, the discovery of a universal cure for disease, and the discovery of a means of indefinitely prolonging life

2: a power or process of transforming something common into something special

3: an inexplicable or mysterious transmuting

When you take back your projections, you pave the way to alchemize all former errors into perfection. The past now has the potential to be purified, and you are free to continue remembering that your means for salvation cannot possibly come in the form of something as impermanent as a "special relationship" (where he is the savior Prince and you are the one being saved). This is a time for faith. You can see the horizon, but you don't have a clue what is on the other side. As you are waking up to what is truly going on, you realize that the shaky, unstable conditions have a potential for changing to sunny and calm. However, things could be precarious. It is a time of trial and promise. It is also a time to take a close look at the dynamics of the relationship, notice what's working and what's not, and then decide if the benefit of staying together outweighs the cost.

The "special relationship" in which you may have engaged in order to be saved from your longing and loneliness (whether knowingly or not) cannot exist in the form of a fairy tale. He is not equipped to save you. And, even if he could, it is unfair to ask him for the salvation that only you are capable of providing. Keep asking what you really want from this relationship. Be radically truthful. Do not condemn any answer. Does this connection give both of you the potential for growth and expansion? If the answer is yes, then it is definitely worth pursuing. If the answer is absolutely no, well—you know what to do. And, if you are not sure, keep digging.

Seeing What Triggers You as a Gift

By facing ourselves and beginning to take a look at what is happening when his behavior triggers a certain emotion within us, we can start to uncover all of our inner treasures. Ultimately what we are attempting to do is end needless suffering in our lives. Right? In order to accomplish that, we have to eliminate whatever is interrupting us from our *happily ever after... right now.* Of course, if we don't know what it is, it is impossible to stop it. Disturbance and dis-ease give us important clues. Admittedly, uncovering the truth can be tedious. Remember, our conditioning is deeply tucked in the trenches of our minds. So, if we're going to move beyond whatever is limiting us now, we will have to continue working to create some new circuits in our hard-wiring by extinguishing the old patterns that have kept us stuck. This process does require patience and care. We don't want to blow a fuse or overload the breakers. The best way to avoid causing an electrical surge and potential power outage is to pay attention to the warning signs.

An intense reaction to something is always a red flag telling you that underneath this trigger are some unresolved issues. The intensity of the response to an event is the key. The more severe the reaction, the more we need to take a look at what's up for us. On a scale of one to ten, if your feelings of panic, grief, abandonment, or loss of control are at a ten or close to it, you need to *stop yourself from doing anything immediately.* You are not in a position to exercise your best judgment when you are hot with rage or upset. Use whatever methods known to you to get yourself back to some balance and stability and *then* you can decide what to do.

Here are some common events that may signal your feelings of despair:

1. *He frequently seems emotionally distant, shut down, and moody.*

2. *He does not appear to be at all interested in things you care about.*

3. *He notices other women and comments on how "good" they look, but he rarely, if ever, compliments you.*

4. *He would rather play golf or be with "the guys" than spend time with you.*

5. *He doesn't check in or call like he used to.*

6. *His body is there, but he isn't.*

7. *He leaves altogether, body and all.*

Level I: Modify Your Responses

Projections can bolt like an arrow and pierce in an instant. Something happens, and we react (our old, rugged brain has kicked in). And when we act quickly on our instincts, we don't take the time to stop and consider the consequences. Reversing our words, actions, and deeds is much more difficult than stopping to interrupt a potentially disastrous outburst before it gets out of hand. Use the following suggestions to help unwind your reactive inclinations.

1. *Notice that you've been triggered.* Stop before you speak or act.

He is an hour late for the romantic feast that you have been preparing for two days. When he finally calls to apologize and to tell you he is on his way, your alarm goes off. The heat rises in your body and you start to fume. You feel like screaming at him, "Where the hell have you been?" Stop yourself now, before you go into the vapors and create worse problems for yourself. Take a deep breath, bite your tongue if you have to, politely thank him for the heads-up, and tell him you would appreciate an explanation for his tardiness when he arrives.

Look into your magic mirror (actually any mirror will do) and ask yourself a few questions before sharing your feelings with him: First and foremost, does he have a good reason for being this late? Be fair to him and fair to yourself when you define what qualifies as a good reason. What messages have you given him about how okay or not okay it is to be delayed? Are you prompt? Have you ever kept him waiting? Do you communicate openly and honestly with him, or do you withhold your feelings because of your concern for how he might respond? Is tardiness a habit of his? Have you talked to him about it before, or is this an isolated event? Are you willing to listen to what his day has been like? Have you made him aware of how important this evening is for you and the work that has gone into the preparation? Use the interaction as an opportunity to communicate the truth. This situation has gotten your attention, and you don't want to let it slide.

2. *Feel what you are feeling*: Don't resist. Allow what is there to be there.

As the feelings emerge, avoid the impulse to withdraw or lash out (anything that resembles passive or aggressive behavior is not appropriate). Rather, permit whatever is bubbling up in you to expose itself (but keep it to yourself at this point). Identify what emotion is most prevalent: Do you feel mad, glad, sad, or scared? Is anything happening in your body? Is your chest tight or is your heart pounding? To be successful in shifting this situation to the positive, keep inquiring. What is really going on here?

Whenever we experience an adverse response to something or someone, almost always fear is the culprit. And we have to realize that fear can often be a fierce opponent. It is clever and manipulative and will always go for our weakest spot. Fear starts in the mind, beginning with doubt, and then grows into full-blown anxiety. When it reaches paranoia, reason doesn't help. Our anxiety turns into dread, despair, and eventual desolation. And so, we have to learn to manage our fear before it takes over and manages us. One way is to sit still in what may appear to be the virtual prison of fear. Strange as it may seem, it is in this place of confinement that you can actually begin to become detached. There is no right or wrong way to do this. Just practice allowing whatever feeling arises to be there without having the need to react to it, change it, or judge it. Focus on your breath. Feel your nostrils expand as you inhale and the warm air on your lips as you exhale. Keep doing this (difficult as it may seem) until your clammy hands and pounding heart have normalized. Now, ask yourself if you can communicate without projecting blame. If you are not there yet, keep your mouth shut until you can. This is all about patience and practice. This exercise is for you and your growth. Take the potion, bitter as it may seem, and remember that the beautiful pearl that forms inside the oyster begins as an irritant.

3. *Dig*: Go deep and ask yourself if this situation and your reactions trigger some memory from the past.

While experiencing anger, terror, sadness, or even possible relief, start to let go of the suffering, even if for only a moment. Try to tolerate some internal inquiries. What does the possibility of his waning interest remind you of that may have happened before? Then make note of the first thing that comes to mind. It could be as simple as never having been picked for the kickball team, or as pervasive as your father leaving the family when you were sixteen. Your mother became clinically depressed. You never felt you had a safe place to process what was going on. You took care of everyone else without ever tending to yourself.

It is important for you to realize that *your parents' patterns of relating to each other had nothing to do with you*. What happened in their lives was a result of the choices *they* made. Even so, because they had significant influence on your conditioning, it is possible that you may unknowingly repeat some of their patterns. This is particularly true if you have not had the opportunity to heal from the buried feelings left over from long ago. (Don't think you are alone here. Rare is the person who doesn't have some hidden hurt that has resulted from a painful situation in the past.) When things get really uncomfortable and we are ready to take a look at why we feel the way we do, we can usually cite something from our history that feels familiar. It may be time to uncover unconscious patterns *without* shame or blame. Your willingness to face the truth is a really healthy sign. Congratulate yourself.

4. *Focus on context vs. content*: Get out of your story.

Our feelings are triggered by thoughts, which, if left uncensored and unrestricted, are like the Sorcerer's apprentice. If we go too deeply into the story, our runaway thoughts can convince us of anything. *He doesn't love me. He doesn't care. He's going to leave me. I am not good enough for him.* Begin to notice these thoughts and then the actions that may result from them. What stories are you telling others? Are they focused on what he did and what he may be thinking or not thinking? Or are they focused on what is going on with you? Don't bore people with endless details of your despair.

When sharing the events of your life, keep it short and simple. Monitor carefully what you say, especially when you are feeling upset. Do not cause harm by letting words slip out that you will later regret having said. When you are feeling vulnerable, limit your conversation to the measurable facts, ("He stopped calling") and the feelings that accompany those ("I feel sad and confused"). A true friend or good therapist will be able to help you process the context of the situation without going into the story (content). Do not permit yourself to be in the company of anyone who allows you to go into the dramatic negative when you are upset. And then discipline yourself to notice when you are about to fall into the trance of a long, sad, story and be faithful to whatever it is that stops you from doing so.

5. *Choose happiness instead of righteousness: A Course in Miracles* **asks us: "Do you want to be happy or do you want to be right? Give up the need to control outcomes.**

Most of us would rather be right. This desire is directly linked to our survival instinct. And, being happy is not part of survival. In moving beyond the Brute and the Babe syndrome where survival was key (and happiness *wasn't*), we can spend more time on developing effective ways to be *happy*. Being right is not one of them. When we are grounded in our truth, what difference does it make if anyone else believes it to be "right?" If it's right for us, it's right enough. Having to *prove* that we are right is a different matter. In holding on to the position of righteousness, we relinquish the opportunity to clear the patterns that have kept us glued to the past by staying stuck in the story that has caused our misery. If we decide to quit playing, however, the game stops. It takes two to participate in a verbal exchange that includes accusatory comments such as, "you did it," or "it wasn't my fault," or "you shouldn't have." When no one responds to these attacks, the accuser eventually loses interest in trying to justify their behavior.

Real Queens do not have a need to be right or to participate in any kind of dialogue where they might need to prove their point. They don't have to. Their powerful presence says it all. *You* are a Queen. You have value and worth. You don't have to have anyone else's approval to maintain your sense of self-respect. If someone doesn't agree with you or like you, it may feel uncomfortable, but you *can* learn to accept their opinions and feelings. Focus your attention now on attracting all of the people into your life who can support your growth and expansion. If it feels like the current primary players are constantly invested in setting you up to be wrong, notice how this behavior can chip away at your soul. Communicate your concerns (respectfully) once again, taking responsibility for what is yours. And, when things don't change, remove yourself (or them) from the situation. Painful as it may seem now, you will eventually understand the benefit of such a choice, even if you still feel a pinprick of sadness whenever you think of them. Sooner or later, you won't. And eventually, as you continue to practice self-advocacy, you will no longer be attracted to people who have the potential to belittle or berate you. You get the lesson. They were just reflecting to you how you envisioned yourself. And you don't see yourself that way anymore. You are waking up to your Queenly, *Regal* nature.

6. *Surrender the shame*: Remember that blame = shame.

If you are blaming (projecting onto) someone else, there are more than likely some remnants of shame buried within you. If you can feel yourself wanting to dump on him, *stop* and go a little deeper. There may be something inside that is trying to get your attention. Rather than making him the culprit, take time to look at *your* behaviors and practice letting go of the ones that no longer serve you. If you feel you have been in error in the past, remember that it was not your intention to cause harm. Be easy on yourself. Let it go. Finish it. And when you do, chances are you won't be tempted to focus on what he is doing anymore. You will be much less tempted to blame when you can face and let go of your inner shame. *It doesn't serve you.* As you release it, your communication patterns will be *much* healthier, and the issues that you have with him *will* resolve one way or another, *for the better.*

Level II: Take on a New View/Perspective

Why is it so difficult for us to *truly* love and be loved? Perhaps it is because we cannot love ourselves and the moment enough. If someone has come into your life who isn't respectful, loving, and supportive of you, then chances are you have not mastered the art of becoming all of those things for yourself. The gift that he is presenting to you is that he may be reflecting back your own image.

7. *Assume his behavior mirrors your own.*

It is way too easy to get into the "he is a jerk" game. When we become irritated, it takes courage to look at the situation from an objective point of view, but if you are willing to do so you might see what bothers him about you. If you can view the situation from his perspective *without judging yourself,* you are laying the foundation to take the relationship to a whole new level, whatever that may be. Be willing to *really* see what is going on. If you perceive your partner to be immature and still acting like a boy in some ways, ask yourself how you are still acting like a girl instead of a woman, a princess instead of a Queen. If he is bossy and controlling, ask yourself if it is possible that you might be acting out these traits in some way, even if they appear less pronounced or in a different form. If you want a commitment and he seems ambivalent, assume that, on some level, you feel ambivalent, too. When you are willing to look at the situation with a different perspective, the results can be transformational, for you, for him, and for the relationship.

8. *Watch for familiar patterns.*

If what's played out between you and your partner feels familiar, it probably is. Be vigilant. It is critical that you notice the behavioral patterns showing up here that haven't worked for you before, so that you can clearly see what you want to change in yourself.

9. *Remember:* **As without, so within.**

Psychologist Carl Gustav Jung introduced the idea of "active imagination" in dream interpretation. His exercises consist of listing each person who shows up in a dream. Who is visiting and what messages do they bring me? Is there any part of me that is trying to get my attention here through them? Could they all be representing some aspect of me?

Use this technique with your partner. If you wish he would tell you he loves you, assume you need to tell yourself the same thing more often. If you want him to call more frequently, ask how you're not tuning in to your own calling. If you want him to be more successful, make sure you are focusing on your goals. What's your main complaint about the man in your life (or about not having a man) right now? Be brave. Generalize it and apply it to yourself.

10. *Assume you are an active participant in what is going on.*

You have been invited to the ball, and both of you are dancing here. It may look as if it is all about him, but it isn't. Be clear on your part in getting out of rhythm and discover what you can do to shift it if you aren't comfortable with the tempo anymore.

11. *Watch your words.*

Do not cause harm by your words, actions, and deeds. Make certain there are no hidden agendas in what you are presenting. Look at the facts from a place of observation instead of judgment and state them clearly. *Do say,* "I noticed that when you were an hour late for dinner it seemed to really bother me. Can you help me understand what caused your delay? How can we communicate more clearly next time? I am willing to be more adaptable, but in order for that to happen, I will need more information."

Don't say, "I was extremely disappointed when you were so late for dinner. I had worked really hard to make it a nice evening for us and now everything is ruined because of your insensitivity and lack of caring about my feelings."

The first scenario simply relates the facts without judgment. It also shows that the speaker has respect for both parties and that she takes responsibility for her feelings/reactions. The second situation is full of complaints, projections, and attempts to make him feel guilty. It also includes a judgment that he doesn't care about you or the relationship. Can you see how quickly he will lose interest in listening to you when all you are doing is building a case against him? Begin with facts and declarative statements. "You are late." "I am upset." If he starts to defend himself and his behavior, stop him by encouraging him to stick to the facts as well. Assure him that your intention is to avoid judgment. Invite his cooperation by doing the same.

Level III: Take Back Your Projections and Love Them

All of the Queen's jewels have a foundation in self-love. As you become aware of how you might have projected onto others in the past, you may feel embarrassment, regret, or shame. Instead, as you take back each projection, have compassion for yourself. You were doing the best you could at the time. Congratulate yourself for recognizing the patterns that no longer work for you. Love that you are willing to learn how to transform yourself from the scared princess hopeful to the powerful reigning Queen. It can feel extraordinarily uncomfortable to notice the maladaptive, subtle, or even obviously dysfunctional behaviors that we ourselves contribute to an unhealthy connection. If you are even willing to take a look at them, you are making tremendous progress.

In the past, the lover who "betrayed" us ranked high on the list of our foes. Ultimately, what we must come to realize is that we ourselves are the enemy, when we can't take back our blame. Still, we must find a way to love the saboteur, while gently redirecting her into becoming a better self-advocate/self-savior.

When Is It a Projection and When Is It a Valid Complaint?

Projections do not occur without some grain of truth. However, we tend to concentrate on building a case against him when we are hurting. Have courage and follow these steps:

1. *Be willing to look at both sides.*

Look at what *you* are doing and how *you* participated. And when you do, watch your world magically transform. Prepare to claim the Queendom that is yours to celebrate, and realize that it is always within your reach.

2. *Don't engage in any way with someone who is projecting onto you.*

Like the mythical chimera, made of different animal parts, projection has many facets that aren't what they appear. Don't react to the aspect you are perceiving, because it doesn't show the whole story. If you are being triggered by what someone else is saying to you, and you are feeling intense emotions, you are likely experiencing a projection. *Remember, it will not help you to retaliate here.* If the other person has gone into blaming and projecting, they will not hear you if you build a case for being right (this is why righteousness is so useless and will always serve to perpetuate an unhealthy pattern, both with individuals and with nations). Their only interest now is to prove you wrong. If you participate in the argument, you have reverted back to your ancestors' behavior where survival was the only issue at stake. *Don't take the bait.* Stay in your power by ending the conversation in a way that shows respect for both of you. If you are on the phone, politely say good-bye and hang up. If you are in the same room with the individual attacking you, quickly take your leave. If you are in the car, get out at the next safe opportunity, or if you are the driver, firmly state your intent that they are either stop the conversation or remove themself at the next stop. Respectfully let them know that you mean it. When you set firm boundaries both for yourself and for others, your life will take on a major shift for the better. And if you keep at it, eventually, the dramas will cease.

3. Don't try to solve a problem the same way it started.

When an unhealthy pattern manifests itself in a relationship, it is impossible to interrupt it with the same behaviors that produced it. If two people find themselves in a power struggle, a passive-aggressive exchange, toxic dumping, or projection, continuing to engage in those behaviors will not serve to resolve the dilemma at hand. Somebody has to wave the magic "time out" wand and it is likely going to have to be you if it isn't happening any other way. You have to call a halt to this nonsense. How do you do this? Stop participating. And, don't go anywhere without your magic wand *from now on.*

4. Listen to your inner Fairy Godmother—your intuition.

If you exercise your insight like a muscle, it will grow stronger and become clearer over time. You will intuitively know when something isn't quite right. Learn how to distinguish between fear (instinct) and truth (insight). You do know the difference. If your insight is telling you that things are out of balance, then you have to address your concerns. Become aware of what it is that is not working, and then be willing to share your observations with him. Offering your insight does not mean telling him how wrong he has been (projecting) and how right you are. He won't be able to listen to you unless you are willing to take responsibility for your part. Invite him to share what is going on with him. Be clear about what you are willing to do (and not do) in order to grow together. Chances are, this action on your part will cause things to shift in a positive direction and expand into more freedom and growth for both of you.

Should I Stay or Should I Go?

As you master the art of taking back your projections, a decision to leave a relationship that's not working will be less fraught with conflict. In our updated version of the Cinderella story, our heroine Queen has some options. When things get dicey, she can attempt to change the circumstances by communicating openly and honestly about what is going on for her. She can invite her partner to share his feelings, and the two can negotiate. However, if their attempts repeatedly fail and she consistently forfeits her sense of freedom and peacefulness, she may decide that exiting the situation is the only loving choice for both her and her partner. Of course, he has the same options.

Maintaining harmony is the key to all healthy relationships. Feelings of balance create the most favorable environment for any connection to grow and flourish. And when harmony is not forthcoming and finally fades despite your best efforts, it may be time to walk away from the relationship, *without* being tempted to project or blame. When you can leave with loving detachment, you are liberating yourself and your partner (if he is willing to see it this way) from the dysfunction that has kept you both stuck.

If he should flee while you are in the midst of attempting to balance the relationship with him, then heave a sigh of relief. It was going to happen eventually anyway. The only way to go forward now is to *let go*. Even in his absence, you can access and use all of the tools and resources you are developing to help you create the healthy relationships that you deserve. And eventually, the soul's voice *will* emerge and begin to penetrate the wall of fear that has shrouded your heart's true longing. Love yourself for being willing to take a truthful look at your fantasies, illusions, and shortcomings. You are *amazing*. Celebrate!

New Stories, New Enchantment

"Each time you are presented with the opportunity to make an enlightened choice, know that the results of that choice will be felt throughout all of creation."

—*Rasha*

Here are some questions that may be helpful when finding your way through the tangled vines of projection:

- *Have I been conscious in this relationship?*

- *What healthy/unhealthy behaviors are predominant?*

- *Have I been authentic with him? With myself?*

- *Have I attempted to become all of the qualities that I expected him to possess?*

- *In what ways have I benefited the relationship? What challenges have I brought into it?*

- *Have I been able to remember that he is not responsible for my happiness?*

- *Have I communicated lovingly and without projection, even when I am upset?*

- *Have I been able to avoid defensive behavior?*

- *Have I felt empowered or "less than" in this relationship?*

- *Have I been self-sacrificing in anyway?*

- *Have I been able to emphasize the positive in him and in myself, or do I tend to go more toward the negative?*

Don't judge yourself if you didn't like some of your responses. Just be proud that you are at least willing to take a look at your behavior. You are progressing and you can always begin again at any time.

❧ EXERCISE ❧

Here are some thoughts to ponder as you add Sardonyx, the jewel symbolizing harmony, to your crown:

I will begin each day with the intention of releasing the demons of my past projections until each one has been fully alchemized toward supporting my conscious, aware state of being. It is my desire from this moment forward to live my life from a place of loving compassion, starting with myself. If I notice that I am moving into blame or righteousness, I will seek to catch this behavior quickly and move back to my center of peace. Above all, I will have patience with myself. I am a work in progress. My desire is to grow. I will not be denied. I will move forward confidently, knowing that my positive momentum cannot be interrupted. I have the power to turn something common into something special ... to turn base metal into gold. I am a Queen.

SEVEN

REGALITY—
BE ATTACHED TO NOTHING

Jewel: Aquamarine for Invoking High States of Consciousness

"Breathe. Let go, surrender, forgive. Be attached to nothing. Wait for no one."

—*LRH*

A woman (Queen) who has trained herself to be in a peaceful state chooses to stay in peace regardless of what is going on in her environment. If a tree falls on her car, she experiences the upset and inconvenience—and returns to peace. If she receives a new diamond necklace, she allows herself to delight in the gift without making it overly significant—and returns to peace. If she catches a nasty cold, she allows it to run its course—and returns to peace. If the King is in a nasty mood, she avoids taking it personally—and returns to peace. Even when circumstances appear intolerable, the Queen finds a way through. And when life appears more glorious than she ever could have imagined, she accepts the experience joyously—and returns to peace. The Queen has a secret formula for allowing this peaceful state to be the foundation of her existence. No matter what, it always works like a magic spell. Whenever she uses it, she is happy ... *right now*.

Breathe.
Let go, surrender, forgive.
Be attached to nothing.
Wait for no one.

Think for a moment about how this magic spell could transform all of *your* life's upsets, frustrations, disappointments, and feelings of betrayal.

Breathe

Imagine what it would be like if every single human on the planet would take the time to consciously inhale and exhale before acting or speaking. You can practice this technique yourself. The next time you have an unexpected encounter with someone who is behaving unconsciously (for example, suppose your boyfriend projects some angry comment at you), use this opportunity as a reminder to focus on your breath. Rather than taking his searing words and inappropriate behavior to heart, *immediately* instruct yourself to concentrate on breathing instead of reacting. Do you really have a response for someone who is choosing to act out his anger in this way? Is there anything that you could say or do that would be helpful here? Remember, the conversation stops when you refuse to participate. The kind of exchange that you want to encourage comes from your *Regal* nature. If someone cannot meet you on that level, then *you* will have to take charge and decide the most effective means of communication. Often this type of "dialogue" requires silence—or that you *do nothing* other than to repeat the four-part exercise above until you have come to experience peace within yourself.

The best course of action will probably be to remove yourself from the situation, using whatever tools you can access to stay calm. When you feel that your equilibrium cannot be disturbed, you may then proceed with the next step, which could be an attempt to communicate. If, when you share your assessment of the scenario *without judgment or blame*, and you find that he starts pestering you again, *do not engage*. Rather, simply say what you are willing to do (you won't have a conversation with him until he decides to meet you in a peaceful state). If it is clear to you that he isn't choosing to go there, don't even *try* to "fix it." Maintain your royal resolve to protect yourself, whatever that decision requires. *Let go.*

Webster defines regality as: "of or relating to, or suitable for a king [queen]." In not being attached to having the last word whenever someone is rude to us, we are free to proceed with *Regality*. Interacting with anyone who is not operating out of integrity wouldn't be *suitable* for a Queen and therefore, it isn't a consideration. Clearly, the angry, raging boyfriend is choosing to project his misery onto you, *but you do not have to accept it*. No matter what he is doing, you can choose peace and ultimate happiness for yourself, in this moment and all subsequent moments by following the four-part formula, starting with your breath. This formula will guide you to the unconditional love within yourself—the foundation of your *Regality*. When you are completely on your own side, it is literally *inconceivable* for you to receive anything that will not support this unconditional love in you. *Breathe.*

Inhalation is our first autonomous act at birth, and exhalation is our final farewell as we transition from this world to the next one. As long as we are drawing breath—even if we lose everything else—we have a companion. Inhaling and exhaling is what keeps us alive. Breathing also acts as a metaphor for the cycles of life, which are to begin, end, start, finish, arrive, or leave. As we breathe in and then release that breath, we create a natural rhythm of letting go, dying to the old, and making room for the new. In exhaling, you cannot bring back the same breath that you just discharged. Think of the effort it would take to retrieve that breath, and yet so often we try. We revert to the past for the memories we want to maintain, and we look to the future for the relief that can only be accessed *now*. When we turn our full attention to whatever preceded or will follow the precious present, we have forfeited our peace—because peace can only be accessed in whatever is happening *here*, in *this* moment.

If your boyfriend, husband, or partner starts to blast off out of nowhere, stop, breathe and *silently* send back to him what he is dishing out. This is done by simply *visualizing* the attack being spun around and returned in his direction. It is *his* to deal with, not yours, and no *active* communication is necessary at this point to make sure that he gets it ... *only* your dynamic imagination is at play. *Don't react.* Just leave the room and remind yourself that whatever is upsetting him has *nothing* to do with you. Even if it may *feel* personal, make a conscious decision to avoid allowing yourself to make it so. Do not scan for what you might have done wrong or assume you are at fault here. When you are calm enough to speak, set your boundaries, and only take responsibility for what is yours. Refuse to have a conversation with him until he can respect your perimeters. The more you practice, the easier it will become. *Breathe.*

Our breath punctuates our lives. We take it in sharply when we are surprised. We sigh deeply when we are disappointed. And we exhale with laughter or disdain when we are amused or irritated. Our breath functions as the barometer of our inner world. It is deep and slow when we're at peace and high and shallow when we're not. The breath is the free and portable sorcerer's tool that we always carry with us. Artists and writers use it to be inspired. According to Webster, the word "inspiration" literally means "to breathe in."

Therefore, when we are stuck and don't know what to do, a few deep breaths can open the way to new perspectives, brilliant solutions, and flashes of genius. Likewise, when we are hurting and imagine ourselves breathing into that pain regardless of whether it is in our body, mind, or spirit, the discomfort will ease.

Our heads are filled with slippery thoughts that race through our heads with a constant ebb and flow—even so, the mind *can* be quieted. If you concentrate on your breath, it will help to free you from its menacing ways. That's why spiritual masters and mystics suggest using the breath as the focal point for meditation, and many religious practices consider breathing a form of prayer and an act that connects us with God. Spiritual leader Thich Nhat Hanh tells us that in breathing consciously once or twice you can recover your smile.

Letting Go

The act of letting go is unequivocally the most effective means to end suffering. It provides the ultimate relief from all of life's challenges ... although often it is the most difficult behavior to put into practice. And yet the process of letting go is absolutely natural. We let go of our mother's womb when we are born into this world. When we become mothers ourselves, we are definitely ready to let go of our bulging bellies and aching backs at the end of nine months. Our toddlers leap from our laps and go off to pre-school. We heave a sigh of relief in one breath and catch ourselves choking on tears in another. When our children leave home for the first time, we will experience more of the same mixture of anguish and liberation, and when they marry or go off on their own, we will again revisit the paradoxical feeling that is triggered by the anticipation of good-bye. This cycle will occur over and over until one of us lets go of life itself.

There really is no alternative to saying good-bye to our children at some point (and ultimately everyone we come to know and love). When the time for farewell approaches, a part of us knows that we have an opportunity to open the door to other possibilities—even while the dread of departure lurks in the shadows. If we can just be aware that this feeling of doom is connected to a signal conditioned by our ancient past, we may be able to reason with it a little. No, this good-bye does not necessarily signify *the end*. In fact, it could actually mean the beginning of new adventures and discoveries for everyone involved. And even if it is the final farewell, we will be given the strength to deal with that, too.

Observing the mating patterns of the penguins shown in the stunning 2005 film, *March of the Penguins,* provides us with an astonishing example of loving and letting go. This remarkable breed of birds demonstrates extraordinary tenacity, courage, and wisdom as they are repeatedly tested in the harsh habitat that is their home. While enduring the daily challenges of survival, they manage to mate and rear their young in the midst of what appears to be near insurmountable odds. They bond together in order to stay alive and then, just as naturally as they have connected, they will say farewell. Shortly after the couples produce their miracle offspring, the little critters are nudged and then pushed off by their parents to fend for themselves. The adult penguins know that this is how the cycle works. They do not hesitate to proceed with the send-off, and yet in watching them, you can almost feel the anguish in their souls.

How can they so gracefully surrender to this process? They have an innate understanding that to hold on would mean certain death and eventual extinction. They are wise. They know that letting go is necessary and so they do not question the need for impermanence. They live their transitory lives with a quiet, extraordinary elegance.

The "dread response," which humans often associate with the anticipation of saying good-bye, is rarely an accurate barometer for measuring what is *really* going on. Most often, the apprehension around leave-taking is connected to our ancient, conditioned fears of abandonment and ultimate survival. As we become more conscious and aware of our true Essence, we realize that there is actually nothing to get sentimental and scared about. We are *always* connected to those we love. It's just that our mind has been patterned to believe that in order to really be with someone, they have to be physically in our presence. This is not necessarily so. Visualize the person and she will be there. Look at her picture and you will feel her. Imagine the sound of his laughter and he is right next to you. Send him a message of your love and caring right now—directly from your soul—to his.

How can we better understand the nature of parting from the ones we love when it appears to cause despair and anxiety in even the most benign and simple situations? Where did the term "good-bye" originate? For the expression to be so widely used as a common means for bidding farewell, surely there must be something "good" about the experience. When our children embark upon an independent life, we say good-bye. When our parents die, we say good-bye. When the love of our life marries someone else, we say good-bye. When we look at nature, we see that saying good-bye is intrinsic to the cycle of life. The green leaves of spring will inevitably turn golden, then brown, and eventually shrivel and fall to the ground. And sooner or later, we will say good-bye to the bodies that have housed us on our brief journey here. All of these changes are predictable, necessary, and in harmony with the natural cycles and rhythms of life. And yet our conditioning tells us that bidding farewell is *never* good and that saying good-bye should be avoided at any cost. Why? Because we have come to define ourselves around our physical, impermanent, Earthly state.

Each time we say good-bye, we face our own mortality. We are reminded of the constantly changing circumstances that are the very foundation of our existence in this life-form. Our catastrophic conditioning has programmed us to resist change. And when we operate from this primal patterning, even the preparation for bidding farewell can evoke a somber mood.

Consider the departure lounge at any airport. It has a markedly different atmosphere than the gate of arrival. Saying "hello" appears to be a far more popular greeting than "good-bye." It would seem that in many ways we just don't want to let go, even though we know that ultimately, we will have to leave behind even life itself (or at least life as we have come to know it). We are the only species on this planet who can actually conceptualize our own death. Animals instinctively understand, yet we have *both* instinct and awareness.

Perhaps there is a way to perceive this uniquely human predicament as a blessing rather than a curse. Maybe there is something special about being creatures of the great good-bye. If this is the case, how can we quit resisting this mysterious gift so vigorously? In order to stop the endless suffering created by the anticipation of good-bye, perhaps we can use the heart-mind to provide some education in the art of *letting go.*

Forgiveness—A Forward Giving

"Peace isn't determined by circumstances outside us. Peace stems from forgiveness. Pain doesn't stem from the love we're denied by others, but rather from the love that we deny them."

—*Marianne Williamson*

One of the most powerful acts of letting go is to forgive. St. Francis reminds us that the man or woman who has not learned to forgive others has forfeited a great source of joy. Forgiveness (forward giving, letting go, releasing) is the systematic suspension of all guilt, shame, and feelings of personal and universal betrayal. In order to be able to completely forgive another person, we must be willing to repeatedly forgive ourselves by releasing our perceived mistakes. We do this by intending that the necessary wisdom be gleaned from the experience, so that the error will not be repeated. We can then ask that everything be corrected and purified for the highest good of all involved. Now, we can let go of the entire situation, *forever.* No going back. If we hold on to our guilt and pain, eventually it will decay the very spirit we came here to nourish. We simply cannot be fully committed to the path that will guide us to our *Regal,* radiant, and loving nature until we are ready to see all of the events that have contributed to the tapestry of our lives as miraculous blessings. Every person, place, circumstance, and event has had the potential to contribute to our growth in extraordinary ways.

When we harbor resentments, our hearts will freeze and eventually harden. In becoming embittered by bearing grudges against ourselves and others, we will be so concerned with maintaining our defensive, righteous positions that we will lose the lesson in the experience. This situation has the potential to awaken us to more love and more compassion. By practicing forgiveness, we have the opportunity to open our hearts. Even so, we must avoid skimming over our pain. For if we can actually *feel* what we are experiencing, we can move *through* the upset—not away from it. Then when we can let go and offer the whole state of affairs up for the most expanded good of all involved (a literal forward giving to God)—miracles will happen. Regardless of how extreme the situation may seem, it *is* possible to cultivate a forgiving heart. We *can* let go, and we *can* move onward and upward.

Spiritual teacher Jack Kornfield offers a stunning example of practicing forgiveness by sharing the story of a fourteen year-old boy who was murdered as a part of another youth's initiation into a gang. The perpetrator, too young to be tried as an adult, was sentenced to a few years in a juvenile facility. After several months, the mother of the deceased began visiting her son's assassin, who had no family and no support system. Over the months, her visits to see the boy became more regular. Near the end of his three-year term, the woman invited him to come and stay in her late son's room for a while. Eventually, she adopted the young man, who had brutally murdered her child, and provided him with a sense of family that he had never known. She made a conscious choice to forgive her son's killer rather than to keep herself (and him) captive with bitterness and anger. Through her compassion and kindness, she made meaning out of her beloved boy's devastating death by resurrecting the life of another.

The well-known story of a Vietnamese orphan girl provides another remarkable illustration of the miraculous effects of letting go. The girl is pictured in one of the most famous and startling photographs that emerged from that long, terrible war. Horrified, the child is seen tearing down a lonely road with her clothes singed off. Her innocent, frail body had been badly scorched and burned. The village where she had resided with her family had just been raided and she was one of the few to survive. Her parents found her later in the morgue, presumed dead. Her name was Phan Thi Kim Phuc Oont, known as Kim Phuc, who said, "I had not died yet. God had a plan for me."

Kim has survived many surgeries and endured years of physical pain. She married, moved to Canada and had two sons, avoiding publicity for decades until agreeing to speak at the Memorial Wall on Veteran's Day, 1996. While sharing her life's journey on stage, she remarked that if she could speak to the pilot who dropped the bombs she would say they could not change history—when suddenly a note was handed to her from someone in the crowd. The note was from now Reverend John Plummer, who publicly accepted her forgiveness and collapsed in her arms.

Plummer's story as the commander who lived with unbearable guilt and shame for so long became the subject of many stories about the power of mercy and compassion. In fact, he turned out to be a staff officer at the time of the attack, later admitting to the press that he was not the pilot nor the commander that day, but caught up in overwhelming emotion during Kim's speech at the Wall. In an affirmation of her feelings, Kim later said that "whether or not he played a major or a minor role, the point is I forgive him."

What mattered was that Thi Kim Phuc opened her heart, let go of the past, and changed both of their lives forever. Think what the world would be like if every single human on the planet could embrace the philosophy of this remarkable woman. No more war, no more hatred, no more bombs. If we should ever find ourselves being stuck in the victim/villain game, we can remember the stories of Thi Kim Phuc, John Plummer, the mother of the murdered son, and the amazing effects of a forgiving heart.

We are all fellow travelers just doing what we do—including the saints and the scoundrels. Every relationship, every encounter, every simple connection with another—no matter how profound or insignificant it may seem—is meant to help us become more fully ourselves. We can choose to come from a place of loving compassion or from a place of fear and constriction in responding to the circumstances that these opportunities create. The person who has put you in touch with your pain or joy—regardless of which one—has provided a chance for you to be more connected to your compassionate, loving nature.

Anne Frank, the famous young Jewish girl whose treasured diary was retrieved following her demise from the unconscionable crimes of the Holocaust, demonstrated the remarkable effects of choosing a positive outlook. Even though she and her family faced the ongoing threat of capture by the dreaded German Gestapo, Anne made a decision to be happy each day, *no matter what*. By refusing to entertain negativity, she was able to focus on love instead of hatred, and happiness rather than dread—regardless of her horrifying circumstances. We, too, have a choice—happiness or suffering? Allow your *Regal* nature to decide.

Occasionally, it can seem impossible to let go of our anger, hurt, or feelings of betrayal. Depending on the level of intensity, it could take a while, and we must be patient with ourselves. Even so, as Thi Kim Phuc has so elegantly demonstrated, we *can* forgive—even the most horrific of situations. It also helps to remember that there is something *much larger* than our local, little selves—taking care of it all for us. All we have to do is remember to release it for Divine resolution. And when we do, it is best if we don't interfere. Whoever "betrayed" us *will* have their lesson from the experience. *We don't have to do a thing* other than to expand and emerge wiser and stronger than before. If we do harbor our wounds and upsets, they may eventually eat away at our injured hearts, creating a wedge from the wisdom that could be gleaned from the experience.

When we are caught off guard by the unconscious "slam" of another, we are reminded that it is time to polish our practice and skill at avoiding trouble. One way is to actually visualize being constantly protected from harm by an invisible shield of exquisitely gilded mirrors designed to constantly safeguard our *Regality*. There is only one royal opening (located in the center of your crown) that receives and gives love. This is an especially sacred and special portal. Any personal intent from you that does not have the essence of pure love and integrity as its primary goal will be automatically withheld by your conscious spirit (while you continually seek to transform all thought into pure, unconditional love). Only then can your words, actions, or deeds be released. Conversely, anything that is directed *to* you that is not sent with loving integrity and compassion will be reflected back to the sender by the mirrors of protection (a perfect visualization to help with the angry boyfriend mentioned earlier). The dispatcher will then have the choice to deal appropriately with their actions, words, or deeds. Your Queenly good judgment advises that you will not engage with this individual again, unless they choose to act with complete love and integrity—whether or not they make that decision is of no concern to you. If they should decide to transcend their original aim into beneficence and love, you will receive it through the same opening in your crown that you use to send love and compassion to others.

So, if you find that you still have a hook or an uncomfortable feeling when you unexpectedly run into the "friend" who projected her garbage onto you months before, reflect that garbage back to her to deal with, while simultaneously sending her love through the opening at the top of your skull. This technique is quite effective. As you continue to practice it, you will eventually realize that whatever your friend dumps onto you cannot affect you anymore. But remember not to seek righteousness in this situation. If she slammed you, she will not be able to hear you if you try to defend your position. It felt as though you were her target. You weren't. In pointing the finger at you, she actually directed three fingers back at herself, exposing her own unresolved issues. Whether or not she is ever willing to look at what caused her to project her pain onto you is up to her. The point here is *your* healing, *your* truth, and *your* justice-making. There is no room in your life for people who cannot treat you with respect, love, and care. As you let her go without a need to be right by telling her how completely out of line she was (or by trying to make her look wrong to others), you will break the pattern of even engaging with someone who does not operate from a foundation of authenticity, integrity, and love.

Be Attached to Nothing

> "*He who binds to himself a joy, does the winged life destroy; He who kisses the joy as it flies, lives in eternity's sunrise.*"
>
> —*William Blake*

We have been conditioned to believe that if we *let go*, we will somehow be left, stripped down, naked, and alone. When we are in such a mindset, we have forgotten that *nothing* can really exist in and of itself, and so it is impossible to be alone. All of life is interdependent. To illustrate the point, imagine that you are walking through a grove of aspen trees in the mountains of Colorado. You may see each tree as a free-standing entity. Ah, but you forget (or perhaps you never knew) that all of these trees are part of one of the largest living organisms, because they are all connected by their root system. What affects one affects another. And the trees are all influenced by other conditions like sun, rain, snow, and wind. The trees live, the trees die. Just like the aspen trees, so do we live and die in all of the moments of now. If we keep ourselves attached to those moments, and all that accompanies them, we will suffer. In accepting our role as *creatures of the great goodbye*, we must continue to train ourselves to be attached to nothing.

We can look to the aspen trees for guidance. They know without knowing that they do not have to make an effort in order to be linked. In fact, imagine these trees straining to cling to each other. What would the aspen grove look like if the trees that freely rustle with the wind were suddenly entwined, gnarled, and stuck together? How would such a development affect the ecosystem that supports them? The trees have a simple understanding of the Oneness that connects them to all that is. They don't try to make that connection happen. It just does so on its own. The relationship always existed naturally, and the trees *know it*. We know it, too. We just forget sometimes.

Wait For No One

Do you recall the childhood expression, "wait up"? Now imagine yourself as a young girl watching everyone else advance to the agreed upon destination. Yet you can't keep up with the pace of the others. You start to panic. What if you lose your way? You can almost feel the terror starting to overtake you. What if you are completely left behind? Clearly, if you are reading the words on this page, your worst fears did not come to pass. Truth be known, the times you charted your own course and avoided depending on anyone else to get you to where you were going were the least anxiety producing of all.

Think of the people you admire most—of any age. Did they seek to follow someone else? Did they wait for others to catch up before fully expressing themselves and their gifts to the world? Those who forge ahead, following their own compass and timeline, are the ones that we most admire. Artists, inventors, and pathfinders all move confidently into unexplored territory to express their genius. How many tries did it take Thomas Edison before he invented the light bulb? What would have happened if he had listened to the skeptical voices of his peers?

Mother Teresa did not wait for someone else to resolve the challenges of her mission. Ana-Perez Chisti, Ph.D., a beloved professor and friend, shared a story about her experience with the late, modern-day saint during class one day. In the midst of a cold Northern California winter, Mother Teresa and other volunteers were attempting to organize a soup kitchen for the homeless. Just prior to the scheduled opening, the team was informed that the city would not allow the facility to operate. It was believed that the antiquated heating system in the building might be a fire hazard. When Mother Teresa was told the news, she did not blink or even appear disturbed. Instead, she firmly stated, "We will open the kitchen. Heat will not be necessary." And so, the staff and volunteers sprung wide the doors. They gathered blankets and made hot soup. The warmth of love and care was all that was important. *Mother Teresa did not wait* for someone to grant her permission to go ahead with her plan. She courageously went on about offering her service, despite the challenges. She chose to be a living demonstration of *Regality*. So can you. All you have to do is *decide* to follow your own divine compass and timeline.

Learning to Love the Questions

How can we train ourselves to welcome change; to be attached to nothing; to wait for no one; to breathe; and to let go? The silent and powerful voice that guides us in this training is unmistakable.

It is the voice of love. It speaks softly. That's the reason so many of us don't hear it. Yet when we are willing to listen, its messages are concise and clear. It doesn't berate you, argue with you, shame you, or call you any names. It does not seek to frighten you out of your wits, but rather it serves to provide comfort as it gently guides you toward strengthening the shafts of your heart. This voice is ever available. If you listen, it will direct you toward the full actualization of your *Regal* nature where you will learn to love the questions and the mystery, more than the answers and the familiar. The German poet Rainer Maria Rilke elegantly captures the essence of living in the blissful unknown with one of his inspirational letters to a young student seeking his literary advice:

> Be patient toward all that is unsolved in your heart
>
> and try to love the questions themselves
>
> like locked rooms or books
>
> that are written in a foreign tongue.
>
> Live the questions now.
>
> Perhaps you will then gradually, without noticing it,
>
> live your way some distant day into the answers.

"If you go into your garden and tread on a thorn, say thank you though it may cause you blood and tears. Though it is well disguised, this thorn is given you in the same way as the perfume of the rose."

—*Reshad Feild*

If we can just allow whatever is happening in our lives to unfold without the need to label it as pain or pleasure, we have more of a chance for revealing the underlying happiness in *all* of it. Such an art requires patience, which can only be learned when we are willing to go with an open heart into every situation—particularly those where tolerance is required.

If you can think of your life as being like a "Guest House," the nature of which Rumi so elegantly describes for us below, we can begin to take on a bit of a different perspective. In order to help yourself see the point, look back on your life and witness a time that you thought was a disaster. Recall the circumstances that brought you to that conclusion. Make a personal inquiry now, noticing if this period really was so catastrophic. Might you even go so far as to call it a "hidden delight?"

> *The Guest House*
> This being human is a guest house.
> Every morning a new arrival.
>
> A joy, a depression, a meanness,
> Some momentary awareness comes
> As an unexpected visitor.
>
> Welcome and entertain them all!
> Even if it is a crowd of sorrows,
> Who violently sweep your house
> Empty of furniture,
> Still, treat each guest honorably,
> He may be clearing you out for some new delight.
>
> The dark thought, the shame, the malice,
> Meet them at the door laughing,
> And invite them in.

Be grateful for whoever comes,
Because each has been sent
As a guide from beyond.

—*Rumi*

New Stories, New Enchantments

Acknowledge where you are stuck and slowly pry yourself open. Nurture and care for yourself in this place of constriction. Breathe in and be empathic with everyone else who might be experiencing this tight, hot spot just like you are. Open your heart and send out joy, love, compassion, peace, and forgiveness. Now, be open to receiving all of this bounty back into your beautiful open heart—in abundant supply. Let go. Breathe.

⚡ EXERCISE ⚡

Gifted Creatures of the Great Good-Bye

Be disciplined and determined in your willingness to let go. The final reason for practicing the art of saying good-bye is to familiarize ourselves with the process, so that when the ultimate farewell (our own death or that of a loved one) is at hand and we (or they) are close to dissolving, we are familiar with the process.

Become intimate with the experience of letting go. The more you feel attached to something, the greater the opportunity to practice non-attachment. If you think you absolutely cannot tolerate having to say good-bye to someone, *immediately* practice saying good-bye. If you are set on being right, be intimate with not being right.

In all circumstances, practice loving compassion, both for yourself and for the others in your life. Cause no harm. Do not deceive others. Do not deceive yourself. Intend that the highest good will occur for all involved in every situation. This includes everything from the experience with your angry boyfriend to celebrating a festive occasion with cherished friends and family. These experiences are part of the grand, glorious mosaic of your life—none actually more important than the other. For each uniquely contributes to the masterpiece.

Do not wait. Move forward fearlessly. Be vigilant. Watch your choices. Which alternative causes you to experience more freedom? More pain? Don't get hooked on the suffering game. Clue: Victim thoughts will take you there immediately. Move on, out, and up into your *Regality.* You cannot be a victim if you are going to reign as Queen over your life.

EIGHT

PASSION— FULLY EXPRESS YOUR GIFTS TO THE WORLD

Jewel: Beryl for actualizing Potential and Having Unconditional Love

"Our deepest fear is not that we are inadequate. Our deepest fear is that we are powerful beyond measure."

—Marianne Williamson

Being Is Becoming

As you continue opening your heart and soul more fully to the *Passions* that will guide you to your most creative nature, the moments of clarity will likely intensify and then wane, over and over again. What will happen if you go forward toward all that sparks the fire in your soul? Should you listen to the silent voice that keeps whispering sweet messages on the *unprecedented joy* that will accompany you when you commit to fulfilling your purpose on this planet? You *know* this voice is guiding you in the right direction. And yet, what about your protection? If you give up the safety nets in your life, regardless of how suffocating they can feel at times, what will happen? Couldn't you fail? Isn't it frivolous and clichéd to think of "following your heart"? What about being practical? And what will everyone think if you decide to go forward with the changes (possibly radical) that following your *Passions* would require?

How much are you willing to be absolutely unwavering in your commitment to yourself? In honoring the *Passions* that will guide you to your true and lasting purpose in this life-form, you will have to listen to the laser-sharp clarity that bleeps across your radar screen from time to time. Tune in to these alerts, brief as they may be. If you are willing to give them your full and undivided attention, they will continue to provide you with valuable information. Refine your skill in understanding the difference between *insight* and *instinct*. The instinct wants you to run back to your safety zone and forget all about your dreams, *Passions,* and inspirations. If you should get smacked with the suspicions of your fears, immediately instruct yourself to *stop* for a minute. Breathe into your anxiety and then remember this: once you are linked to the insights that are guiding you to the truth, *you cannot regress,* even though your ego may want you to think otherwise. And so, proceed. Move *through* your fear and not away from it. In doing so, you will always be given a helping hand in one form or another, no matter how elusive the assistance may seem at times. Have faith, and when you are tempted to doubt, turn to the miracles of nature for confirmation that you are on the right track. Animals and insects don't have to think about becoming more fully who they are. They just naturally proceed into each phase of development.

When a caterpillar moves into the final stages of becoming a butterfly, it literally melts down in its own cocoon. The caterpillar doesn't stop to ponder the risk of melting down. It just advances right into the cooker without hesitation. Guided by the simple wisdom that there is something else beyond being a caterpillar, it eagerly engages in everything that will facilitate the process of transformation. This little creature follows the forces of nature and goes forward, despite the daunting progression of events that must occur in order for it to grow into the butterfly that it is destined to become. It willingly allows whatever is necessary for this metamorphosis to occur. The caterpillar is in complete alignment with the flow and current of the Life Force that guides it, and because it is ready to accept the dramatic changes that will inevitably occur as it enters the cocoon, it somehow understands that the reward (total transformation) far outweighs any inconvenience. And so the caterpillar surrenders to whatever is required for the final result. It eventually becomes an exquisite, elegant creature—no longer bound to the ground. Replete with a set of wings, it now has the potential to fly for several thousands of miles—across the land and the sea. The unfolding of this miracle is just one stunning example of the marvels that you, too, can experience as you develop your own willingness to go with the flow that is ever-present in the undertow of your consciousness. This Life Force patiently awaits your readiness to melt into *your* process of transformation. You and the caterpillar have something in common. You each have within you the potential to transcend and transform. All that is required of you is your willingness, faith, patience, and persistence.

The butterfly in you is born from the garden of your heart and soul. And she can only emerge when you are ready to risk entering your own chrysalis phase. You can move into this stage of your unique development by actually melting into the *Passions* that ache in your heart to be birthed. As you accept the mission to go forward in uncovering your purpose, you must make a commitment to cultivate the kind of garden that will nurture your growth. Then as you develop your expertise in tending this landscape of yours, you will be able to identify the tangled, overgrown "vegetation." With meticulous care and patience, you will separate the flowers from the weeds—all the while being more and more alert on how to distinguish the two.

The weakest plants are intimately woven together with the sturdiest, and part of your development is learning to appreciate the beauty of your soul-garden in its entirety. Still, in order for it to grow and flourish, you will have to carefully let go of what is no longer needed—all the while remembering to love the collective compost of everything that has nourished its growth up until this very moment. Every single particle, however minute, has contributed to germinating the seeds of your soul. *All* of the relationships, experiences, and events of your life can strengthen and potentiate the "caterpillar you" so that you can have the courage to proceed with whatever it takes to eventually fly. Becoming the butterfly is your destiny. And the root word of become is "be." "Be" is not an action word. Rather, it implies motionlessness. And so in order to *become*, we must first go to the core meaning of the expression and embrace the stillness within. It is there that we will find what the caterpillar is able to access without a menacing mind to interfere. The unmoved Mover is ever-present to guide this innocent creature into its next phase of development. This same Voice is available to all who want to listen. And the Voice's message is universal. All we have to do is *be* still enough to listen.

Your Genius Zone

It is time for you to light up the corners of your soul and ignite the sparks in your spirit that will combust and then catapult you into the grandest version of yourself. Remember, it is not up to you to decide how worthy your *Passion* is. The caterpillar doesn't stop to contemplate if they are good enough to become a butterfly prior to entering the cocoon. Your only responsibility is to discover what makes your heart sing and then decide that you are now attracting all of the most expanded resources to assist you in bringing forward this song of yours. Once you have started to reveal the truth of who you really are, you have uncovered the capacity to move into your genius zone where there is absolutely no end to the creativity that awaits you. Albert Einstein, Rumi (the great thirteenth century Sufi mystic and visionary), Michelangelo, and Claude Monet (extraordinary French Impressionist artist) mostly hung out in such a zone. They were completely tuned in to the Flow that took them directly to their most expanded potential. They listened to the inspirations that guided them straight to the source of their brilliance. You, too, can do this. The same spark that ignited their souls came from the Unified Field of Energy to which we are all connected. All we have to do is flip the switch. Now is the time.

Your *willingness* to be open to the inspirations that have been incubating in your soul is all that matters. Once you have made the personal commitment to dispatch what has been brewing within, there is absolutely no limit to what you can create. *Do not play small*. It is time to shine. Iyanla Vanzant is the author of five *New York Times* best-selling books. She has shared stories of challenge and victory about being a teenage welfare mother and battered wife, which have touched a multitude of souls. When she was a young girl, she was told that she would never amount to anything. Iyanla did not listen. And look what happened. As you approach the frontier of possibilities that await you, your only blocks to success are the ones that you yourself create. What you did up until this very second is immaterial. You can choose to see the past events, situations, and accomplishments in your life as "good" or "bad." However, such labeling will probably *not* be useful. Nonetheless, if you must make a fuss, then allow yourself five minutes or so to wallow in the past. Then *move on*. Remember that the perceived pace at which you travel in this earthly time/space continuum is of no consequence. Our little, local selves can only speculate on what is really going on here, so time is actually of no consequence (though our training in insufficiency would have us believe otherwise). All we have to do is be willing to move on down the road, wherever it may be leading us. The rest will take care of itself. *The intention to go forward from this moment on is what counts.* Whether you are twenty-four or eighty-four, it makes absolutely no difference. As long as you are drawing breath, you still have an opportunity to live at your most optimal level of creativity. And you can utilize everything that has brought you to *now* as the foundation on which you will build your glory. Every fresh, new moment is a chance to *begin again.*

Here are some soulful inquiries to consider as you step onto the launching pad of your *Passionate* journey:

> Do you typically awaken in the morning eager to dive into whatever awaits you? Or do you feel flat, drained, and exhausted when you contemplate the beginning of another day? Are you somewhere in between these states, feeling apathetic and just going through the motions of a mundane existence? Do you ever dream about someone or something rescuing you from this humdrum state? Can you identify your strengths? What has the potential to be developed in you? Remember, Einstein had to start somewhere. Get out a sheet of paper and don't quit writing until you have identified ten personal attributes. Anything counts. No cheating. Go.

> Can you identify the feeling of inspiration? According to Webster, the word "inspire" means: to influence, move, or be guided by divine or supernatural forces." Write down what accompanies this feeling

of "being guided by divine and supernatural forces." Don't accept any personal response, like "I don't really know what that feels like." You do. Everyone does because we were all born from Divinity. Quiet your mind and let this Divinity brew and bubble from the center of your being.

The slogan for the special services of the British Air Force goes something like this, "Those who risk, win." Not that we are necessarily trying to replicate the Air Force here. However, we can't ignore the fact that the British have been enormously influential throughout history. Are you willing to take some risks to be the winner of your dreams? Surmount your own odds. Embrace the "no obstacle can stop me" attitude. Identify what you are willing to do to move forward. Notice where you may get stuck. Then remove, or step around, whatever it is that keeps you from proceeding.

Are you ready to forgo any regrets about squandered time and lost opportunities and instead make a commitment to yourself to go forward from here? As you do, not only will *you* be inspired, but you also will inspire everyone you meet along the way.

Identify your opportunity costs and opportunity benefits. The cost of pursuing your *Passions* equals whatever you feel you will have to "pay" to move into your genius zone. Naturally, the benefit is the reward. Be careful here. Be fair. Weigh everything. If the costs outweigh the benefits, start over. Ask yourself which part of you is "talking" here. Your fret and fear or your guts and genius?

Make a mental list of what it will take for you to begin opening yourself to your creativity. For example, let's say you have a *Passion* for painting birds. You love everything about these creatures. From hummingbird to crow (the hybrid doesn't matter) you are utterly fascinated. You have always wanted to pursue taking a class in watercolor. Up until now, you've had excuses. Something else has always come first, like your job, your kids, your boyfriend, or husband. Or you don't think you have any talent and you would embarrass yourself if you actually committed to taking a class. Even so, something inside of you is now ready to investigate how you can ease into pursuing this *Passion* of yours. Poke around and make some discoveries. Who knows, before long, you might be showing your art in a local gallery, being commissioned by the Audubon Society, or designing greeting cards for Hallmark. *Nothing* is impossible as long as you are willing to stay open.

It does not matter whether you are baking cookies (as in Mrs. Fields, who started her multi-million dollar cookie business by peddling freshly baked morsels door to door) or sitting on a launching pad waiting to embark into outer space. All that is important is that you absolutely *love* what you are doing. Your true *happily ever after ... right now* is directly linked to this love of yours. It is the guide to your truth, your creativity, and your genius. It will take you everywhere you really want to go, including into the arms of your beloved—without even trying.

Real joy comes from your earnest desire to create your own cookie, whatever that is. Happiness is not elusive nor does it evade you. Only you can evade it. Receive the bounty of joy that is yours right here, right now. Allow the sheer rapture of it all to overtake your spirit and soul. *This* is who you are. *This* is how you should feel. Fully embody this feeling.

All-out Happiness: a Checklist

In making the personal commitment to bring forward your *passions* and inspirations, you are developing the art of becoming intimate with your own heart and soul. As you do that, the knack of nurturing your spirit will naturally overflow into your relationships with others. The foundation of self-love that you are creating will magnetically draw to you people who are choosing to live with similar values and ideals. Your combined assets will serve to strengthen the means and expand the possibilities of whatever you can give of your life, from the personal to the communal to the global.

As you proceed on this path of passion, you are learning to balance your independence with interdependence. Dependency is a thing of the past. You now understand that *real* success is about greatness. It isn't about competing or winning. Rather, it is about being willing to catch the wave of your own unique genius and ride it to shore, over and over again. It is about noticing what is genuine in your life and developing your creativity, wisdom, and brilliance from that foundation. It is about realizing that there is no one else on the planet who can provide you with the magic potion that will awaken your authentic personal *Passion* —other than your own glorious self. (And, of course, I don't mean the kind of passion that dazes and dazzles you when you are dreaming about *him* and what *he* is going to bring to the table). Now you are beginning to understand that this *Passion* is ripe in you, and that there is no other person, place, or thing that is capable of reaping the unique harvest that can be yielded from your very own field of dreams—except you. You are all about being fired up over what it is that you are going to *give* to the world, because you have faith that everything you could ever need or want will come to you now without effort or struggle. You are now *becoming* everything that you might at one time have been seeking somewhere else. You are discovering the real meaning of what Gandhi was saying when he encouraged people to "... *be the change you want to see in the world.*"

In continuing to expose yourself to the true glories of who you *really* are, realize that you will probably have some lingering fears. Are you willing to address those as they arise? Are you ready to do whatever it takes to move your brain from the primal to the cerebral to the spiritual? Are you willing to live a life of purpose inspired by your *Passions*, which are unique to your personal versions of genius? Are you willing to claim your *Magnificence* now and stop playing small? Can you start to comprehend that the Universe actually aches to open the floodgates of abundance for you, so that you can live in the riches that are yours to enjoy whenever you are ready to *claim* them? Can you thoroughly and completely love and accept yourself and recognize that this is the life *you chose* to assist you in bringing forward your most expanded potential? Can you always attempt to take the higher ground and be "temporarily more" for those who are "temporarily less?" Can you have patience with anyone who may not be as aware as you are that the true path to freedom and happiness requires you to come from a place of love and compassion? Can you let go of the fairy-tale fantasy of being rescued by Prince Charming and enjoy the glorious reality that is yours to embrace right now? Can you let go of the *relationship* if you notice that your repeated attempts to *live* and *communicate* the *truth* continue to end in frustration and despair?

What about your attachments or addictions? (Everyone on the planet is subject to these behaviors. You and I are not exceptions.) Can you begin to identify all that is keeping you stuck because you fear abandonment or being alone? Can you start to notice when you are creating ways to avoid dealing with challenges and are therefore producing even more difficulties and chaos for yourself? Do you know the difference between dependence and interdependence? *Real love* vs. *romantic love*?

Do you remember that you have three choices in any given scenario? You can resist, change, or accept your current circumstances. Ask yourself which choice is the most likely to create peace? Which one will produce pain and chaos? Can you remember to be present long enough to begin to identify your *feelings* and then go fully into them rather than running away? Can you accept responsibility for your past, both the "good" and the "bad," take neither too seriously, and continue to commit yourself to being on your own side, *now*? Don't be discouraged if you have some loitering challenges. Just take a peek at what needs to be tweaked, modify, and then go forward. Eventually your obstacles will be fewer and fewer, or you won't see them as impediments anymore. Rather, you will see them as opportunities.

The Cosmic Love Story Revisited

"For a fully enlightened being, the difference between what is neurosis and what is wisdom is very hard to perceive, because somehow the energy underlying both is the same."

–Pema Chodron

Hope and fear are intimately connected. There are things we like and want to keep, and there are things we don't like and want to get rid of. We are attached, and repelled; repelled and attached. It is easy to let go when we don't want something anymore, but letting go of something that we still desire, or even crave on some level, is quite another matter. How can we come to know more intimately the feelings we "like" and the ones we "don't like"? Is it possible that the energy driving each (whether it is neurosis or wisdom) is the same? If so, how can we come to make friends with our shadow-nature, which suffers in the starkness of lack and despair and lives in a constant state of insufficiency? If we can't get used to the idea of impermanence, can we somehow inch our way into becoming at least a little more familiar with it? Could we even bring ourselves at some point to make friends with the mystery that lies just beyond our awareness?

More often than not, you will find that if you actually acknowledge that the darkness is somehow constantly lurking in the shadows, then, when it pops up to show its ugly head, you can shout "Boo!" In not taking the goblin or ghoul too seriously, you instantly break the spell it has had over you. You begin to lighten up. You notice how serious and somber you have been. In maintaining your narrow focus of solemn skepticism, you have skewed your perspective to favor the negative. In attempting to lighten up, you will find that the chain of fear that has kept you locked in the virtual prison of limitation will be broken and eventually disappear.

And once you train yourself to be illuminated in *every* situation regardless of how it appears, you will need less and less effort to embody the spirit of truth—because it will just unfold naturally. And magical things will continue to happen—frequently. When we are *contributing* to the world from the essence of Spirit that guides us directly toward potentiating the grandest version of ourselves, the natural response from the Universe is to give back abundantly. Give and receive; receive and give back. That is how it works. Such a process is an absolute guarantee.

Your Awakened Heart

Keep awakening and opening your heart. Notice when you feel joy. Be present with this feeling and remember that this is your natural state.

Be aware of feelings of pain that may arise. You might react because you instinctively resist this pain. Be willing to sit still with it for a minute. Become intimate with the twinge and tenderness that you are experiencing. See if you can pinpoint where the pain is most acute. Where are you the most sensitive? Where do you feel particularly vulnerable around this ache in your heart? Do you feel jumpy, heavy, restless, or motionless? Can you have a conversation with this pain? If so, what does it have to say to you? Can it teach you anything about yourself? If it has to do with your connection to another person, realize that this connection, and all that accompanies it, is no accident. Everything that has occurred in this relationship has the potential to help you grow and expand your levels of consciousness. Allow yourself to feel any discontent that may be coming to your awareness. Begin to comfort yourself with love and compassion. Notice that these feelings of love and compassion are ever available to you.

Understand that the benefit of allowing yourself to go deeply toward the feeling you want to resist, actually guides you in the direction of opening your heart. Allow yourself to fully feel the gift of compassion that you are offering here. Then permit your compassion to overflow and reach anyone else who may be stuck (including the individual that helped to awaken you to this experience), so that they might benefit from the powerful energy that you are recruiting. You are courageous. *You are Passionate.* You have the ability to dramatically effect positive change, both within yourself and in others. Don't wait. Start now.

We are not separate beings roaming the planet disconnected from one another. Rather, we are *one* with each other and all that exists. What I give to you, will return to me. If I bestow love unto each of my brothers and sisters, so shall I receive back in full bounty the love that I have offered in one way or another. As I become more and more identified with the love that is the root of my being, I will notice that I am blessed with a burning desire to share everything I came here to create. In waking up to the truth, I can recognize the multitude of creative expressions with which I can choose to share my own personal genius with the world. I am part of the whole and yet, ironically, I must differentiate from this whole to become more connected. The joy of endowing the Earth with my own unique imagination is what connects me to expansion. As I offer my gifts to facilitate growth in others, each one can combine what they have received with their own distinct talents and then "pay forward" the entire package. There is no end to the cycle of creativity that begins with your *Passions* and inspirations.

Once I have dabbled in the delight that is the natural result of such a process, I can begin to let go of the conditioning that has produced in me a need-based paradigm of relationships and love. In viewing life through a different lens, I am fully aware that the idea of a Prince Charming, who will come along and save me, is part of a fairy-tale fantasy that no longer serves my true purpose on this planet. Rather, it is in bringing forward my *Passions* that I will quiet the longing, which I once believed could only be satisfied by some external event (like hooking up with the Brute or the Prince).

Higher Ground

The freedom that we seek cleverly evades us because of our conditioned need to maneuver outcomes. Each time we attempt to manipulate a situation for what we perceive to be personal gain, we will actually block the very result we are hoping to procure. Therefore, in awakening to a more conscious state of being, we must relinquish the temptation to operate from a fear-based survival mentality and go courageously toward all that will release us to higher ground. This means we have to embrace the spirit of surrender. Rather than trying to control what happens, we instead begin every single event and encounter with a conscious intention, such as, "Let the most expanded good be the consequence of all of my actions, words, and deeds—from this moment forward." You may decide to offer your intent as a broad, sweeping statement that you make at the beginning of each day—or you can silently say it to yourself all of the time, until it becomes fully integrated into your awareness. You can also make your intentions detailed and specific. For example, if you are interviewing for the job of your dreams, imagine that your very presence in the environment of this jobsite will bring good to all. Every single employee is exponentially enhanced by interacting with you. Now invite all assistance possible from the seen and unseen world. And then surrender and offer up the entire situation for the most optimal benefit of everyone involved. This job (or something far grander than you can imagine) —*is coming to you now.*

The key is to remember that the only way to fully ensure the best outcome is to surrender your intentions to all that will produce the most optimal good for everyone involved. The result may be completely different from what you had perceived from your limited, local perspective. Nonetheless, the Divine outcome will *always* be better than what you had originally pictured, even though the improved version may initially come well-disguised. If you look back on your life right now, you will more than likely be able to recall at least one situation, or possibly multiple events, where you put out an intention or a prayer and something entirely different occurred. Yet eventually you were able to see that the final result was much better than your original idea. The very example that you are calling to mind right now helps you to remember what surrender is all about. It always works when we just allow the magical process to unfold. Why resist?

Let Go of Forever and Live for Now

"The only authentic responsibility is toward your own potential,
your own intelligence and awareness-and to act accordingly ...

if you act according to your past, that is reaction .... Response is moment to moment. It has nothing to do with memory, it has something to do with your awareness. You see the situation with clarity; you are clean, silent, serene. Out of this serenity, you act spontaneously. It is not reaction, it is action. You have never done it before. And the beauty of it is that it will suit the situation."

—*Osho*

How can we give up our conditioned worries, fears, and insecurities while allowing ourselves to be with whatever is happening now? Staying focused more and more on this moment, instead of fretting over the past or worrying about the future, you will begin to notice some significant shifting in your awareness on what is really true. When you are no longer occupied by needless regret over the past or anxious anticipation of the future—you create an opening from your emerging wisdom for your full creativity, gifts, and talents to emerge.

As we continue to peel off the layers of dread and doubt that have kept us from noticing who we truly are, we might meet up with some of our old, outdated belief systems along the way. These will be reminders of how far you have come. Every single awareness that has assisted you in accessing your most expanded potential is permanently recorded. Nothing can change that. Further, once you begin to identify what you *truly* long for, stop grasping for it and simply allow it to emerge by letting go of any need to control—you will be endowed with treasures beyond your most favorable imaginings.

Learning to Sit with What is There

Sit really still for a moment. If you are willing, bring to mind an event, either current or in the past, that is tugging at your heart. Even if just for a moment, experience the stinging sensation. Allow it to be there without a need to change it. Rather than running away from the feeling, stay with it for a while, and *breathe into* it. If you can, give gratitude for this opportunity to heal a part of yourself that has been awakened here. Then, offer thanks to the Divine for helping you to heal the lingering wound. Ask that everything and everyone involved be purified of any error for the good of all. Now—let everything go, and repeat the exercise again on occasion, until you feel the entire situation being released.

If you are suffering from an extreme loss, such as the death of a loved one, or the physical release of someone in *any* form, let go of the need to blame or judge yourself about what you may or may not have done "right" or "wrong." Remember that the concept of "guilt" is a thought form, rooted in a punitive belief system based on the idea of penalty and retaliation, which has no place in the developing consciousness of a species moving from *Homo Sapiens* to *Homo Luminous.* There are plenty of signs (both the internal and external hurricanes and tsunamis) that are warning us to evolve or be wiped out altogether.

Operating from the outdated survival mode *is not working anymore.* As we move toward the spirit of unity, we can begin to recognize that every single action, word, deed, and event can hold a seed for positive intent, regardless of how small. In coming from a place of Oneness, there really can be no "right" or "wrong." When people act based on their primitive nature, which has a foundation in insufficiency and survival, they are behaving unconsciously. In our desire for conscious living, it is our responsibility to take the "higher road." We need to slay the selfish streak that wants to rise and be noticed, and instead move to a place of humility, summoning the strength to avoid taking personally whatever has happened. Our courage is exponentially enhanced when we remember that something much greater than this little wrinkle in the grand scheme of things is busy cleansing the entire situation for the highest good of everyone involved.

If you are experiencing difficulty in a relationship, whether it is with a significant other, a friend, or family member—try not to move into the future or back to the past. Rather, just be aware of whatever is happening right now. It takes enormous courage to look deeply into what's going on, tell the truth about it to yourself, and then tell the truth to the other.

As living, breathing beings, we are still plugged into the planet with all of its illusions of doubt, fear, and panic. Therefore, if we choose to come from a place of truth, our ego mind will try to tempt us into believing that if we reveal this truth, we will surely be abandoned— something we want to avoid at any cost. So, our ego mind snarls, "Put up or shut up." When this voice emerges, it is time to amplify our strength and courage. In calling forth the inner hero, they can step in and quiet our fears, while helping to put things into perspective. *This inner strength will never fail us.* All we have to do is to decide to summon it.

New Stories, New Enchantments

If your pain is intense and fresh, be patient. It takes time for the frequency, intensity, and duration of any episode of grief, anger, or despair to diminish and soften. The only way to weaken the hold that these feelings appear to have on us is to simply allow ourselves to experience and then move through them.

Here is an exercise to assist you in dealing with feelings of pain, anger, or grief:

> Set aside ten minutes at least once a day (twice is better) and tell yourself you are going to allow any feelings that are incongruent with your peace to wash over you. Stare them in the face. Fully feel what is

happening. Give yourself the freedom to cry, laugh, scream, or shout. Write everything down if you want, without censorship. Spit it all out. Do whatever you need to do to allow what is there to be there. Then, get rid of it. When the time is up, it's up. You only have ten minutes. It is now your duty to go on with your day. Any time those feelings start to arise again, tell yourself you will revisit them only during the allotted time at the end of your day (ten minutes ... max). If you adhere to this exercise for a minimum of twenty-one days (the amount of time that has been proven to change or break a habit), you will begin to notice something magical happening. Your feelings of pain/despair/grief are not as intense anymore. They don't have as much of an effect on you as they used to. You are opening your heart to your *Passions* and inspirations again, and the pain, which you thought was your enemy, was the very vehicle that provided this expansion.

In your willingness to approach your fear with an awakened heart, you can continue to expand and grow beyond it. When everything is said and done, the ripened, open heart is all that really matters. Did we love enough while we were here in this brief, physical form? What will you take with you when you go—your house, your car, your children, your lover? It is only the *love* burning in your soul that will accompany you into the next realm of being where you will harvest the seeds that you sprouted from your inspirations, here, now. Open and melt into your very own heart. When you do, you will have cracked the code to peace, everlasting. You can go there *right now, and be happy forever—in this moment.*

Silent Shadows

Sit there like a stone.

Sit there in the sweetness and the sorrow.

Steep yourself in the stew of your past, present, and future, here and now.

Don't move.

Allow any dark demons that arise to do their dance,

In the scary shadows of your menacing mind.

The pest that growls and grumbles and keeps you from your peace.

Stop. Don't move.

Witness your slippery thoughts as they begin to surge and gather force.

Stop. Stare at all that is seething in your skull as it rises and rages from the stormy sloth.

Watch yourself being swept up, swirled, and hurled in this stunning illusion.

Sit there like a stone.

Now, join the One, Who, in silence, sees the light as it shimmers through.

Dazzling, sparkling with delight, dispersing the illusory shadows,

And replacing them with the marriage of rain and sun.

You participated in creating this miracle-rainbow.

Move, stir, awaken.

Realize that all of the jewels you have been chasing

Are the glittering gemstones,

Shimmering within your very own heart.

—Luann Robinson Hull

❧ EXERCISE ❧

Create your existence from your own center of Power and Passion. Take responsibility for how you want your life to be and then make a daily decision that you will create every possible opportunity for yourself to move into and live from the genius zone that will effortlessly guide you toward the most regal regions of your being. If you are on, celebrate. If you are off, flip the switch and reactivate yourself. No remorse or self-doubt. Just begin again—all of the time. Be obedient and faithful to this way of being. Now, detach yourself from every outcome across all areas of your life and decide that you will be supplied with the most expanded good imaginable from this moment forward. You are Queen of your world. Bring forward your Passions and inspirations. As you make a conscious commitment to this magical path, add the next jewel to your crown. You now have acquired beryl, which opens you to your full and optimal potential as you continue awakening the passions within. Continue watching yourself sparkle into the radiance of your very own rainbow of gems. Anything is possible because now you realize that you are the miracle that you always thought was just out of your reach.

NINE

PREEMINENCE—
LIVE LIKE A QUEEN EVERY DAY

Jewel: Rose Quartz for Attracting Unconditional Love

"Genuine happiness is a profound and lasting sense of peace and fulfillment that deeply satisfies and enlarges the soul. It doesn't go away when circumstances get difficult. It survives and even grows through hardship and struggle. True happiness is our entire reason to live, and that kind of happiness can only be obtained as we find Real Love and share it with others. With Real Love, nothing else matters; without it, nothing else is enough."

—Greg Baer, M.D.

Real Love

Most of us have a desire to eliminate suffering in our lives. In order to open into our full and most radiant joy, we have *got* to show up each day with a *conscious decision* to become the joy we are waiting to receive. To cultivate such an attitude requires commitment, responsibility, and discernment. A significant part of the process involves learning to distinguish the difference between happiness (peace, fulfillment) and pleasure (immediate gratification, or short-lived ecstasy). Identifying how to experience and then live our lives from a foundation of *real love* is a critical component of the formula for *happily ever after ... right now.*

What does *real love* feel like? How can you be sure when you are truly experiencing it? *A Course in Miracles* tells us that "Real love has no lurking shadows or dark corners for it is bathed in light. It does not seek power because it is power. And it does not search for freedom because it is already free." In accessing this *real love*, which is ever available to us, we must be strictly committed to and completely firm in letting go of everything that does not mirror back to us the most expanded possibilities for our growth and ultimate freedom.

Real love is multifaceted. To have passion for another can be fitting when kept in the proper perspective—as long as this passion is balanced with self-love, care, patience, and *freedom,* both for yourself and for the beloved. Freedom is one of the most important elements of *real love.* In order to know your beloved, you must be willing to dissolve and melt into a new way of being, in a sense, to become one with him. Yet, to genuinely experience a sense of oneness with this other, you cannot seek to possess him, because *he is not yours to own.* You have joined him (for now), so that the two of you can become more familiar with the circular nature of love through your mutual growth and exploration. It is in such an exploration that you will come to know and experience feelings of:

> Rapture (How dearly you will want to hold on to those moments of bliss that take you there—*let go, there is more to come. Embrace the mystery).*

> Heartache (You want to blame him—don't. *If you do, you are projecting).*

Joy (You adore him—*balance*—*remember he is only human*).

Defeat (He has "won" the disagreement—your ego has gone into competition. *Stop*. Remember where your peace is. *Go there*).

Devastation (He is leaving, he marries someone else, or he dies. *Have faith*. As you allow yourself to go through whatever is necessary to experience your grief and sadness, you will transcend this temporary pain, and when you do, you will have attained another important rite of passage in your life, preparing you for some new delight).

Patience (Sometimes his behaviors totally frustrate you. When you are tempted to be short-tempered, *breathe*, and remember that he has to put up with your idio-syncrasies, too).

Compassion (He lost his job and you must be there to support him. *No matter what fears this situation may provoke in you, treat him as you would want to be treated*).

Freedom (If his developing passion requires him to be away from you for long periods of time—*allow space for his growth*, while sharing with him your genuine enthusiasm. Then communicate your fears and concerns. *Be fair*. You will be rewarded—*abundantly*).

Your beloved is the one who will teach you more of what you need to know about yourself, and who you are becoming. It is crucial for you to always remember that without him, you will still be yourself, and you can still be happy. And with him, you have the potential to expand and grow into other versions of happiness and fulfillment. Remember, he is not Prince Charming. He has come into your life to join you. Not to save you.

Learning to Love Liberty

The more freedom you allow him (and yourself), the more you will contribute to the stability of the relationship. When you try to hold on, or restrict him in any way, you will cause him to feel limited and confined. He must be given the freedom to pursue his purpose with your full support, even if it means the two of you will go your separate ways at some point. Learn to accept *his truth as your truth*, and expect the same from him. Making such a personal and collective commitment requires that you continue developing trust, first in yourself, and then in him.

When you are feeling threatened by his desire for more freedom, don't cave in to your survival instincts. Be strong and keep giving him more rope. And if he wants to take the rope and go, release him—with your blessing. The Divine example, which is wanting freedom of choice for those you love, is the best or only model to follow for obvious reasons.

If at any time you feel that he is restricting *your* purpose (however conscious or unconscious his actions may appear), you must speak up and immediately seek to resolve the situation. In firmly staying true to your commitment to grow toward all that will open you into your natural state of peace and happiness, you must be fiercely *dedicated to the truth (wherever that truth takes you—even if it is out the door)*. Such a commitment must be the foundation of your relationship. It is the only way. To hang on and cling to each other when your goals and the energy behind those are no longer a fit, will not do. In your quest for *real love*, you are choosing to expand and grow beyond the confines and constrictions of emotional separation, fear, anguish, hatred, and resentment, both in your individual souls, as well as the soul of the relationship, however that may take form.

Probably about ninety-nine percent of the human race is still acting out traits that exemplify emotional aberrations, which result from a fear-based paradigm. You and I are no exceptions. Just because we may consider ourselves to be engaged in a process of growth and transformation does not mean we are off the hook. We must stay vigilant at rooting out the old prototypes still *deeply* engrained in our psyche.

Listen for just one minute to the daily news or read a random paragraph from the front page of your local newspaper and then ask yourself, "Is the foundation of this information based on love, unity, connection, and oneness? Or are the qualities of fear and emotional dysfunction more evident?" The influences of our ancestral patterns are still with us, and so we are not exempt from their fierce persuasion. If we want to live in a world without fear, hatred, war, and separation from our Divine heritage, it is up to us to carry the torch for transformation. Anyone who is willing to pay attention can see the signs. And *you* have paid attention and seen the signs. Even so, it is not up to you to save the world. Just do your part.

Self-Love: The Launch Pad

The journey of loving and being loved requires making a lifelong commitment to self-love and self-respect. Admit to yourself that you have made mistakes, celebrate your willingness to learn from these errors, and honor your desire to discover and develop your dreams. Be as tender, patient, compassionate, and kind to yourself as you would be to an aging, beloved elder or a tiny, helpless newborn. Learn to love who you are without exceptions. Regard your mistakes as opportunities (I know, it sounds clichéd, but it really is the only decent way to live). Remember that you have strength and stamina. Don't allow the pitfalls to throw you off the path. Avoid putting too much emphasis on perceived shortcomings or attributes. If you wallow in either one too long, you will miss the guideposts that have the potential to broaden your exploration. Above all, have a grateful heart for every single event, person, place, or circumstance that has brought you to this very moment.

Liberating Ourselves, Liberating Our Ancestors

In opening to the possibility of *real love,* we must continue transforming the texture of our hearts from the coarseness of our ancestry into a smoother, more pliable state. Our predecessors maintained their tough demeanor in order to survive. As we decide to unplug from the highly charged emotional patterns that they established to endure, these patterns will no longer be recognized because our ancient conditioning will have atrophied and fallen away. In letting go of our reactions, we will weaken and eventually dismantle the "docking stations," which formerly conducted the charges in producing their high-voltage effect. Our commitment to neutralize these surges triggered in our "old brain" by external events will eventually result in liberation from our fearful past. As we release ourselves, so do we set free our ancestors, allowing them to finally rest in peace. They made stunning contributions to the future of the human race—paving the way for our own participation in being of service. As we proceed, we can recruit some of their determination, will, and resolve, while oscillating outward and beyond the limitations of their crude, primal world.

Until we can firmly establish new thought forms, we must be on constant alert so that we can notice and eliminate the outdated tendencies that no longer serve us. Start to catch the fear before it catches you. Be crystal clear on what is true and what you are making up or exaggerating. If you start to clam up because he is feeling detached or distant, watch yourself. His behavior may be exacerbated by the energy that you are creating in your attempts to hold on to him. Now is the time to stop, be still, and take a personal inventory. How would you want to be treated? Wouldn't you want freedom? Ask yourself who is out of line here. Be fair. If it is *you*, take responsibility and act accordingly. If he is the one off-center, *communicate with him openly and honestly without judgment.* Silently flood yourself with encouraging, constructive affirmations to boost your strength. As you continue rebuilding your confidence and courage, allow yourself to be vulnerable by sharing some of your fears and concerns with him. Keep on *opening your heart.* In your willingness to do so, regardless of the outcome, you will be feeding and watering the seeds of *real love* with the nutrients that will not only nurture and grow your own soul and spirit, but also the soul and spirit of everything and everyone you touch (including him).

The task before us is to begin noticing how our accumulated impressions of love have evolved over time. Sometimes we can be overwhelmed and swept away. This type of "love" is more concerned with what it can get, rather than what it can offer (an ideology of love that is linked to our primal patterning). Another approach to love is more focused, thoughtful, responsible, and compassionate, having its roots in conscious awareness and a desire for the most expanded good of all involved. Such an attitude is the proper path to *real love*— the type of love that has the potential to move us along and away from our primitive patterning.

The multitude of brain waves in our heads travel on pathways that have been programmed over time. This process is what conditioning is all about. And when we give in to our conditioned responses, we strengthen the conduits that reinforce old behaviors *over and over again* (such as what we perceive *real love* to be). The brain is not selective. It will copy and replicate any information received. Think of the brain like the hard drive of a computer, which will receive whatever software is inserted. It does not censor or use a process of selection. It simply allows for data input when inserted, and then assimilates and regurgitates whatever is downloaded.

When we behave like a computer, we can become robotic and mechanical. Reverting to the programming of our personal and ancestral history, like rats in a maze, we will respond to triggers and stimuli. Thus, if we believe we smell the cheese, we'll keep chasing after it. Never mind that with every step we are becoming dizzier and dumber. In following our instincts instead of our *insight*, we will be driven by forces that feel like they are beyond our control. Insight is always available to you through your willingness to be aware of your conditioned reactions to events. Learn to discern what is useful and what is not, and begin to emancipate yourself from the control of your conditioning. Instead of acting based on instinct, practice operating from your own central base of power (or the eternal Inner Love-Light, which can never be extinguished). In focusing on this light, you will be guided toward all that will open you to *real love* both in yourself, and in others.

As long as the grooves and crevasses in our heads are repeatedly reinforced by the perpetuation of conditioned responses ("good" or "bad"), we will not escape their influence, and the ruts that these behaviors produce will deepen. Nonetheless, we *can* alter the deep ditches that linger in our minds. All we need to do is fill them with the thought forms that will *support* our growth, rather than prevent it. The brain is malleable. It will enthusiastically receive new information. And when repeatedly introduced, this different data will be permanently stored to such a degree that the old, outdated patterns will be deleted.

The Look of *Real Love*

Understanding how this process of changing our conditioned responses works is a beginning, but awareness alone does not cause change. Change can only occur when you make a conscious decision to do whatever it takes to go boldly toward all that will help you to first *become* the love of your own life, prior to searching for love in other places. You have to be able to recognize *real love* by first experiencing it through a conscious commitment to loving yourself. And once you do, you will know from every awakening cell in your being that *you don't need someone else to provide what you already have.* Then when a potential partner appears (or is already beside you), you will see him as someone significant in your life who will join you in extending and opening this love of yours—outward, upward, and beyond.

Remember Sara, who decided to spend almost a year alone to get to know herself better? In her ensuing journey toward real love, she spent many years learning how to be a self-advocate, taking responsibility for her life, discovering the true principles of *real love*, practicing this authentic love on herself, and then extending it to others. Through education, self-improvement, and spiritual growth, she continues to be engaged in altering the former patterns of behavior that repeatedly found her wallowing in want and wedged in the "Prince-Charming-will-save-me" syndrome. When she finally became weary of her repeated difficulty and defeat, she fully committed herself to engaging in the practices that it would take to transform. And what she has learned is that it is not necessary to travel the long, winding path to freedom. Rather, she believes that if you are proactive and have a strong commitment to growth, you will start to see immediate results. Sara is choosing to share her story because she *did* take the circuitous route first. In offering what happened as a result of her traveling the back alleys and rocky roads, she hopes to contribute to your commitment in doing whatever it takes to engage in a more streamlined approach to your *happily ever after … right now.* In setting the tone for Sara's story, we will begin with a short and whimsical fairy tale.

Once upon a time, in a land far away, a happy, independent, self-confident Queen came across a rather pitiful, forlorn-looking frog while sitting on the shores of a beautiful lake close to her castle.

To her surprise, the frog jumped on her lap and spoke, "Glorious Queen that you are, I know that you have the power to remove an evil spell, which was cast upon me. If you would just provide one kiss, I am certain to return to the days of my glory when I was the most handsome Prince in the kingdom. Then, I can marry you, and I will be King! Once we unite in marriage, I shall take over all official business (since I am the man) and you can take care of me. You can bear my children, keep the castle looking beautiful, support what I am doing for the world, and be forever grateful and happy that you are by my side."

That night, as the Queen dined on sumptuous, sautéed frog legs seasoned to utter perfection, she recalled the frog's proposal with amusement. "I don't flipping think so ..."

The Princess Turns Queen

In hindsight, Sara wishes she would have had the nerve to think and behave like the Queen in the story, but she didn't have the knowledge she has now and so, she went ahead and accepted the frog's proposal—*big mistake*. Sara admits that it has taken an unwavering commitment to growth and change for her to stay focused on the fine-tuning necessary for transformation. Nonetheless, when she remembers that she once gladly settled for the role of maid, mother, and main support-person for the Frog Prince, she admits that any challenge she has faced as a result of her resolve to grow has been incidental compared to the life she was living while staying stuck in her old ways. Here is Sara's story—still in progress:

When I was in high school, I was pretty much one of those mysteriously invisible creatures. Even though I was attractive and mildly popular, I had little, if any, self-confidence. I saw myself as unremarkable—just an average girl, with average achievements. And so I sort of blended in. I didn't care much about school really, just about what I was going to *wear* to school, so that I could attract boyfriends. And, the only positive result from that preoccupation was to be deemed the "Best Dressed" girl in my senior year. (The boyfriend thing didn't work out too well. But my choices were a perfect reflection of how I saw myself—which was just a shade above miserable). I participated in some class plays and musicals, which I enjoyed immensely, but my near-paralyzing stage fright restricted me from ever being a soloist or having a lead role.

Layton Hedger, a couple of years my senior, was unequivocally one of the most popular guys at Martin Luther King High. He was an all-American hunk (football star and all). Naturally, in taking on the role of the invisible underachiever, it *never* occurred to me during those lonely, hollow, high-school days that Layton and I would hook up someday. To my surprise, just following my twentieth birthday, and after a broken engagement to Ed, he found his way to my heart through a mutual friend.

It took hours for me to prepare for our first evening together. In attempting to organize myself for the occasion, I felt like I was about to take the most challenging exam of my life for which I was completely and utterly unprepared. He had carefully put together an elaborate picnic and optional swim (the picnic extended into the wee hours and the pool was closed, but we broke in and swam anyway).

Layton Hedger was the essence of charm and charisma, in other words, he was the *ultimate* Prince. *Dear God.* I could barely breathe for most of the evening, during which I recall never relieving my bulging bladder *one single time* (an absolute first—and come to think of it, it hasn't happened since). What would he think if I just started whizzing in the grass? Never mind that Layton frequently took his leave for the make-shift urinal in the bushes—underneath which was that very same grass. And yet, somehow it was perfectly natural for him to do so. He was exonerated from any embarrassment as far as I was concerned. He was Layton.

About as quickly as it had started, probably the most memorable evening of my life came to a screeching halt. Just like Cinderella after midnight, I was left standing in the garden, completely disheveled. My make-up and hair were a mess from the swim, and they served as a perfect representation for the intense spin I was in from the wake (or was it the undertow?) of an evening spent with Layton Hedger. This would-be Prince vanished just as quickly as he had appeared. As I watched him circle the driveway in his red corvette, I wondered if I would ever lay eyes on this glorious creature again. He waved good-bye (that famed, familiar last-look farewell, which we all know and *hate*) and that was that. No, "I had a great time." No, "I will call you tomorrow." Just, "See ya." (Perhaps I should have taken this cue to be a warning. I didn't). Layton Hedger had become the magnet (enticer) and I, the magnetized (enticed). This was to be the beginning of a dizzying dance that would move me to the heights, and to many, many dark and dismal depths.

It has taken me a long time to understand the simple yet profound lyrics of the once familiar song from the sixties, which obviously was a little ahead of its time, *and* mine: "Got along without you before I met you, gonna get along without you now." I remained stuck in the magnetic draw of Layton Hedger, which at times was consuming, for a period that would exceed long after we ended our relationship—at least as we had known it.

And so, on that fateful romantic summer's night, Layton Hedger became a legend, who would ever be locked in my memory, even as the fairy tale would transcend and change over time.

He did show up the next night at my door (unannounced). I was actually entertaining another young man, (having already moved on since I thought Layton was a one night thing and had disappeared from my life). When I sent my brother to the door to cover for me (who obediently took the instruction to do whatever it took to keep Layton from discovering that one of his old high-school chums was in our living room), Layton must have been a bit put off. Perhaps his suspicious irritation inspired a pursuit. Maybe I wasn't so available after all—and so began the hunting and chasing between Layton Hedger and Sara Hopper in a funky little Mississippi swamp town, so many, many years ago.

Layton was the perfect Brute/Prince Charming. And since I was the Babe/Princess, I spent most of the time we were "together" occupied with attempts to "keep" Layton, so as to ensure that he would remain faithfully by my side. I was always afraid and constantly vigilant. What would become of me if he *did* actually decide to take off? Naturally, my varying degrees of insecurity would peak when he noticed other women. Those of you who were trained as Princess-hopefuls (as in go to college if you want, but your primary focus is to become someone's wife) might understand my dismay when Layton continually ogled over my sister-in-law's trim body and Audrey Hepburn looks. What did he think of me? I would never really know for sure. Can you feel what that was like? If you can, you were likely a Princess-hopeful, too.

And, I waited in vain for him to say those three words that I so longed to hear. The silence was utterly deafening. Layton Hedger did not speak of love—*ever.* To my overwhelming dismay, the word did not appear to be in his vocabulary. What I was to learn much, much later is that Layton was the one who finally helped me to realize that there was nothing he, or anyone else, could say or do that would fill the bottomless pit of my longing. I had to find my own formula for resolving that desperate dilemma —though it would take many years of looking for the answers elsewhere before I finally would understand what was really true. The *real love* that I had been seeking was patiently waiting to be discovered in the warmth of my very own heart.

There were some pretty interesting times with Layton. Like early on in our relationship, when his "other" girlfriend came rushing to his side upon word of a family crisis. (We can only assume that Layton had to have been the informant—and hence had been maintaining communication with her during our developing relationship). I was the local and she was the non-local. It was clear that there wouldn't be room for both of us in the life of Layton and that *she* was going to be the one to go. So, I decided to take action and enter myself into a self-imposed contest with this young woman, whom I perceived to be trampling on *my* territory, *my* town, and *my* guy. I had gone into full possession mode—clearly having not a clue about the vitally important component of *freedom* necessary in *real love*. The Babe/Princess in me was fully operative. And, like any good Babe-Princess would do, I waited—rather than walking away upon hearing that Martha was anything but out of the picture. Not too bright, but, then, Princess-hopefuls aren't necessarily known for developing their brains and bravado. Which one of us would win the heart (however deeply hidden and disguised it may have appeared) of Layton Hedger? Hi-De-Ho. Guess who got the prize? Of course, this award was not granted without some significant maneuvering on my part—the gotcha-with-guilt-thing was the ploy that probably tugged at his conscience and caused him to be influenced in my direction, though we will never know for sure.

My cue that I might have been "chosen" on that fateful eve when Layton came to deliver the news, was his reference to the then popular Carol King song, "It's Too Late, Baby" (What did that mean? Was it too late for me, or too late for her?). In hindsight, I'm not certain I ever really knew for sure. This method of sharing was to be a foreshadowing of the developing communication style between us that was *anything* but direct. In hindsight, to have exited the Layton Hedger scene altogether (Prince, Brute and all) upon hearing the news of the "Martha invasion," would have been a much more appropriate move. However, back then, I was insufficiently equipped with the courage or fortitude necessary for such a bold maneuver. And so I did not advocate, or set any limits or boundaries, I just manipulated—like all Babes do, which contributes to the already-southward direction of our communication style. And in keeping with our developing mastery at the "silence is golden" theme, Layton and I did not speak again of the Martha debacle—and so I never revealed my permanent loss of trust in him and the personal devastation her untimely, surprise visit had caused.

In my mind, this boy (man?) was a perfect combination of hunk and heartbreaker. Gorgeous, sexy, clever, and utterly brilliant—it appeared he could have anything he wanted. He was well on his way to becoming an esteemed professional, and I had pegged myself as the absolute perfect "stand by your man" girl. Doing everything I could to be good enough to maintain that role, I cooked, I cleaned, I dressed up, I did my hair, and I put *lots* of make-up on, and then—I watched, and I waited. Upon my infrequent, coveted visits to see him (he was in medical school during most of the time we dated), I remained vigilant while lingering in the wings of his tiny Tucson apartment, ever hopeful that he would emerge from his study cubicle—which was off-limits to me—and seek respite in my company, even if only for a moment.

I often convinced myself (of course, we never discussed our feelings) that he had little, if any, interest in anything having to do with me, other than sex or support (pretty much in that order), which I attempted to make faithfully available to supply *at all times possible.* I did not complain or advocate for myself because I did not know how. I didn't understand that I, too, had passion, potential, and something to offer to the world. But I wouldn't discover or come to follow that passion and potential until much, much later. And so I just kept mindlessly doing what I was doing, that is, trying to be as good as I could in the Babe/Princess role, until I was so utterly emotionally and physically drained and exhausted that I finally fizzled out.

That's when I knew that something had to change, and I had pretty much figured out that Layton Hedger would not be the one to do the changing. So, I made change happen in the only way that I knew how at that tender, vulnerable, and mostly unconscious time of my life. I went and I found another Prince Charming to replace him, even though I was utterly and completely heartbroken at the mere thought of living my life without Layton, and I would remain in that state for a long time. As fate would have it, the time frame of my departure occurred just prior to his graduation from medical school. In that tiny makeshift modular, Layton Hedger had managed to mastermind his way into becoming number one in his class. Years later, I would wonder if my presence during that critical time in his life had been more of a distraction or crutch, rather than a source of love and support, which, from my perspective, I believed I had provided using everything earthly possible that was available to me at that time.

I did end up marrying the other version of Prince Charming, and unlike our heroine in the amusing anecdote that preceded this story, I never once said, "I don't flipping think so," to the duties expected of me that would accompany the union. I cooked, I cleaned, I smiled, and I looked pretty in my Princess clothes. And, I supported *his* growth and *his* achievements to the point of near emotional breakdown. Predictably, the time came once again for me to make a change, and not unlike before, I believed the solution to my dilemma was to trade in the demanding, stern Prince Charming #2 for yet another model (admittedly, I can be a slow learner). So, I divorced Prince Charming #2 and promptly found Prince Charming #3. The drama deepened and the cycle of pain and pleasure became more dizzying and defeating, until eventually I became so severely anxious and depressed that I had to be hospitalized.

I think it was the trip to the nut farm and the compassionate physician with the bow tie that finally got my attention. This kind and caring man gently and masterfully facilitated a stunning awakening in me. I started to become aware that the ache of longing, which perpetually tugged at my soul, might just have something to do with what was unresolved in *me*. It wasn't the Brute/Prince who was going to come to my rescue after all. *I had to do it.* What a lousy twist of fate! My years in training as a Babe/Princess had all been in vain. Alas, I had to start over. And so slowly and carefully, I began the long, arduous process of taking responsibility for my own life and my own happiness. Eventually, I came to understand that I could use all of those years in training as a Princess-Hopeful for guidance (but if I were you, I would skip that part and go for taking responsibility *now*).

On my wedding day to Prince Charming #2 (PC2), I realized that I had made a disastrous mistake. Layton would not be there to meet me at the end of that very short aisle. Instead, there would be a stranger who came from a world that I barely knew and little understood. Maybe Layton would come before or during the ceremony, like in the classic movie, *The Graduate*, sweep me up and carry me away from this nightmare. My fantasy did not materialize. Layton Hedger did not come.

Somehow I made it through the hurricane reception. I saw PC2 for a sum total of about ten minutes during the entire event (a foreshadowing of what was to come in our marriage) and that included the ride in the car from the church. The rest of the time was spent in trying to keep from fainting in a room filled with a trillion people that I had never met and didn't care to ever see again. Then there was the honeymoon to some remote island that might as well have been the moon. I secretly spent time plotting how to flee and return to Layton, but alas, that was not to be. For twelve years I continued to stop myself short of leaving my miserable marriage to PC2. When I finally did go and subsequently set out to find Layton, he was more unavailable than ever. And one more time, I would find myself saddened and longing for an illusion that could never possibly materialize.

Admittedly, I screwed up. I didn't mean to, and I did anyway. Did I make a mistake in not marrying Layton Hedger? No, I don't think so. Rather, the mistake was in how I *handled* not marrying him. (Oh yes, Layton did finally ask, but that was *after* I had told him I would be going off with PC2—not exactly the best timing on his part). Layton and I were not meant to be together. I was consumed with him, and he was consumed with his developing career (the focus on which, incidentally, *did* result in a stunning professional future). Somehow I had been destined to learn the meaning of *real love*, and even though Layton contributed enormously to that discovery, I doubt I would have been able to notice *real love* at that time of my life, let alone be able to live it. After many years, I believe I finally know how to love Layton Hedger—by setting him free and loving myself.

It is important that I make one thing very clear. Even though I have great respect for Layton's contributions to the world (he is now making a significantly positive global impact with his own version of *Preeminence*), I have not elevated him to sainthood—at least not yet. I do not exonerate him from his part in the dysfunction that we both created. He was distant, and insensitive. He was unavailable, aloof, and noncommittal, at least until he thought I was going to marry someone else (the marker of a true Brute). Now, once again, I don't doubt that I aggravated those qualities in him by my poorly disguised neediness. Nonetheless, Layton *did* act out his role in the classic drama and demise of our relationship (we played our respective parts of the Brute and Babe dance *exquisitely*). Hopefully by now, he has made some of his own discoveries and based on those is living his own version of *happily ever after ... right now*. But maybe I will never know.

Today, many years since that fateful picnic and swim, I am finding my way through the mysteries while moving into the joys of *real love*. I have benefited enormously from my years in training with Layton (and a host of others, whom I have undoubtedly wounded and harmed, even as I focused on how I was being injured or victimized by them.) Finally, I understand that playing "less than" and taking on an inferior role, or trying to be good so that I will be significant in someone else's life, does not support my *Magnificence*. And I have come to embrace the true qualities of a *real love*, which have nothing to do with need and dependency—just pure, unconditional care and concern for another's (*and* my own) growth, joy, happiness, freedom, fulfillment, and peace. Lovers have come and gone, my partner *may* endure, and yet, I know one love that will never leave. It is the *real love* that lives in me.

Here are a few of the beginning inquiries to which I was guided that created the foundation for bringing me out of the wicked spell of the "trench trolls" (those nasty little creatures who continued doing the digs in my skull that kept me stuck). What is it that makes me feel diminished in another's presence? Does this feeling have to do with my conditioning or my insights? Why am I so hard on myself? What is it that I think someone else can do for me that I can't do for myself? What will it take for me to move from a need-based paradigm to a choice-based paradigm? What are the components necessary for me to create a foundation of freedom? How can I come to love and care about myself unconditionally, thereby creating a foundation for me to love others in the same way? Who am I anyway? And as I keep discovering and uncovering my essence (a lifelong process to be sure), can I continue to be okay with who I am and not have to prove my worth to others by endlessly trying to be loved?

These questions were enough to get me started, though I certainly didn't move into my rising wisdom unaccompanied. I saw an extraordinarily wise therapist. I studied self-help books until I was saturated with spirit up to my crown chakra. I went to workshops, joined meditation groups and women's circles, and went back to school, climbed mountains, walked beaches, engaged in physical/emotional release work, did cleanses, experienced energy healing, and worked with a host of brilliant spiritual teachers. But most importantly, I continue to do everything I can to scour out and cleanse away any and everything that is chipping away at my soul. It has been a complex process. *And yours absolutely does not have to be so complicated. Keep it simple.*

Through everything, my willingness to be honest with myself has been one of the most growth-enhancing, albeit humbling, techniques of all. In facing the truth, I have had to admit the following: I've screwed up a lot—not just a little, but a lot. I have been insensitive and uncaring, at times getting caught in the web of my own desires and wants. There have been occasions where I have been tempted to be a victim. While attempting to be both mother and father to my children, often I have over-functioned, which has definitely caused some back-lash. I have spent more money than I have made—definitely being less than a conscious steward of my resources on occasion. There's more, but you get the point, which is that I have failed, even in the midst of my successes. And through it all, I have finally been able to embrace every part of it: the good, the bad, and the ugly. Rather than keeping score of the victories and breakdowns, I choose to focus now on whatever is happening *in this moment* and then going forward with the selected ideology (following many years of trial and error) that I know will carry me into the next octave of conscious awareness. My past is my past. I cannot retrieve or change it. But I *can* be accepting. And so I have done my very best to make amends both to myself and to others when possible (though I must admit the nasty phantoms of guilt and projection still crop up from time to time).

One of the most important lessons I have learned is that there is still a part of me that wants the fairy tale, and who operates out of conditioning. Even though that part's influence is weakening (this work in the trenches is definitely paying off), it can be quite persuasive on occasion. And I am particularly influenced when feeling vulnerable (yes, it still happens—I just know how to manage it better now). The good news is that I have learned how to turn up the voice of the soul and when I do, without exception sooner or later (mostly sooner), I will be soothed and guided back into the safety of my own skin. Old patterns of behavior are rigid and fixed. If we have spent most of our lives believing that the Prince will come to the rescue, we must be gentle with ourselves as we allow education and awareness to overcome our deeply conditioned fears and insecurities.

The Sara and Layton Who Live in Us All

Is Sara Hopper real? Yes, because she represents the collective idea of heartbreak and hope that lives in us all. And as for Layton, does he exist? Perhaps, but he is truly brought to life through the lens of our own unique experiences. Each of us will more than likely encounter a Layton Hedger in some shape or form at one time or another in our lives. What matters is not how we can come to possess, long for, blame, or discard him, but rather how we can more fully come to love through the experiences that his presence in our lives awakens.

Your version of Layton Hedger has the potential to guide you to the miraculous in yourself. And so, no matter how much you think he has hurt you or caused you heartbreak in the past, it is time to lose the sad story and realize that it is *you*, in your own glorious state of *Preeminence*, that will rescue the fragile part of yourself still waiting in the lonely tower of trials and tribulations, longing and hoping to be saved by Prince Charming. If he *never* says, "I love you," you must be the one to stand in front of your magic mirror and repeat those three words to yourself over and over again, until you actually *believe* them. And how will you know when you do? You will know when you are no longer waiting for Layton Hedger or anyone else to validate that you are worthy of being loved because you hear those beautiful words—"I love you"—echoing back to you from every corner of your universe.

And, as for your rescue of Prince Layton from his frog-curse with a kiss from your Queenly lips? Naturally, that particular formula is part of the fairy-tale myth. You must realize that your kiss won't really help much. Alas, it is up to him to break the spell that has kept him cast in the shadows of a shut-down heart. He is in full possession of the key to the padlock that has perpetuated his separation from the love that is waiting to be discovered in his own soul. He can easily lift the dark enchantment that has kept him removed and distant from everything that aches to be awakened in him. All he has to do is decide to unlock the dead bolt and liberate himself from his own bondage. Whether or not he ever decides to do that is of no concern to you. Your responsibility is to *go on loving him anyway*, however his spirit may manifest in the world. Love, love, love. That is all. That is it. Now then, we have already been through the drill of how to honor yourself. If he cannot meet you where you are, ya gotta let him go, or if he is already history, dissociate yourself from that part of your life. Do not allow him *near* you unless you are completely convinced (from your developing Queen consciousness) that he is willing to explore with you the true meaning of *real love*. And if he won't, then keep loving him with all of your heart and soul—always and forever—*from a distance*.

It is time now, wherever your version of Layton Hedger may be, to bless him and set him free, and as you do, he will feel the ripple of your generosity expanding and reaching out to touch him, even if he is on the moon. He has made a tremendous contribution to your developing awareness of *real love*. So this is the moment to shower *him* with *real love*, freely, and in a way that is appropriate, considering both of your current circumstances. (Use your insight here. You will know what to do). What he does with that *real love* simply does not matter, because it has come to him from the purest of intentions. At last, you give your love without any expectation of what you will receive. You simply love for the joy of loving. Now, set *yourself* free and claim your *Preeminence*. Add Rose Quartz to your crown of jewels, and consider your heart fully activated. You know the meaning of *real love*.

New Stories, New Enchantments

Be still and see if you can sense the beating of your own heart. Just sit there until you can feel it. Now, realize that this rhythm is created from a Force that lives through you but is not of you. It has chosen you as the vehicle through which real love can uniquely be expressed. It is ever there to guide and support you as you embark on the mysterious adventures that will open you fully to the Essence in you that connects you to this Force. It does not seek to receive anything from you, for it is already complete in and of Itself. Rather does It yearn for the experience of offering the current and texture of Its flow as you share It with the world? In opening yourself to receive this abiding Love in its purest form, be aware that infinite possibilities for joy and happiness await you. All you have to do is decide to embark on the journey that will take you there. Let real love be your guide. Begin.

❧ EXERCISE ❧

Look in your magic mirror three times daily and repeat, "I love you"—indefinitely.

TEN

PARTNERSHIP— REVAMP YOUR RELATIONSHIP WITH MEN

Jewel: Angelite for Speaking Your Truth and Acceptance of Others

"What is necessary to the growth of the partnership is identical to your own growth ... each of you holds a piece that the other is missing."

—Gary Zukav

Soul Sister

If we really want to experience true intimacy with a partner, then we have to be willing to tune in to our very own heart and soul. What is the secret to finding happiness, finding the right partner, the right career, enough money, better looks, more energy, and greater health? You must begin by making a commitment to loving *yourself*. The soul sister that lives in your essence will never leave or forsake you. *Marry her first* (or marry her *now* if you are already married). Go and buy yourself a simple, little eternity ring. Slip it on the third finger of your left hand, and make a personal pledge to begin (or continue) learning how to provide for *yourself* absolutely everything that you think (or thought) you would require from someone else in a conscious, loving relationship. Every time you look at the ring, be reminded of what it symbolizes: a lasting commitment to *you.*

What will it take to recruit all of the love, compassion, forgiveness, understanding, support, affirmation, and patience you can muster on a daily (hourly) basis, and then give it to *yourself*? For many of us, this is an unfamiliar inquiry. We have been trained to believe that *self-love* is selfish. It isn't. Understand that if you cannot fully love and accept yourself, it will be impossible for others to love and accept you. The magnitude of love that exists within your very own being is *infinite.* And if we are not experiencing this love in bountiful supply, then we have to look inside and ask ourselves what it is that is keeping the lid on. Maybe we will never know. It doesn't matter. What does matter is your willingness to discover in yourself everything that you may have been waiting for someone else to provide.

Be absolutely vigilant around any negative thoughts that are self-directed, and turn these thoughts into loving kindness. Notice how deeply conditioned negativity is. Here is a simple example. Suppose you are in school and you just have done poorly on a test (by your standards). What is your first inclination? Is it to tell yourself how wonderful you are for even trying to do your best on the test (compassion)? Is it to find all of the ways that you have been successful in this situation (loving kindness)? Or are you more inclined to belittle and berate yourself for not measuring up, for not being good enough (self-degradation)? Unless we have been trained to the contrary, when we experience a perceived failure, we will jump to feelings of shame and disgrace almost immediately, because of our conditioning. It won't even occur to us to look at the positive aspects of the situation. And each time we tell ourselves how wrong we are, or how miserably we have fallen short, guess what happens in our computer brain? It records and stores the data as unsuccessful and then the idea of failure gets triggered every time we think we haven't measured up.

It is high time for our brains to be programmed with new information. Catch yourself before you go into the dramatic negative (or if you have already slipped into that mode, wake up now, and stop what you are doing). Try having a list available for referencing, either in your head or on hard copy, of all the ways that you are utterly *Magnificent*—even if it is how you floss your teeth. It doesn't matter what it is as long as you *believe* it. *Just find everything possible to love about yourself.* Every single person on the planet has something extraordinary to offer. And *not bringing forward whatever that is,* which of course, cannot be done in the absence of self-love, is the root of all misery and suffering. So, start practicing how to *love yourself,* bunions, warts, and all.

Love Lamp

Realize that you have an inexhaustible inner light that glows even in your darkest moments. This light is eternal. It can never be extinguished. And the only way for you to actually experience its full, radiant brilliance is to embrace all of those attributes in yourself that you love, and then accept the qualities that you would rather not acknowledge. How is this possible? By opening our hearts and allowing ourselves to be vulnerable, over and over again. Eventually, what you will come to realize as you proceed with such a practice, is that all of your suffering is actually just a result of your perceptions, having nothing whatsoever to do with facts.

As you face your fears, insecurities, dreads, dangers, and heart-aches, you are actually providing direct access to the heart-voice that will never forsake or abandon you. It is always available to rescue you from your imagined dread of being deserted, neglected, and *alone*. Eventually, if you persist in facing all that scares you (within reason that is—you don't have to jump off the cliff to prove your point here), you will become immunized from your fears. Then it won't matter to you whether Mr. Wonderful ever shows up (or sticks around if he is already there). In becoming your own best advocate, no longer driven by your insecurities, you realize that there is only one reason to be in a relationship—to enhance who you are, spiritually, emotionally, intellectually, and physically—and then to contribute *your* gifts so that the beloved has the opportunity to grow and expand as well.

In your increasing state of awareness, you realize that your happiness comes from sharing all of that which has been contained in you. You want others to experience a greater abundance of love and joy because you are present in their lives. As you continue opening your heart, you can do so from a place of power, using love as your anchor. You give for the joy of giving without expectation of what you will receive in return. Because you already know you will always be protected and taken care of. The thought of scarcity no longer exists in your consciousness. You are opening to your *happily ever after ... right now.*

You also no longer feel the need to control, dominate, limit, restrict, or hinder yourself (or another) in any way. Rather, you nurture in yourself everything that will bring forward your most creative expression, in whatever form it may show up. Your very presence in the world serves as a constant source of enrichment and blessing, bringing happiness and joy to all you meet. You do not allow yourself to go into competition or judgment because you realize that these qualities produce suffering and feelings of insufficiency. You are constantly opening to a state of freedom as you seek to balance all that will assist you in accessing the best combination of everything that represents the truth of who you are. Naturally, the voice of trepidation can compromise this balance. Even so, you have awakened to the perfect immunization from fear's influence as you continue to remember that your own inner light is the love lamp that will shine away your anxious imagination.

Connection: A Paradox

As we concentrate on balancing whatever appears to be out of whack in ourselves, at some point we come to understand that our capacity to love, create, and reach our most expanded potential cannot be complete without experiencing human relationships. And the paradox inherent in this realization is that we won't be truly balanced until we are willing to *let go* of everything we believe we must be connected to in order to survive. Often our attachments and addictions are subtle. We can rationalize them, particularly when we don't want to take a look at what we might be doing to create our own misery. Frequently we feel that it is impossible to detach from our harmful habits, at least until nothing else works. *You do not have to wait for that moment.* You can start now, even if you begin by just admitting to yourself that there is one little aspect of your life that isn't working. Dare to stare at that detail, whatever it is, even if only for a moment. What keeps you from changing it?

Now, ask yourself a few more questions. What is it that you most want to hold on to? Is it your identity, your man, your children, your friends, your parents, or your career? Are these "things" or people really yours to possess? What does the word "identity" or "personality" mean to you? Are you your job, your car, your house, your role as a partner or a parent? Conversely, if you are not these things, who are you, then?

The truth is, who you *really* are does not crave happiness, connection, joy, love, peace, health, money, or freedom. Because the *real you* knows that "it" already is these things. And when you are operating fully from this essential "youness," you are moved from "That" which moves all things. While in such a state of awareness, you don't need to evaluate why this is so, or ask questions about what is happening. You don't allow the voice of fear to manipulate you or to make you doubt who you really are. You are just simply living life. You are not driven by your social and cultural conditioning. Rather, you are effortlessly moved by the ocean of spirit that stirs within you, above you, beside you, and beneath you.

We cannot depend on our partners to generate the breakthroughs that are going to create in us the simple, profound awareness that will set us free from our suffering and longing. Only we ourselves are capable of discovering what truly connects us to the heart of our very own soul. And we make this discovery by bravely turning to face all that has kept us from seeing our hidden wholeness. But first, we must connect with our own true Self. When we ignore or defy her, we will suffer. In partnering with our own authentic Essence, we prepare the way to partner with another.

Balance

Practically everyone on the planet has the same goal in one form or another. We want to be happy, find meaning in our lives, and then join with someone significant to share our discoveries (not necessarily in that order). It is when we reverse the arrangement of this process (that is, if we join someone else in expectation of finding happiness and fulfillment, we can cause ourselves—and our partners—enormous suffering. By entering into relationships with a developed sense of self, we are positioned to eliminate struggle and projection (as it applies to both ourselves and others). Most of us are works in progress in that regard, and yet, if we are at least *aware* of what is happening on some level, then we are headed in the right direction. Grounded in an awareness of who we are, we can adapt to the relationship while maintaining our central base of power (love). Such a foundation has the capacity to flawlessly advise us (if we listen) of when we should flip the switch, set limits, or push the surge button. It does not matter whether we are heterosexual, bisexual, gay, or lesbian. We must first have a strong understanding of *who we are* if we are going to be able to contribute and receive the powerful exchange of mystery and magic that is the marker of a truly loving, sincere partnership.

Practicing Our Powers

The process of "practicing our powers" requires that we are fully engaged in the life we are destined to live. It doesn't mean that we need to have everything all figured out right now in order to be happy. It just means that we must be open to all possibilities that will allow us to develop and grow in ourselves the very thing that we came here to share with the world. When we are concerned for our survival, we can lose touch with our souls, disappearing into who we think we should be (rather than who we are) in order to make sure we will endure. In allowing our inner and outer worlds to merge, we can start to uncover the sense of magic and enchantment that was once so natural for us to experience, even if it is only a twinkle or blink at a time.

As we become more balanced and whole, this stability will be reflected in our relationships. In being loving, compassionate, and powerful, we will attract those qualities in our partners and friends. And when two people are coming from a place of personal power (not to be confused with force or control), there is no need to dominate or manipulate. Feelings are easily identified and then articulated, clearly and without judgment, regardless of the circumstances. We must maintain a strong commitment to our ongoing development (never resting on our laurels) until we draw the last breath. The minute we relax, believing we have arrived, we will probably have to go back and start all over again. So, remember: discipline, detachment, obedience, and surrender. Practice, practice, practice.

Equal Opportunity

Equality means different things to different people. What is important in a relationship is not that each party has the same job, earns the same amount of money, or makes the bed the same way. What does matter is how each person is *valued*. How are decisions made? Who makes plans? Is there an equal voice in important matters? Is *your* behavior induced by a sense of sacrifice or generosity? Does he appreciate you and show it? And how do you demonstrate your appreciation of him? What are your contributions? What are his? Are there any noticeable imbalances? Do you feel that you add significantly to his growth? Does he contribute significantly to yours? Where are the imbalances and how can you address those without projection or blame?

When both people are admired and respected for who they are, the relationship flourishes. No one feels inferior or superior. There is little risk for burying feelings or not speaking up. Issues arise, are dealt with, and then fall away. Each party continues to practice paying attention to his or her own behavior first, rather than focusing on the other. The relationship continues to provide a fascinating opportunity for growth and exploration. It is a daily process of discovery and expansion.

In a truly conscious partnership, all levels of intimacy continue to deepen. Naturally, this includes the physical aspects of the relationship. And, it is up to each individual to respond and to be responsive to his or her own physical needs and desires, and to activate physical intimacy and deactivate it when it is not appropriate for you (or him). This doesn't mean that you don't love him when you need some space. You really *may* have a headache sometimes, in which case having sex wouldn't be a good thing for either of you. We must be very honest about our wants and desires (first with ourselves and then with the others in our lives). Most women have been trained to be coquettish, seductive, and pleasing to our partners, while silently gritting our teeth and on occasion, even hoping whatever is happening will be soon over. We fake orgasm or enjoyment in order to bring pleasure to our partners, setting aside our own desires. This is the 21st century, girlfriends. Surrender the self-sacrifice routine, and *tell him what you want.* If he doesn't get it, explain it again. And if things don't improve, then keep trying to communicate as long as it feels true. If things do not change, you will have to consider your options. Can you adapt, or would it be jeopardizing your integrity to do so? Only you can decide, and ultimately, you *will* know what to do. Trust that.

Any woman who is playing the part of the Geisha had better re-evaluate her life. Start to identify what kind of physical intimacy you prefer *now* (if you haven't already). Be clear on what you want, and then find ways to be direct and honest with your partner regarding your preferences. If your libido is low, attempt to uncover the basis for the difficulty and then take the appropriate action to ameliorate the situation. The cause could be physical, mental, or both.

If you have a healthy sex drive, use it to your advantage. Once you and your partner have explored and communicated openly, be willing to negotiate, but *do not sacrifice* yourself or your needs. Don't take responsibility for his difficulties (naturally, not just in the case of physical intimacy, but across all areas of the relationship). If he is having problems with *his* libido or physical functions, chances are this situation has absolutely *nothing* to do with you. So, don't jump to conclusions and immediately assume that you aren't appealing or sexy enough. There may be some physical and emotional challenges that need to be addressed. Work it out together. Get your ego out of the way. When you let go of the drama, then whatever is happening isn't a crisis anymore. It's just another situation to be addressed by both of you. Don't make it a big deal, or it will become one.

Myopic to Modern-Minded

In revisiting the star-crossed romance of Sara Hopper and Layton Hedger, it might be useful to take a look at what went wrong. One obvious difficulty was Sara's myopic vision. She had little, if any, focus on her own life. Her eyes were predominantly focused on Layton and what *he* was doing. Even though her behavior was extreme and many modern women consider themselves to be beyond such deportment, it is vitally important to notice even the *slightest* inclination that might move you off-center (where you begin to shift your attention to him). Remember. Women have been exquisitely molded, shaped, and conditioned to look in his direction. This training is subtle and sneaky, *and it can show up in any one of us.* It doesn't matter if you are the CEO of a Fortune 500 company or immersed in the details of domesticity.

If you are preoccupied with what *he* is doing more than what is going on with *your* growth and expansion, *it is time to take a long, hard look* at yourself *and* the relationship.

Maybe you have been single for a while, focusing on your own goals and expansion. Please *be aware* of any changes in your behavior if PC (Prince Charming) or Mr. Perfect lights upon your life when he appears and distracts you even for a nanosecond. You need to remember that *his role is to encourage and open you to even more possibilities for yourself.* Sure, it's okay to daydream a bit, but if the majority of your time together doesn't contribute to expanding you into grander parts of who you are, put the brakes on and ask yourself what is *really* happening here.

Pride and Prejudice

Jane Austen's sublimely humorous novel *Pride and Prejudice* takes place in late eighteenth-century England. During this time, men had virtually all the power, and women were at the mercy of a patriarchal world. Groomed nearly from birth to be chosen for marriage (their only hope for survival), women did whatever they could to make themselves appealing for prospective suitors. Then, they waited, and watched. The rank and dowry of a woman were of primary importance in the decision-making process. Love and romance weren't typically considered. Marriage was a business arrangement, designed around issues of survival (not so different from the Brute and the Babe). Women required protection and men needed to have someone tending the hearth and to keep the family tree going (hopefully by having male children). The women's education and cultural development (most always confined to the upper classes) was primarily aimed at amusing and entertaining the men they served. If a woman was born into a family that wasn't considered socially acceptable to the "higher ranks" (as was the case of the heroine, Elizabeth Bennet, in *Pride and Prejudice*), she was more than likely doomed to remain in her "station," destined to a life of mediocrity at best, assuming someone would have her.

One of Elizabeth Bennet's suitors, Mr. Darcy, meets our heroine and finds himself "bewitched" by her—regardless of his "elevated social status" Eventually, he asks for her hand in marriage. But Elizabeth is uncompromising in her self-advocacy (I wonder if such a woman really might have existed during those times) and refuses, repelled by his arrogance. Eventually, as one might predict (after all, it *is* a novel), things turn out swell for Elizabeth Bennet in the fairy-tale ending. Nonetheless, we are left wondering if the situation could have possibly been quite so splendid in the real world of late-eighteenth-century England.

Keep in mind that the setting of Jane Austen's story was only a few generations ago, and even though it *is* fiction, we know that the book is based on the social norms of the time. So there are sure to be some remnants of truth to the tale. Not *that* much time has elapsed between now and late eighteenth-century England. So, let us have compassion for ourselves when we slip into the longing and waiting mode. *Look at our heritage.* To "wait" and to "long" is what has been *endlessly* emphasized. Yet isn't it possible that there is a part of Elizabeth Bennet in all of us? Maybe she represented more than just a character in a novel. She certainly has something to teach us about ourselves. When we rise up from our fear-based reality, move into full-fledged power mode, and say *no* to anything or anyone that cannot fully celebrate the depth and breadth of our *Magnificence,* we clear the way for everyone who *does* recognize our splendor and brilliance to come to us in *droves.* And sometimes, the very one that we refused will awaken in the face of our relentless dedication for self-advocacy. Then, we can decide whether or not we might be inclined to give him another chance.

Opportunity: The Shifting Point Is Now

Sara Hopper came into the world around 1960, a pivotal time in human history. Born just before the war in Vietnam began to brew, and the women's liberation movement started to gain momentum, she had been exposed to many changing thought forms around a women's role, both in her culture and in her relationships. Even though she's now in her fifties, her age is of no consequence. What matters is her decision to be her own best advocate; to lose the drama; and to grasp the opportunities that await her. For the first time in history, more and more women and men are being seen on equal ground (*even though women still have a ways to go*). Sara is keenly aware of all the conditioning that has shaped her perceptions and beliefs. Still, she knows she has a chance to break the patterns that do not serve her growth, expansion, and most radiant joy in this life-form—and the time to bring about this change is *now*.

When Sara Hopper is in a state of balanced awareness, she knows that, ultimately, she is the one responsible for making change happen for herself. And, she will not have to do it alone. The resources and support for her transformation are more plentiful than ever before. It is time for Sara to let go of her own pride and prejudice, lose the drama, and go forward. If her own version of Mr. Darcy shows up (or is already there), then he can join her. But with or without him, it is the dawning of a new day, and she is the one who will light up the sky with her own internal brilliance.

Another Picnic

Let's pick up where Sara meets Layton again (the picnic in the park, minus public washrooms). Suppose that at the tender age of twenty she has decided, for whatever reason, to make a commitment to her own growth, with or without Layton. She might allow herself to be swept off her feet a bit on their first date. After all, Layton Hedger appears to be the Prince of all Princes. Nonetheless, she stays grounded and balanced, all the while watching with amusement whenever she is tempted to drift off to the Neverland fairy tale that lures her into dreaming and fantasizing about a romance. Sara is wise. For not unlike herself, she is aware that Layton is just another human being, no matter how he may appear. And more than likely, he has clay feet—same as her own. While he may seem perfect, there are bound to be some flaws.

Should the relationship continue and Layton's perceived faults start to become more apparent, Sara will realize that it is not up to her to fix these faults, but rather to continue observing how his behaviors may be affecting her—all the while encouraging him to share his feelings. She will communicate openly and honestly, inviting him to do the same. (By now, her shortcomings are bound to have surfaced as well. Needless to say, Sara does not expect Layton to fix her either). Each day she will monitor, in some form or another, how she and Layton are contributing to each other's growth. Whether or not she is in a place of celebration or disturbance, it is up to her to communicate the *truth* to Layton about what is going on for her. They may have grown up in the same town and attended the same schools, experiencing similar cultural and environmental influences. Nonetheless, they came from different families with diverse backgrounds. They must be able to convey their individual ideals, dreams, and hopes for developing a loving, conscious relationship.

If Sara begins to notice that Layton appears evasive or emotionally distant, it is her responsibility to *communicate*. Maybe Layton has different ways of showing his love and affection, and isn't comfortable verbalizing his sentiments. If this is the case, Sara and Layton will have to come to some kind of an agreement on how they will let their feelings be known to one another. And if Sara continues to note that she remains disturbed, she will need to keep finding ways to convey that disturbance. He cannot read her mind. If she repeatedly ignores her feelings and brushes aside her hurt, it will grow to the point of despair, and the relationship will inevitably disintegrate. She must be strong enough in her sense of self to tell him what is going on. If he leaves, then he leaves. If he exits the room—she can't go running after him. If she does, he is likely to quicken his pace. Regardless of what he does, she must stay true to her *sense of self*. Should she ever start to feel subordinate to Layton, Sara must continually ask herself what is triggering these feelings of "less than" and then do the work to heal what is ailing in herself.

Remember. You don't have to embody his strengths in order to be a match for him (nor does he have to personify yours). You have brought him into your life to *compliment* your gifts and talents. It would be utterly boring if the two of you were exactly the same. Keep staying focused on your passions. And if you continue to find repeatedly that this is impossible to do while in a relationship with him, then hit the road. As painful as that decision might be, keep in mind your time with him has brought you more wisdom and guidance than you could ever have had without it. *Bless him for awakening in you the awareness that you simply cannot compromise the glory of who you are for anyone or anything.*

A Different Dream

Let's assume that Sara feels really connected to Layton on their first evening together. However, because she is grounded in who she is, she can actually detach from and then watch the part of herself that is all swept away by the dream of becoming Layton Hedger's girlfriend. She realizes that she can have fun with the fantasy as long as it doesn't consume her. *Balance.* By the end of the evening she is ready to say good night without any expectation of what Layton might do or not do (even if the fairy tale part of her still hopes that they will go on another date—and another, and another). She does not concern herself with apprehension about whether or not he will call, because she realizes if she wants to talk, she doesn't have to wait until he rings her up on a whim. If her curiosity does make her wonder about what he will do or not do, she will just coax herself back to experiencing the enjoyment of what is happening on *this* night—even if she never sees Layton again.

When Layton Hedger *does* call to invite her to spend another evening with him, she is mildly enthusiastic while continuing to maintain her sense of *balance.* (Meanwhile, the fairy tale Princess part of her is all atwitter). This is another day, and she will focus on whatever she would have been doing if Layton hadn't surfaced. She will not spend hours preparing or deciding what to wear (even though she may hear that little voice inside her head that tries to tempt her to do otherwise).

As Layton rings the doorbell, Sara will answer it with the same anticipation and enjoyment she would experience with any new friend or acquaintance. Throughout the evening, she will watch herself with amusement whenever she begins to slip into the "I hope he will choose me" routine, and realize that she is perfectly delighted to choose herself. If he doesn't get her, then so be it. *She* gets who she is and there will be others who can meet her there. She remembers that if she cannot be fully cherished and understood by him, that she cannot compromise her self-advocacy by going forward with the relationship. And, if the evening goes well, there may be another date. Either way, Sara is okay, because *she is okay with herself.*

Another Second Date

Suppose the second date does manifest and by the end of the evening, Layton and Sara have loosened up with a couple of gin and tonics that may have gone down a little too easily. When Layton takes her home (or she takes *him* home), he suggests that they take a walk in the yard and sit down to relax for a while. One thing leads to another and the time has come for Sara to make some choices. First of all, it is always Sara's responsibility to avoid putting herself in a precarious predicament. By now, she is an adult. She knows her tolerance for alcohol and she knows her areas of vulnerability, i.e., anything beyond one gin and tonic and she won't be thinking too clearly (not to mention a weakness for gorgeous men). She is well aware that when she engages in behaviors that weaken her strength, she will inevitably lose her judgment. And when agreeing to a romantic, moonlit walk that results in sitting down, she is creating a set-up for something to happen. So, she better be prepared, or accept the consequences.

In order to avoid an outcome she may later regret, Sara can make a commitment to herself at the onset of the evening. She needs to be clear on what she wants. This is the only body she gets. *It is sacred.* What does physical intimacy mean to her? Is it okay to go with the flow? Or does she want the relationship to be grounded and going deeper before she agrees to explore the physical aspects of the connection with Layton? Maybe she has made some mistakes in the past. Now is the time to correct those errors. Being with Layton provides her with the perfect opportunity for self-awareness. It doesn't matter if he is the sexiest man alive. She has value and worth, and she gets to decide when it is time to become physically intimate.

She must stay grounded in self-respect and personal integrity. If Mr. Gorgeous doesn't get it, then, well—he doesn't get it. Either he will respect her for setting boundaries or not. Chances are, he will. The key is, *there is no hurry.* The best rule in any relationship, whether it is personal or professional, is to *move slowly.* If someone is pushing you beyond what you believe is suitable for you and your needs, take note of the obvious signs, and be uncompromising in your personal boundaries.

Assuming the friendship develops and grows, Sara will continue to observe what is going on. There will come a time (it doesn't really matter whether it is three weeks, three months, or three years) when being physically intimate with Layton will be as natural as drawing breath. She won't be overwhelmed by the act. Rather, she will embrace the sense of wonder, rapture, and awe that the two of them will create as they explore each other in yet another facet of their developing relationship. Perhaps this physical intimacy will come when the two of them are clear that they are ready to take the connection to a different level. While they are both aware that there are no guarantees, they are ready to make a deeper commitment to each other. This will likely mean that the relationship will remain exclusive until one or the other decides that this exclusivity is no longer fitting.

The criteria for discovering how the developing relationship is going are simple, yet slippery. The more appealing the situation seems (as in Layton Hedger is drop-dead gorgeous, brilliant, sexy, and quite possibly the most amazing creature you have ever laid your eyes on), the more challenging it gets. You have real chemistry with this guy. He is perfect for you, etc., etc. *Be careful.*

As we have mentioned before, when something is too good to be true, it *always is.*

Once more, here are the questions you need to ask yourself: How does this relationship contribute to my growth and expanding awareness as a human being? How do I contribute to his growth? Can I maintain a sense of balance between the two? Can he? Is there equanimity between us? Suppose things are going swell, and in the middle of it all, wham—out of the blue, his old college sweetheart appears. If Sara is grounded in personal integrity and self-honor, no matter how glorious 'ole Layton appears, what will be her best course of action?

In determining how to respond to Layton's announcement that Martha will be coming (it seems perfectly normal to him for her to rush to his side—after all—it *is* a crisis)—Sara must do a reality check. How much does she really care for Layton? Assuming they have been physically intimate by now, what is it like for her to imagine him being with someone else in his state of crisis and dismay? How does this feel? Can she convey her feelings honestly and sincerely without attempting to make him wrong? Has he been truthful with her about Martha all along? Or is this a surprise? Whatever discoveries Sara will make based on her careful, grounded inquiries (after she gets her ego, sense of betrayal, and anger, out of the way), she has to stick with the process until she arrives at a peaceful solution—no matter what course of action might be required in order for her to follow her resolve. How will she recognize that solution when it appears? It will keep emerging with more clarity and precision until there is little doubt left.

Keep in mind that *there is always doubt. And, there is always risk.* We are not perfect beings. So, sometimes we just have to go for it, even if we expose our imperfections. And, let's get real here. If Sara is clear that Layton is her guy, and the two of them have been developing a deepening connection, including the physical aspects of the relationship, then she will have to set firm limits (first with herself and then with Layton) about what she is willing to do in this most uncomfortable situation. Is she really going to step aside and let Layton have his little fling with Martha (despite the crisis that precipitated it), or is she going to advise him that she will not be around if he does? No threats, just truth. If Sara believes that she would be disrespecting herself by standing by while Layton makes up his mind about whom he will choose, then she needs to bid Layton farewell. And she needs to do so with a finality that is sincere, unwavering, and irrevocable. Remember—*no waiting.*

Who knows what might happen? Maybe Layton will cave under the pressure and decide to let go of both Sara and Martha. Maybe he will choose Martha, or—maybe he will seize the opportunity to look at what is really true for him, declare that to himself, and then courageously announce it to Martha (who likely has been clueless up until now) or Sara before he allows Martha to comes to town. *The truth*, despite the inconveniences it may appear to cause in the initial phases of delivery, is always the best and most direct path to peace—*for all involved.* Don't be a coward, and don't allow him to be. Cut to the chase, and watch in wonder as your life continues to become more dynamic and glorious by the moment because of your courage to be honest with *both* yourself and him.

Magical Mystery Tour

Let's assume that you and "your" Layton have reached a rite of passage in your relationship. You have taken the risk to discover that the greatest threat to your partnership is the fear each of you may share about completely coming forward with the truth at all times. Naturally, these fears are exacerbated by your deepening affection for one another. The closer you become, the higher the stakes. And this is where the mystery can become more and more magical. Now that you have practiced stepping out into the unknown by fessing up (and I don't mean *always* spilling your guts—there are some things that should remain sacred for a while), you can begin to trust more and more your own ability to know and share the truth. As you proceed in this honest awareness, your confidence level will gain momentum. You realize that you do not need Layton to be complete, happy, and fulfilled in yourself. Rather, you are *choosing* Layton, in *this* moment, to share the happiness and joy you already experience. And the mystery continues. You are watching yourself and your own sense of joy and wonder develop in the presence of this other. As a direct result of the environment you both are creating, you observe in amazement how he, too, is unfolding, ripening, maturing, growing, and expanding.

Conscious Partnership/Conscious Intention

Although Sara and Layton have laid the foundation to grow together from a place of truth and love, they will need to continue observing themselves, paying close attention to their interactions, in order to notice when their conditioning may sway them to the contrary. Their mutual regard and respect for one another is a reflection of their individual groundedness and self-value, which they are both committed to honoring. They have learned to treasure themselves, and from their foundation of self-respect, they naturally will continue to honor each other. They are embracing the principals of being happy right now. They don't have to worry about whether or not there will be a forever, because they know that forever is a concept that is a product of their conditioning. Rather than focus on the future, they are concentrating on *the present*, while tending to all of the obvious practicalities that accompany their deepening commitment. As they continue to be more grounded and balanced, individually and as a couple, they realize that the drama is effortlessly dropped when they can separate a conditioned response or reaction from a conscious one. The more stabilized they become in what is true for them daily, hourly, and minute by minute (and the more anchored they are in the present), the less difficulty they will have as the future unfolds.

If the combined aspects of their practical, conscious partnership should lead them both to discover that they want to merge their lives to form a unit, then they need to come to an agreement on how they will develop and grow that unit. Naturally, this team must have a foundation on which to expand, based on the principles of truth, integrity, compassion, understanding, patience, and balance. They are each well aware that there are no guarantees for tomorrow. And so, they must be committed to making the most out of every moment—no slacking, no cheating, just love, joy, and truth.

Wherever you are in your relationship (with or without a partner), you can start now to create a conscious partnership by using Sara and Layton as examples, or better still, by beginning to develop your own awareness of what works and what doesn't for *you*. If the voice of fear comes in to heckle and haunt you, don't resist. Just catch the feeling that it evokes in you—and stay with the feeling—not the fear. Continue to pay attention to what is true for you, and as you do, you will keep finding your way to the answers you thought could only be resolved somewhere else.

New Stories, New Enchantments/ Exercise:

This section is for you to create in your own words. Reread the chapter and pick out key points. See what resonates with you and tweak the concepts to fit your own developing awareness. Now, write your own set of intentions for a conscious partnership. Think big. Don't leave anything out. Keep developing this list and share it with your partner—or the one you are attracting when he arrives. You know what to do. Begin.

ELEVEN

LEGACY—
FOR OUR SONS AND DAUGHTERS

Jewel: Emerald for Domestic Harmony and Loving
Unconditionally

*"Love is the recognition of beauty. Each of us longs to know and
feel confident in the beauty and goodness that lies within us.
Especially as children, we needed someone else to see the beauty
of our soul and to reflect this beauty back to us, like a mirror, so
we could see and appreciate it ourselves."*

–John Welwood

Despite all of the challenges I have encountered that may be seen as
gender related, I can honestly say that I am *extraordinarily* grateful to
have been born a female. Even so, at times I have whined and moaned
about how unfair it all is. (You, too, may have slipped into this
fruitless behavior at times). And whenever I manage to jolt myself
out of the drama and despair, I realize that the men I have resisted—
while wallowing in my self-pity and pain—have been struggling right
along with me—mired in their own lives of quiet desperation.

I have watched them do whatever they do to avoid feeling what
they feel, and when they can stand it no more, I've watched them

retreat into their caverns of silence. Only those caves are never silent for them. They are crammed in every corner and crevice with the voices of failure and fear that continue to haunt and torture them. I have lived with and loved these cave-dweller men until I thought my guts would fall out. I have watched them occasionally dabble in their vulnerability long enough to be tender and gentle, only to return to their stony, stoic silence. And I've witnessed what they do when they're unsure how to deal with the emotion and judgment that continues to bounce off the walls of their skulls—they lash out and rage their feelings at others, including me. I have experienced this type of projection from my father, brother, former husband, boyfriends, teachers, professors, friends, and—regrettably—even my own glorious sons. Such behavior is universally, collectively male. (Of course, women, too, are certainly not exempt from "expressing" ourselves in this way). From raging, to numbing, to retreating (and I don't mean the kind that happens at an ashram), men do whatever they can to get by. It does not matter whether they use drugs, alcohol, sex, work, gambling, or something else as their method of coping. They are still dancing around their pain, and eventually, their buried feelings will build. Many of us have watched in horror as their accumulated, hidden emotions are unearthed, often in the form of an outburst. It isn't pretty. And, even though they are responsible for what they put out into the world, some of what they have been taught is beyond their control (until or unless they wake up to the conditioned patterning that perpetuates their pain and suffering and then decide to do something about it).

Their spirits have been broken and their emotional lives have been numbed, all in the name of getting ahead, being first, accumulating wealth, and obtaining the most objects in whatever form that may show up or become available to them (from money, to women, to cars to real estate, etc.). The overarching goal is to win. Win what? I wonder if any man in pursuit of "triumph" has ever stopped to ask himself what the grand prize actually is. And when the feelings of exhilaration that accompany the trophy do appear, can they be sustained? If not, are they real?

Naturally, the traditional approach for a man in training requires him to learn the art of competition, which leads to duality and ultimate isolation. This approach of rearing little boys to become men breaks down their hearts and strengthens their heads (which is hardly a good thing if you really think about it). An intense focus on competing to get ahead causes men to fight, go to war, and diminish all feelings other than the anger and rage they must use for momentum as they claw their way to the top of the societal pecking order. When men ascend their ladders of "success," they do so at enormous personal cost—for in many cases, they must use society's standards to get there, which requires that they often neglect their hearts and souls. So in a sense, a man can be hugely accomplished according to the world, but really empty and hollow inside—far from content and happy. A great misfortune, of course, is that many who are "successful" don't even recognize how unhappy, empty, and hollow they actually are—until or unless they are forced to face their reality through a crisis or their own perceived "defeat."

Current Cave Dwellers

The current male archetype is not so different from the Brute back in the real cave days. So it is not surprising why men still want or tend to retreat to their metaphorical grotto when things go awry. They continue to be taught that he who has acquired and accumulated the most in the way of power, possessions (including you), and territory, is the one who rules. Potency and hierarchy can be tantamount to a man's sense of success in the world. And so from the beginning of their tender, beautiful lives, innocent young men are trained and socialized to embody these qualities, which can eventuate in chipping away at their hearts. Often, from the time little boys are old enough to absorb what is going on in their external world, they begin their training to become alpha males. And if you take a look at boy-baby-clothes, this process begins pretty much the minute they are born.

Alpha male training almost always excludes encouragement to be in touch with any emotion other than anger. They are not supposed to cry, or show tenderness. The few men who do make it to the "top" (a well-known real estate billionaire comes to mind) set an impossible standard. The rest spend their lives attempting to ascend, usually setting aside their talents and strengths while in the process. Why do we have such unreasonable expectations of ourselves and the gloriously unique little boys who deserve a chance to create their own magnificent destinies by following *their* passions and dreams?

His Beginning: A Feeling Heart

It is up to us as mothers to teach our sons how to *feel* and to provide for them all the resources that will support them in the process. You can start by *listening* and acknowledging his feelings as soon as he comes out of the womb (and if you didn't then, begin now. It is never too late). This doesn't mean you have to be tending to him 24-7. What it does mean is that when you are there, *be there*. Don't answer the phone or do the dishes. Even if you only give your full time and attention to him for ten minutes a day, this period of your undivided devotion is *critical* to his healthy development and growth as a human being. (And, lugging him around while you get your workout in *does not count*.) By showing up to acknowledge that he is there, you give him the message that regardless of the situation—whether he is happy, sad, crying, or mad, you will stay. As he grows and develops, you will continue to support him in accessing healthy tools to deal with his feelings appropriately (and hopefully, your conscious partner will be joining you in the process).

One of the happy side effects of your genuine, authentic presence is that you are providing your son with a model of how to show up for himself, and ultimately for all the others who will play significant and important roles in his life. And by tending to your own needs in a balanced way, *not* giving him your undivided attention 24-7, you are helping him to understand his own developing capabilities and strengths. Even when he is an infant, he has the capacity to sleep and coo on his own. You do not have to be there all the time. And as you continue letting go of your need to always protect him, you are facilitating in him the art of learning how interdependence works. He can count on you to take care of him when he is hungry, wet, or sick, and he will learn to manage for a while during the in-between times when things are less urgent.

From the minute your son starts drawing his first breath, it is your responsibility as his mother *to teach him how to get along without you.* Ideally, you facilitate his self-sufficiency by showing him (to the best of your ability) all the qualities that will most enhance *his* chances of living *happily ever after ... right now.* And of course, this living happily in each moment has nothing to do with accumulating or acquiring whatever his wants and desires dictate and demand of him, particularly in the way of material possessions and objects. Needless to say, the more balanced and whole you are (not requiring possessions or objects *yourself* in order to be happy), the more you become a true example of conscious living not only for him, but for everyone else as well. You don't have to talk about it or explain how this state is accomplished. In fact, it really isn't an accomplishment at all. You just live according to your genuine nature and in the process, you are showing him how to drop the drama and embrace his own authenticity, which doesn't need a worldly success story attached to it in order to be complete.

Bypassing the Conditioning

In honoring and celebrating your son's feelings, you provide a safe place for him to appropriately experience those feelings before his conditioned reactions have a chance to take over. The world may not support you in this. Hopefully, you will be fortunate enough to have a partner who does. In any case, you have to find ways to permit your son to feel, and then guide him toward the most suitable methods for channeling his feelings. In the beginning of his life, you will do this by comforting him when he cries, feeding him when he needs nourishment, and changing him when he is wet, all the while learning to strike a balance between his needs and your own. Use your impeccable discernment to determine when he *really* needs you and when he is simply testing you. As early as possible, facilitate his independence from you while simultaneously helping him to understand that you will not abandon him. In the deepest parts of your soul, you know how to do this. You don't need to read this book or go to parenting lectures to discover the right methods. Just use your developing awareness to help guide you. Treat him as you would have wanted to be treated when you were a budding infant (or maybe, if you're lucky, you had parents who did just that).

Be creative in helping him to access the right techniques for expressing or dealing with his feelings. For example, as soon as your son is able to hold a pencil or crayon in his little, innocent hands, give him the materials to convey his feelings on paper and then take the time to listen to his interpretation of this expression in whatever form it may appear on the page. He is so tender and vulnerable. Show him how to maintain that tenderness and vulnerability by continuing to be open to your own. As he grows and develops into the man he is destined to become, how you live your own life in the world will continue to influence his own developing consciousness. As you keep mellowing and melting into the stillness that is your natural state, he won't have to emulate you, because your conscious living will awaken him to his own true being. He is actually closer to living this way than you are because he hasn't yet been subjected to the influences of the gloriously chaotic world into which he has recently been born (you have already been here for a while). Somewhere in the profundity of his awareness he has a deep, simple understanding that without the silence in the forest, he would not be able to hear the leaf fall. As you facilitate this ongoing awakening and awareness in him, you will reinforce the same understanding in yourself.

Show him how it is possible to allow the hypnotic human conditioning to dance around in his head while not being captive to its drama. Let him sit with you while you quietly contemplate the day in your own practices that assist you in letting go of the menacing mind. You may do this in the form of mediation, inspirational reading, or other methods. Whatever it is, be serious and disciplined about it. He is watching you.

Becoming Real

Teach your son that *real love* is unchanging and unconditional by helping him to understand that he already embodies these qualities and therefore, he does not have to go looking for someone or something to provide them (including you). Instead, help him to realize that as he embraces this love that is his true Essence, he will attract resonant souls with whom to share it. Together, they will grow and expand this love.

The awareness of the deeper elements of his true nature cannot be taught conceptually through a lecture or homily. Rather, this wakeful state can only be *experienced*. *Real love* must be mentored into being from an atmosphere that recognizes the true nature of love, which has nothing to do with possessions or attachments.

This felt sense of *real love* will be nurtured by an environment that understands that love. It is up to you to participate in facilitating the appropriate foundation for it to emerge, both in yourself and in him.

Naturally, you are human, so you will not be without error as you move toward all that will continue to open you to a life of love, joy, truth, integrity, and compassion. You will simply take responsibility for all the ways in which the grand expression of Life individuates and creates through you. If you have made a mistake, then you will own it, learn from it, and move on. No shame, no wallowing, just accountability. And, when someone else's behavior, such as your son's, is not based on unconditional love, you will forgive him in his moment of ignorance. At the same time, you will maintain your awareness that ultimately, there is nothing to forgive, because you know this behavior does not represent the true Essence of who he is.

Be patient with yourself (or your son) whenever you find it impossible to remember that an error is provoked by the influences of conditioning and that our spirits are easily shrouded by its amnesiac effects. We are all subject to the poison. The only antidote is the *will* to overcome it. Part of the process involves forgiveness (forward giving and letting go), both of ourselves and of others who have become temporarily less than who they really are. According to *A Course in Miracles*, when we are hypnotized by our habituation, we cannot hear our hearts. And so in order to wake up from the trance, we must become "temporarily more" for anything within (or without) that has become "temporarily less." When we decide to do this, we can pierce right through the unconscious action, word, or deed, and see directly into the pure white soul—either our own, or that of another—regardless of how atrocious the situation may seem. If you keep focusing on who he really is (or who you really are, or both), instead of the *behavior,* eventually you will re-adjust your concentration. When you can see through the lens of *real love,* you will be inviting him to open to that love in himself. It won't matter whether he is consciously aware of what you are doing. He will still feel the effect, which, eventually, will be reflected back to you.

Partners in Peace

Help your son to recognize that no matter what is happening in his external world, peace is always available to him. Show him by your own presence that this peace can instantly be accessed when he is willing to drop the stories created by his mind chatter. These ongoing vignettes are exaggerated when we listen to our survival instincts. As you continue to avoid living in your story, or drama, you will demonstrate to him how to avoid living in his (as well as how to avoid future drama addicts). You have an undying devotion to face each new moment with an attitude of peace, no matter what shows up. And your son will be watching in wonder at the magical effects of such an attitude.

You will want to find ways to emphasize for him that one way to contribute to peace in your life (and the lives of others) is to avoid positionality on any subject. You can feel free to have a point of view on things as long as you are not affixed to your opinion. Help your son to see that everyone wants to be happy, and that the only interruption to that happiness is an attachment to pursuing, protecting, or possessing things (or people), as well as attitudes, such as, "You are wrong and I am right." He is ripe and ready to experience the awe and wonder of his developing world. He deserves to be given the best tools to access his own unlimited potential, and you as his mother signed up to be his first guide. You are indeed privileged, for he will likely lead *you* far beyond any experience you could have had without him. And so, every time he attempts to put you through his tests, trials, and tantrums, don't take the bait. Just show up and handle the situation, *consciously.*

It is you who can facilitate in your son the awareness that he is utterly filled to the brim with a special and unique blend of magic and mystery that can only emerge because of his decision to make it so. And it is you who can help to foster his growth beyond the binding forces of patterned conditioning. It is you who can lead him toward the unending possibilities that can only materialize through him and his own extraordinary potential. At the same time, you will notice that in order to be fully engaged in your mentoring role, your love, though constant and unconditional, will take on different forms. Often you will be gentle and tender. In other situations, this love will feel more authoritative. You will be vigilant around your own vulnerability, especially when you notice that you cannot err on the side of popularity if you are going to be a conscious parent. There will be many times when he will not like you. He may even tell you that he hates you or is going to run away. During those times, you will question yourself. You will want to cave in. Be patient. Eventually, he will come to understand your position and why you acted the way you did, although this realization could take a long time, and it may not happen until he himself becomes a parent. It doesn't matter. At this point, you will have done what you needed to do, and that is all that ultimately matters.

The Soul's Song

Use your own creativity and imagination to show your son that the entire universe is singing in his soul right now. And let him come to realize that he is the only one who has the potential to harmonize and blend this song into his own unique cosmic symphony. As he agrees to nurture and grow in himself all that will open and expand him on *his* pilgrimage, he will be automatically endowed with the beneficence and bounty that accompanies his resolve (even though at times this generosity may indeed be well disguised). Nothing can interrupt his commitment to cultivate the glorious fruit that only he has the capacity to ripen.

Your son's journey has no boundaries. And it is unprecedented. Therefore, he will not be able to locate a map from other pilgrims who may have preceded him. There will be those who have taken similar routes, and they can serve as guides in sharing what they know. But ultimately, this is *his* expedition, and he is the only one who can make the trek up, down, across, and through all the mountains, forests, rivers, and streams (metaphorical or otherwise) that will bring him closer to all of the discoveries he is destined to uncover. The more courage, fortitude, and discipline you have by going forward in pursuit of your own passions and dreams, disregarding your fears or the fears of others that may attempt to dissuade you, the more likely your son will be to carve his own way by taking the road that will keep guiding him toward his destiny.

Using you as an example of how to consciously live the exquisite blend of independence and interdependence (regardless of your trials and triumphs), your son will continue to inch toward and then eventually catapult himself into whatever will birth the possibilities that can only potentiate through him. In the process, he will develop a keen sense of discernment in determining the wise from the Merlin imposters. His shrewd discrimination will come from trial and error, which will inevitably accompany the willingness to take risks. By watching you, he will continue to realize that his journey will not be without threat or danger. In addition, he will notice how you negotiate unsettling times. Ultimately, he will come to recognize that the Unmoved Mover within has served him in the form of a constant and flawless compass/companion all along. He will continue to notice that when he listens to Its silent, inner strategies, he remains on course or is guided back effortlessly whenever he goes temporarily astray, no matter how far off track he might wander.

The messages of his conditioning certainly will pop up, and he will take note, but these interruptions, however frequent, won't distract him from his pilgrimage. When it is appropriate, he will make inquiries of others or obtain the necessary information, taking in whatever is helpful and letting the rest go. He will know from his own center how to proceed and who will accompany him along the way as he experiences his trials and triumphs. And eventually, he will recognize the similarities in each—and that neither is really remarkable. Underneath, there is a constant, unwavering Force that has nothing to do with his perceptions. It is in the labeling of the events of our lives as "good" or "bad" and then the underlying, conditioned beliefs that provoke these labels, that will always serve to perpetuate our suffering. If we can learn to discipline ourselves to notice when we are tempted to be caught in the labeling game, we can eventually become disassociated from it. Then, when a label pops in, we can allow it to float past with the wind rather than being caught in a potential gale.

Gracious Giving and Gracious Accepting

No matter how small a gift may appear, your gracious acceptance of whatever is offered to you on your journey will help your son to develop the art of using grace when he receives gifts on his travels. An example of graciously accepting a compliment (gift) would be to respond with a simple yet genuine "Thank you" when someone says "You look beautiful in that dress." In western culture we sometimes find it difficult to receive help or praise. Certainly, our ancestors were rugged individualists. Nonetheless, it would have been impossible for them to overcome the odds of their rocky existence without brotherly and sisterly support. They were readily able to receive. They had to. Their very lives depended on it.

Yet somewhere along the way, we lost the knack for genuine generosity and graceful acceptance when offering and receiving support. We do not seem to be able to engage in either one without at least some level of expectation or exasperation. I know. You may disagree with me here. That's okay, but just ask yourself how you felt the last time your friend requested that you drive her to the airport for a six a.m. flight. We just don't want to be inconvenienced. We have our own agenda for the day, and going to the airport before dawn is not part of the program. I don't care if you are Mother Teresa. At some point during the event, you are going to be annoyed. The exasperation you feel is built into the software that plays out in your head. And you are plugged in to that software, or it is plugged in to you. Ultimately, our human hard drive is wired to receive whatever input we feed it. This floppy flipping around in your head is jabbering messages of survival. It is telling you that you should take care of yourself first and sleep in. *You* are who is important here.

The reptile in you, which has become momentarily operative, doesn't know how to love and be loved. It doesn't realize that there might be a time when *you* will need a ride to the airport at an ungodly hour. It doesn't understand that the *only* way to survive on this planet is to be *connected* to those who share this blessed space with us, even if it means escorting them to the airport before dawn. When you act with a loving heart, regardless of how sleepy and sluggish you are, you would rather be going to the airport than letting your friend take a cab, because you realize that ultimately, you are both flying the same skies—just at different intervals. So it doesn't really matter whether you are the escort or the escorted. It just works out better when we take turns helping each other.

Oh yes, we are big on giving, though almost always not without contingency. (The attitude of contingency has nothing to do with the gift of beneficence from the individual who *really gets* that going to the airport at six a.m. is part of the natural cycle of giving and receiving). When we give with the expectation of what we are going to get in return, we are setting ourselves up for disappointment. And even if we do get the goods, when the gift arrives, often we feel compelled to refuse it because that's the polite thing to do. (If someone *does* compliment you on how nice you look, aren't you often inclined to deny that compliment in the name of modesty)?

How did we ever come to entertain these thought forms of what is polite and acceptable (almost always having nothing to do with the truth)? The politics of giving and receiving in Western civilization is absolutely fascinating to observe. From sending roses to gifting charitable organizations, rarely, if *ever*, do we offer or receive with a pure heart. We do not give without at least some anticipation of what's in it for us. And we do not accept what we are offered without wondering what kind of strings might be attached to the gift. We send roses and we get accolades. We give a contribution and we receive a tax deduction. Ultimately, it is all the same.

Try to ignore the societal messages. Be a living demonstration to your son (and all others in your life) of how to give and receive big—*with grace*. Do this without analysis of possible motives or any attachment to outcomes. Rather, use your heart and soul to guide you toward the deeds that will serve to enhance the ripening of your own spirit. Offer up your love to the world. This love that swells inside of you aches to reach out and touch any and all who could possibly benefit from it, even if only for a second—because you crossed their path. So smile and wave at your garbage collector and thank him regularly for providing a more orderly world. Take your friend to the airport at six a.m., dismissing all conditioned thoughts of inconvenience. Instead, genuinely embrace the gift that she has given you: a chance to show true friendship and kindness to one who has brought joy and happiness to your life. Without any hesitation whatsoever, receive her favors and kindnesses. And, when you win the lottery (literally or figuratively), enjoy it for yourself and then share your bounty, so that others can benefit from your reward.

Discouragement-Heartache-Faith-Hope

Inevitably, there will be times when you will feel despair and heartache. Allow yourself to experience the feelings that accompany the incident that has triggered them. *Do not wallow in self-pity.* Rather, permit whatever you are experiencing to wash over you. *Cry,* for the tears will cleanse you. *Write,* for the words will soften you. *Walk,* for your cadence will connect you to the earth that nourishes you. *Sit still,* for the silence will calm you. *Breathe deeply,* for your inhalation and exhalation will connect you to what is alive in you. Ultimately, you *do* know that whatever is happening *will* pass. It always has. And underneath all of this chaos is the calm and powerful Stillness that forever cradles you in the comfort of Its cozy lap. Show your son that this comfort is always available by consistently going back to the safety of that Stillness whenever you feel distressed or upset. It does not matter what method you choose to access this Stillness, just as long as it is a healthy technique that guides you back to the spirit that runs in your blood and bones. You do not have to explain this process to him. Rather, *live* the process. In watching you, he will pick up everything he needs to know. And he will continue to find his own way, ultimately contributing exponentially to *your* growth. In life, we will experience discouragement and despair. And the conditions, which brought about these feelings, *will* pass. By being available to experience whatever is happening, we are allowing the eventual "new delight" that Rumi so elegantly describes in *The Guest House.* And so, let us continue in our gratitude, for we never can really know who or what has been sent as a "*... guide from beyond.*"

The Death of the Brute and the Birth of the Real Man

It is clear that at some earlier time in the evolution of our species men needed to be brutes in order to effectively factor into the survival of the species. But we have already overcome the perils of the Ice Age. There are no more long freezes and ferocious floods. For the most part, we no longer have to escape from terrifying creatures roaming the planet. So somehow we have *got* to continue mustering all of our determination and will to quit giving our ancient brain so much attention. Operating from a primitive mind simply isn't necessary in the twenty-first century. Through the course of human evolution, we have figured out the survival thing. Therefore, we must keep reminding ourselves that who we are has nothing to do with what we have in the way of material possessions.

Many of our brothers and sisters, who live on this planet with us, suffer from unfathomable hardship. But their apparent endless patterns of difficulty and challenge (from which we are not exempt) do not exist on a planet that is incapable of ameliorating them. Rather, these ways of being persist because many of us have not yet reached the level of awareness that will enable us to eliminate the difficulties. We have all the information and the resources necessary to abolish suffering and move into a higher level of consciousness. *We just have to decide to be conscious.*

We can begin by remembering how intimately connected we all are. What happens to my "enemy" in Iraq is happening to me in some form or another. I am connected with the mother who just lost her son because of the war in which we are now engaged. Our team decided that her team was wrong. But I don't have to buy into that kind of positionality. She is my sister. Her pain is my pain. Her son is my son.

I may not have global empathy in this moment, but it would behoove me to stop a few times a day to count my blessings and remember those who suffer beyond what I can even imagine. We all, each and every one of us, have the capacity to balance our hearts and heads for the purpose of creating heaven on earth right now. We can start by letting go of our positionalities and righteousness. Become a living example of someone who is not attached or identified by her opinions or beliefs.

Don't take yourself too seriously. Be pliable. Lighten up. What's the worst thing that could happen if someone finds out you were "wrong?" And, what is really the marker of truth? Can we be absolutely certain of *anything*? Remember, your son is watching you.

Gentle Strength

The actor Harrison Ford once said that a real man is someone who knows how to be in touch with his tender, gentle side—knowing when to balance it with strength, power, will, determination, and fortitude. If your son's father, grandfather, uncle, or your current partner can model how to demonstrate these qualities, then the examples you are setting with your own conscious lifestyle will be exponentially enhanced. Many of us may not have such men in our lives at the present time. It does not matter. All you have to do is *your* part. That will be enough for this young man, and enough for you. Continue to point out attributes in others (both men and women) whom you admire, particularly those who work to balance their masculine and feminine nature. It can be anyone from Keanu Reeves (who has been known to share his enormous earnings generously with his employees) to Abraham Lincoln. It doesn't matter. You know what resonates with your son. Pick someone with whom he can identify and determine together why this person is outstanding. This person doesn't have to be a rock star. They just have to be someone worth noticing because of how they are balancing their lives in exemplary ways. You know who they are. They are everywhere. Be one of them.

Launching

In many cases, your son's magical rite of passage will be around the age of eighteen (which is usually older in other cultures). However, the moment of his emancipation should not be predetermined just because society makes him legally an adult at that age. For some, emancipation will take place sooner, and for others it will happen much later. Everyone has a different developmental clock. Your son's rhythms are set to a totally unique timepiece. He will be best suited for his individuation process if he is continually nurtured and supported to operate as an *individual* of the whole, regardless of what whole is being referenced. It could be his family of origin, or it could be his school, community, scout troop, or the entire global family. It doesn't matter. He is who he is, and he can only come to know himself in the context of each (and all) of those units.

The current U.S. standard suggests that in order to succeed, one must have a college education, at the very least, a bachelor's degree, (it goes for both sexes, but certainly more so for men). Now, I am a strong advocate of education, which can be evidenced by my own background. Nonetheless, *college* is not for everyone. It may be more difficult for your son to make his way in the world without a college education, but *he will make his way*, and find his *own* methods of edification that will prove ever so much more fruitful toward his vocational choice than if you rammed college down his throat. Many parents have paid the price for such a choice. Their children party, some drinking and drugging their way down the tubes. If college isn't for him, get real with yourself and get real with him. Seek to encourage him toward his strengths and talents by helping to spawn his creativity.

It might not seem convenient for him to try an alternate route (you will both have to put some *real* effort in here). But the process of helping him to discover the best fit for him can be exciting and stimulating for both of you. There are more resources available than you think. Maybe he can be trained in the vocation of his choice via the internet or in a practical setting that provides apprenticeship. Perhaps he wants to be a doctor but would rather launch his medical career by being trained as an X-ray technician first to see if he even likes being around hospitals. Give him room to explore. He lives during a time of limitless possibilities. College is just one way. There are many others. Maybe he will need to try an alternate route before he is convinced that the traditional approach is a better fit after all. Join him in making a viable plan.

Do not force him against his will to do anything because you think it is right. You don't know what his ultimate calling is. What you have been attempting to do all of his life is to help facilitate his awareness that *he is the only one who knows*. Naturally, he will need some help in staying on course. He might tell you that he would like to go backpacking through Europe for a year before going forward with his career goals. In this case, you will have to assist him in making a reasonable plan to arrange for his maintenance during that period, in addition to having some ideas about what he might want to pursue (and how) after the trek. It is your job to help him in setting boundaries and goals. Do your part in offering what is reasonable for you to tender in the way of support (both financial and otherwise) while he is getting on his feet. Keep checking in at predetermined intervals to make note of progress and challenges. He will not fall through the cracks as long as you both maintain clear communication and reasonable objectives. If things aren't working out (you may need to nudge him into realizing this if he doesn't get it), then join him in making the necessary changes that will help him to alter his plan. Whether your son becomes the next president of Microsoft, joins the Peace Corps, or decides he is going to change the entire film and motion picture industry, celebrate daily with him how he is emerging in the world, replete with all of his challenges and victories.

Maybe he will take a more traditional route, graduating from Yale with honors and getting accepted into Harvard Medical School. To become a doctor has always been his passion, and you have been there to support him all the way. He is coming closer and closer to completing the requirements for graduation. Then, as he reaches the final semester, you get a phone call. He tells you that he simply can't go on. He has reached his limit. You will patiently listen to him while he shares his agony, however long it takes. As always, he will feel heard and supported. Then, when he is ready to hear your response, you will gently remind him that he has been preparing for this moment all of his life. There have been other crossroads during which he experienced trial, doubt, and difficulty. And you will point out specific examples of how he always managed to overcome those times. This experience will be no exception.

Remind your son that he is the captain of his "life-ship." Help him to understand that while captains can enjoy and admire their ships in the harbor, they are much happier when sailing in the unknown seas. The vessels in their command are meant to be ocean bound. Having set sail on a particular course, he has encountered a violent storm. What are his choices? Should he abandon ship, crew, and cargo in the midst of this storm, causing his own certain demise together with those who have served him on the voyage? What would happen if he just took a moment and dropped into the inner Stillness? This Voice that will most definitely help to guide him to safety. The crew will be fortified by his strength and courage. He knows what to do, what resources to use, and how to stay afloat, even in the most perilous of waters. He is unsinkable. He realizes that he must unload any unnecessary cargo and go forward, taking with him only what is necessary to reach the destination. There is no need to panic. He cannot fail. One step at a time, he rises to meet the challenge of this relentless storm. Eventually, he makes his way to the calmer waters that will take him to safety, and the harbor, which awaits him. Because you have prepared him for these times, all you have to do is nudge him into remembering that he already knows what to do.

Kings Who Rear Queens

See the beauty of the soul within your children and reflect that beauty back to them, so that someday, they will carry on that legacy with their own children.

When your son becomes a father himself, he will have learned how to celebrate and support his daughter (and son) during all of her tender, vulnerable times—together with each joyous rite of passage that marks the cornerstone of her life. As she continues to move through the physical, emotional, and spiritual stages of maturing into adulthood, he will facilitate the strengthening of her spirit by helping her to notice her *Magnificence* along the way. When she gets her first period, he will take her to tea and together they will celebrate the glorious and monumental changes that await her as a result of this natural event. He may even decide to present her with a special gift—perhaps a pair of earrings or a pendant to commemorate the occasion.

Whatever the case, she will always remember this day with her father. He is a source of strength and courage, all the while helping her to facilitate those qualities in herself. While she knows on all levels that she can depend on him, what she continues to learn is that it is she, herself, who will ultimately become completely responsible for her own way of being in the world. He will celebrate her femininity, while supporting her in developing all of the qualities necessary for her to bring forward the most optimal expression of her gifts—whatever they are. He will support her in her dream to become an astronaut, race car driver, or a professional baker, all the while continuing to treat her with the love, tenderness, and care that she will need to fulfill her passions in this life form.

Conscious Partnership Revisited

Do not settle for anyone less than the man whom you will (or already have) reared as your son. If you are currently married and have children that you want to nourish in a conscious environment, continue taking note of your partner. Should you, at any time, notice that he is unwilling or unable to offer what you have deemed appropriate for both your growth and that of your daughter and son, you will go through the necessary steps that will bring your concerns to his awareness. If he responds positively and maintains that response— excellent. However, if he repeatedly persists in patterns that you know are not supportive of you and your children, you will do what you need to do to extricate yourself (and your kids) or him from the situation. You will not make him wrong. And you will do everything possible to find ways for ongoing healthy co-parenting. We will not detail them here, but if you embrace the principles that are outlined in this material while consciously continuing to develop your way, you won't have any difficulties in establishing the guidelines that best suit your children's and your own needs. You do know what to do. Go forward and open yourself and your daughter and son to grander possibilities. And, if you quit enabling your partner's unconscious behavior by allowing him to stay when it is time for him to go, you are helping to show what to do if they encounter a similar dilemma in the future with their partner. Your daughter is watching. And your son is witnessing how to be in the world not only by observing you—but by witnessing him as well.

New Stories, New Enchantments

In parenting our children, we have the opportunity to become our own parents. Our mothers and fathers had some successes and failures. Regardless of our perception of how well they might have handled our upbringing, we do owe them tremendous gratitude for the gift of life that they gave us. They did the best they could. Now it is our turn and our responsibility to give our children every possible resource that will guide them into their happily ever after ... *right now.*

❧ EXERCISE ☙

Take a few moments to visualize how you would have wanted to be parented if you could re-invent your childhood experience. Now, create the perfect mother and father in your mind. If there were qualities of both of your parents that you particularly admired, add those to the profile of the imaginary parents you are now envisioning. Be expansive in your creation. There are no limits. These people are *Magnificent.* They are wonderfully balanced in both their feminine and masculine nature. They are conscious, loving spirits. There is no end to their wisdom, strength, love, and compassion. Keep creating. Keep contributing to their profile. Take some time with this activity. Write it all down.

Perhaps you will want to extend the exercise for several days. When you are satisfied with the results, look over the material. Now, decide to embody everything you have written or imagined. It doesn't matter how you were parented. Let it go. Celebrate the good with the bad and go forward to become the best version of a mother (or father) you can possibly be—both for yourself and for your children.

TWELVE

ASCENDANCY—
TAKE YOUR QUEENLINESS TO NEW
LEVELS FOR AS LONG AS YOU LIVE

Jewel: Diamond for Light and Illumination

How to create your happily ever after ... right now

Many of you have been on the pilgrimage toward happiness and health for a while. Time and again, you have felt the ecstasy after making measurable progress followed by the agony of slipping back into old behavioral patterns. You have been connected to the sense of freedom and peace that you've so desperately wanted to sustain, only to watch that state of bliss evade and elude you yet another time. You have discovered certain things that work; let go of things that don't; stuck to some stuff for a while; slacked off; gone back to old patterns; started new ones; picked up the latest book; gone to another workshop; hired therapists, healers, coaches, spiritual mentors, doctors, and others, all in looking for the answers.

And, more than once, you have been disillusioned by these various approaches—similar to the disappointment you experienced from the men you positioned into princedom. Alas, they were not able to deliver your ticket to "happily ever after" either. So when things in your external world continue to fall apart—together with all of your unresolved hopes and desires—you may be more inclined to keep directing your attention *inward* for the answers. As has been repeatedly emphasized in this material, it is through the internal exploration that you will access lasting support for your most optimal destiny in this life form. Despite any feelings of personal inadequacy, which may arise as you continue to dig, you are your own best guru. Put aside all of the unnecessary chatter of your mind about how you have fallen short, and instead, take note of the messages coming from a more peaceful, stable place in your heart. This place is your Essence. It will steadily guide you to the truth. How will you recognize the "voice" of this silent whisperer? It is ever supportive, encouraging, and resonate with your highest and best good. And deep in your soul, you *do* know what is best for you—regardless of the perceived inconvenience this may cause. Others can guide, encourage, and cheer you on, but ultimately, dear hearts, it is you who must go forward "confidently in the direction of your dreams." And listening to the heart-voice will definitely provide the most direct route—regardless of how things may appear.

If there is even a tiny part of you that can start to believe, and then actually begin to *know* that you deserve excellence across every area of your life, the heart-voice will become more and more audible. Remember. You were born to be loved, appreciated, and celebrated. And as you can continue to love, appreciate, and celebrate *yourself* (regardless of your perceived mistakes), so then can others see you in your state of grandeur. No matter how your personality may have taken form, you are still part of the royal bloodline that launched us all on this mysterious, earthly adventure. You have sprouted from the Divine seed that is the Source of everything—the Heavens, the Earth, and whatever else is "out there." So, regardless of whether you recognize it or not, you have endless potential and infinite appeal. These qualities are etched in your spirit and soul. It is time that you shine them brilliantly out into the world—and if you are already glowing, then expand your luster.

I realize for some of us that recognizing our own personal divinity can be challenging at times. So often we believe ourselves to be unworthy. We have repeatedly listened to the banter in our heads on how miserably we have failed—how we should be younger, thinner, prettier, and smarter. Our shortcomings and mistakes can glare at us like a gawking stalker. Good news. These humiliating messages are not coming from the *real* you. They have originated in a part of your biology that is hooked up to your primal existence. And guess what? You are never going to get it right according to that "informant." So you might as well give it up and go for emphasizing everything that already knows you are amazing. Even if you have accidentally tricked yourself into thinking you are the most despicable human on the planet, somewhere inside, you get that you are a Godling in progress. Your job is to strengthen your own awareness that this is so—regardless of how diminished you may feel at times.

Of course, as we have repeatedly discussed before, you are going to have to muster some pretty significant self-compassion in order to recognize that on *every* level. We can be guided by another passage from *A Course in Miracles:* "… all of your past, except it's beauty, is gone, and nothing is left but a blessing. All your kindnesses and every loving thought you ever had … are purified of the errors that hid their light, and have been kept for you in their own perfect radiance. They are beyond destruction and beyond guilt. They came from the Holy Spirit within you, and we know what God creates is eternal."

Yes, you have screwed up. And more than likely you will screw up again. This is so, dear hearts, because you are operating out of an imperfect instrument, while simultaneously living on a seriously flawed planet. When you stop to consider all that you have endured, is it any wonder that you've had some considerable challenges along the way? Nonetheless, regardless of the past, you now have an opportunity to deliberately cause your most optimal destiny to unfold in magical ways.

And as you step into the unknown, your next action toward growth could feel more than a little scary. Even so, realize that when you are in alignment with the Subject (God-Force) of your life that has always known how to resolve your heart's deepest longing (regardless of whether or not you have resisted receiving the information), there is absolutely *no end to how your magnificent potential can take form.* As you finally come to recognize the infinite possibilities that await you when you quit genuflecting to an illusory sage (including "your" man), your happiness meter will start going off the charts! Yes, it is time to take the leap of faith necessary *to trust yourself.* Understand that this Subject (God, Creator, Source, or whatever you want to call Her/Him) is *operating through you.* And so therefore, you are not the helpless object of anything. Rather, you are empowered by this Divine instrument to fully become the grandest version of yourself *now*—not some distant day in the future. All you have to do is *pay attention.*

Yes, I know. As you approach yet another "dangerous" edge on the landscape of your soul while the Voice of Truth is advising you to come to the edge, the prospect of going forward can seem dangerous and daunting. If you jump, you might crash, crumble and croak, or at least become seriously maimed and mutilated. Even so you *know you can't go back.* How can you resolve this seemingly impossible dilemma? Remember Indiana Jones as he was just about to reach the entrance of the cave containing the Holy Grail? He had overcome outrageous obstacles on his quest for this prize— and now, it was nearly in his grasp. Yet getting to it from the other side of the deep, endless abyss that separated him from the cave's entrance seemed a physical impossibility. What to do? He stopped, took a breath, and consulted his heart-voice for direction. Almost immediately he was advised to take a *leap of faith.* And as he put his foot out into thin air, miraculously, what paved the way beneath him was *solid ground.*

Not unlike Indiana, as you proceed on your journey toward happiness and peace, you will at times find yourself in what appears to be scary, uncharted territory. In addition, you may become unpopular with your friends and family, who, God love them, wish you would stay being who you were, rather than becoming more fully who you *are.* You can't blame them. They just want the comfort of "sameness," not realizing that the only way to permanently end suffering is to accept that change is immanent. Therefore, the only *real* chance we have to grow is to go forward in the whole leap of faith thing, whatever that may look like for each of us. Remember. You *are* Indiana Jones. Otherwise, you wouldn't be curious about the subjects under discussion here. So trudge on. And could anything stop Indiana? Hardly. He is an endlessly curious, cutting-edge-creative—just like you. So, continue to be alert while waking up to the endless possibilities that can become more than just mere potentialities—all because you decided to *really* be you, here, now, in this moment. Don't you just *love* that?

The reason why we are challenged in listening to the true voice of our hearts is because it is often shrouded by the ongoing prattle in our minds that is ever prying us away from our peace. We have been so deeply conditioned to focus on our fears that we have forgotten how to tune into the channel of love. Even though this "love station" is available *at all times,* if we don't deliberately choose it, we won't be able to hear the peaceful lullabies always available to soothe and comfort away our anxious thoughts and imaginations.

It is no one's fault that you aren't inclined to listen to the love channel—not your own, your parent's, your teacher's, your partner's or the world, which you are temporarily calling home. It is just that you are simply a product of the repeated "fear" messages that have conditioned you away from the truth. Nonetheless, you are exquisitely unique. Each part that contributes to the combination of the whole "you" package is utterly *Magnificent* regardless of how you may believe yourself to *appear*. As you continue your pilgrimage toward truth and ultimate enlightenment, it will be less fraught with pain and suffering if you can be more accepting of this *Magnificence* of yours.

You are an exquisitely crafted instrument of creation, designed to constantly reinvent yourself. The cells with which you awakened this morning will morph into something else by the time you are ready to retire tonight. When you put your head on the pillow, you may *think* you are still the same person you were when you woke up, yet most definitely you are not. So the possibilities for change and transformation are endless. You certainly do not have to be stuck in the conditioned patterns of your past, no matter how entrapped you believe you are by them. You *can* begin again, at any moment you choose.

Radical Simplicity

If you pay attention, you will begin to notice that you do not have to look for the ecstasy or wait for the agony anymore. The more you travel toward your heart and the truth of your being, the more you realize that your balanced, peaceful, happy state has *nothing to do* with the agony or the ecstasy anyway. *Good news.* In order to be in touch with ongoing feelings of freedom and harmony, you will not be required to spend months in an ashram or meditating in a cave; follow a specific religious tradition; attend regular retreats; or "om" for hours on end. (Though if these practices assist you, by all means use them). *When you breathe each breath as if it were your last, and are happy when it wasn't,* you are well on your way to conscious living. Really *look* at the flowers in your garden or the grocery store and notice what a miracle they are, and then realize that the miraculous starts with you.

In order to end the longing and be in your state of *happily ever after ... right now,* you will not be required to stand on your head or sit in the lotus position for hours on end—though feel free to do so should you be inspired. If you want to be youthful and energetic, you won't have to drink mushed-up greens, gulp down wheat grass, give up fat or carbs, become a vegetarian, or exercise until your guts fall out. Of course, if these activities *contribute* to your vigor and vitality (*be really careful here*), then go right ahead. There will be no need for you to slather on expensive face creams; inject toxic chemicals into your forehead; tuck in your tummy; lift your face; plump up your boobs; or suck the fat out of your thighs—in order to feel that you are absolutely the most *Magnificent* Queenly being in the Universe, *regardless of* your age. Your smile is destined to be brilliant and luminous no matter what shade of white or yellow, jagged or straight your teeth are, because this gleam of yours is radiating a beam of happiness that's shining from the *inside*. Your teeth have nothing to do with what is truly glowing here. In following your heart-voice (which is ever-available to guide you), you are stepping into your own version of royal, ruby-red slippers—regardless of how they look to anyone else. This pilgrimage is uniquely your own, and the more you are willing to explore what fits for you (even if *no one else on the planet* is in agreement), the more your free and happy spirit will continue to soar.

Peace Is the Way—Tools for Transformation.

In the famous words of Civil Rights activist A. J. Muste, "There is no way to peace. Peace is the way." And this way to peace is quite simple, although it can *seem* otherwise. You do not have to make the experience of accessing peace difficult or tedious. Your consciousness is already ripe for a shift to take place in you—one where (when complete) you will always be operating from this peace of yours, which has heretofore seemed to cleverly evade you. How do I know about this ripened state that is unfolding in you? Because you would not be attracted to this material if you weren't ready for change.

Most of us are weary of being chained to the pain and pleasure cycle. Of course we believe our captor to be merciless at times. Actually, we have always had the power to release ourselves from this unfortunate pest. Remember our friend Dorothy in the Wizard of Oz? Three clicks of *her* ruby-red slippers and, *poof*—she was home! Just like Dorothy, we already have the formula to be taken *immediately* "home" to peace. We don't have to go looking for it. It's just that our fear-based conditioning has made it *seem* so complicated. So having some version of the Good Witch around to jog our memory can be quite beneficial. If we pay attention, those people, situations, events, and circumstances, replete with their reminders, *are* showing up. And as they do, it helps to keep remembering that peace is the way—while we are *shown the way to peace.*

It doesn't matter what religious traditions, values, or philosophies you subscribe to or uphold. If you have stayed with me this far into the material, you are more than likely in agreement that the world of appearances, which has been viewed through the distortion of a mind that provokes unnecessary reactions and fears, has *got* to be addressed in order for you to enjoy more happiness, peace, and tranquility—*right now*. And so, you must begin (or continue) your quest to notice what works to quiet the voices that keep running in your head, which no longer serve your growth and expansion. Your practices for transformation can be as simple or as complex as you want. All that is necessary is *committing* to what will help you unplug from the nonstop talking machine to which you have been involuntarily attached. And, when whatever you are practicing doesn't seem to be working, invoke the Universal Divine (heart/mind) to guide you to whatever *will* be effective in moving you beyond your primal past.

This primitive programming is powerful. It has trained us to become fixated on what *it* thinks we need to know in order to be safe. Only most of the things that the mind believes are still a threat—like big, bad dinosaurs or saber-toothed-tigers—no longer exist. More than likely, you aren't going to be killed if someone blasts their horn should you happen to inconvenience his driving agenda. Nonetheless, in not being aware of what our mind will automatically do when alerted with this or that, we are more at risk for going into some kind of a spin or drama about it all. Fortunately, we have instant effects in our bodies to remind us—the sweaty palms, racing heart, etc. This is all happening because our ancient mind, which seems to have a significant impact on how we function, is still operating out of threat and ultimate disaster. This sucker is old, stubborn, and mean—like a big bully who keeps trying to frighten and intimidate us. Isn't it high time we put it in its place?

What Are You Afraid Of?

Is it how you are going to survive? Is it death? Is it being abandoned and alone? What *really* is your deepest, darkest fear? Do you even know? Having been a single woman for the majority of my adult life, and conditioned for being taken care of from the time I was old enough to know that boys and girls had a different agenda and anatomy, I get why I've spent a lot of time being petrified that I wouldn't be saved. Saved from what, I honestly do not know. Though I have needlessly exhausted a good portion of my existence being scared out of my wits, I am still not altogether clear on what it is that I was so afraid of—particularly since nothing I ever thought was going to happen to me in the way of catastrophe has actually come to pass.

It's interesting. I mean the whole wanting to survive thing. If you think about it, even if you are an atheist, you more than likely believe that when you die you're pretty much done and you won't know what hit you. So, what's the big deal? If the atheist thinks he or she is going to be reduced to soil and the spiritual seeker believes their soul survives the body to go onto a "better place," how can any of us really, logically dread "death" or fear for our survival? I mean worst case, we are dust, and best case we are floating, happy, and free, right?

Of course there is the whole Heaven vs. Hell philosophy firmly positioned in the belief system of some. One version of that philosophy may go like this: If we're not careful in this life form, we might end up in eternal misery (Hell) in the next. However, there *is* an escape hatch from such an ill-fated calamity. If you ask for forgiveness from God for whatever wrong you believe yourself to have committed, repent, and then move forward with more favorable actions, words, and deeds, you are all but guaranteed a ticket into the more preferable eternity (Heaven). And if you should "mess up" again, just repeat the "asking for forgiveness" exercise with an intention to correct the behavior in the future.

So, I have to ask myself, after contemplating the three aforementioned possibilities, i.e. happy, floating and free; Heaven; or nothingness? What is it that we are trying to survive, anyway? We absolutely *do* know that we are going to leave our current location at some point, so it would appear that either we will become free spirits, angels, or fertilizer. Yes, I know, there is a rather daunting finality to the latter option, though if "you" have vanished from the scene, what difference does it make, anyway?

As far as our final departure being painful—well in all of the aforementioned scenarios at the exact moment of your transition into whatever you will become after you croak, you are either going to be out of your body or no longer anything, so how *can* it hurt if *you* aren't there anymore, or are on your way to becoming dirt? Rather than feeling any discomfort, you will be hovering above the corpse that was never you in the first place—or evaporating into non-existence. Either way, you aren't going to feel a thing because that which you have always *thought* was you is simply not there anymore.

Your Molecules Are Always in Motion

When we arrive on planet Earth, we are a mixture of neurons, subatomic particles, DNA sequences, genetic programming, and who knows what else, all of which keeps constantly moving and changing. And, at the current time, this "wiring" of ours seems to be subject to massive error—resulting in short circuits, power outages, and a tremendous fluctuation in frequencies. The mind, being a part of all of this, is an imperfect instrument. It will lose the keys, forget people's names, and try to trick you into thinking you are going to be eaten by monsters, when there are none in sight. All it really wants is relief from its imperfection, as well as to avoid its worst fear—death. When overcome with the drive to survive, it doesn't remember its rightful inheritance, as well as what it's doing here in the first place. It may even convince you that you are being guided by little green men that show up occasionally on your wall. *Good news.* You are not your mind.

The hardware (or the innocent bystander that is you) is blank. This hardware can be encoded by the mind (software), which is then conditioned to tell it what to do. A fear-event signals you to insert the software for "what-to-do-when-you-get-scared." Once you inject the survival-reptile program, which reeks of narcissism and separation, you will experience some version of those qualities, depending on the strength and potency of your customized curriculum. This software, by the way, is pretty outdated—by about a few billion years. And so it would appear that we have been kinda slow on the uptake in developing alternatives. Nonetheless, we can start at any time.

In your forebrain, you have something that reptiles don't have—a cerebral cortex, which holds the higher levels of reasoning, as well as the ability to neutralize a fear-based reality, strongly influenced by our ancient conditioning. As mentioned in the prologue of this manuscript, there is now empirical evidence to demonstrate that when we are operating specifically from the left pre-frontal cortex (as studies on deep states of meditation suggest), we are predisposed for enlightenment, or the state of being that allows us to witness our mind and thoughts without being "freaked out" by them.

In simple terms, our evolution goes like this: Reptile (three-and-a-half billion years old), mammal (160 million years old), us (100,000 years old). So, the reptile (no heart/strictly survival based) and mammal (some heart, though still steeped in separation) have been around awhile longer than the current version of ourselves, which is why we are inclined to use their programs instead of inventing our own. Though there are some cutting-edge-creatives out there developing different methods of operating—like the monks who have been meditating for over ten thousand hours (as discussed in Professor Davidson's studies in the prologue).

The ego/reptile/mammal mind wants you to keep playing out the familiar—even though it is obsolete survival stuff. It still thinks your only mission here is to keep from getting killed. So if you can just begin (if you haven't done so already) to notice when you are in its grasp, and then remember it is time to develop or employ new software, you are well on your way to freedom. Knowing how the lizard operates and witnessing its behavior, like having no heart (as in compassion or love), and wanting to kill for survival, you don't really want it to be in charge anymore, do you?

Studies now show that there are actual neurobiological events that can shift us into conscious awareness—among these (again) are practicing meditation over time. Now I am not suggesting, nor do I believe, that this method is the only way to peace and the transcendence of suffering. *My* passion, following a life-long career of witnessing enormous suffering, both my own and others, is to encourage you to access your own inner peace, happiness and joy in the most timely, effective way possible—to prioritize the discovery of a personalized path to peace that will be the most supportive for you.

That path is available. All you have to do is decide it is time to start (or continue) the journey home to your heart. I'm not just talking about getting to neutral here. I am talking about getting to *happy* ... **right now.**

New Software: Practices for Transcendence

In the examples below, you will find some exercises that may be helpful for you in your journey. These are only meant to be suggestions or guidelines. Many of you have established techniques, including meditation, yoga, breath-work and so on, which are already working well for you. As far as I know, there is no one, magical, right formula for unwinding from our ancient conditioning that is right for everyone. For some of us, it may take ninety-nine interventions, and whatever happens during the one-hundredth (it could be as simple as inhaling) will be the action (or non-action) that tips our consciousness in the right direction toward operating from a foundation of peace and happiness. The following are practices designed to support you in shifting your consciousness to a joy based reality. See what fits, let the rest go, and be inspired to create more tools of your own.

I. Begin (or continue) accumulating your way to that 10,000 hours of meditation, which seemed to put the monks (in the study described at the beginning of this manuscript) into *really* peaceful, happy states. If you are not familiar with how to meditate, there are a multitude of resources available to help support you. Whatever you do or do not do in your day, consider the benefits of developing some kind of a contemplative practice. It could be yoga, sitting meditation, walking meditation, staring off into space, or focusing on keeping a hula hoop circulating around your middle. It doesn't matter what it is, just so long as this practice helps you disengage from your monkey mind. Further, when you set aside this time to support such a practice, you are proclaiming to yourself, and to the Universe, that *you are committed to becoming conscious, aware, happy, and free.*

II. (**Five to forty-five minutes**) Upon arising first thing, think of something for which you are truly grateful (even if you were unwillingly awakened by your alarm). Cultivate this sense of gratitude all day (doing so will accelerate your happiness quotient exponentially). Next, either seat yourself or go for a walk. Visualize a bright, golden, healing light penetrating the crown of your head and then surrounding your entire body, creating a shimmering, translucent egg. Imagine that the Divine energy generating this light is creating a prayer field of protection as well as a manifestation tool, which will exaggerate all possibilities for Providence to deliver your very best destiny into form. See this happening now and from this moment forward. Ask that you be given the wisdom and discernment on whether to take action or just allow Divine Grace to coordinate the details for you as you relax and let it all effortlessly unfold. Decide that everything is now being synchronized for your highest and best good. Invoke support from both the seen and unseen world (in the form of angels and guides) to help exaggerate this field in all ways possible. Now see the field helping others—helping everyone you touch (and of course, as they are assisted by your love and support, so does all of this come back to you in kind). And if you are inclined, extend your prayer field to help uplift the entire world, the Universe, and beyond. Now relax as you release it all to Creator. Then move along with your day (for more information on how to work with prayer fields, be sure to read *The Secret of Shambhala,* by James Redfield).

III. (**Two minutes**) It may help to have some ideas (either general or specific) on what your "best destiny" would look like. Here are some suggestions:

1. I am fully awake, conscious, empowered, and free.

2. I am fully protected and safe from any harm at all times.

3. I release all fear. I let go of any feelings of betrayal or guilt. I forgive myself and others for all past mistakes and errors.

4. I am free of any past patterns of dysfunction or abnormality. I operate from love, peace, and compassion at all times. The flood-gates of radiant blessings are opening to me now so that all of my strengths and gifts are being utilized while I operate at my most optimal potential.

5. All of my past interactions and connections with others, as well as all of my previous actions, words, and deeds, are purified to provide the most favorable benefit for all involved now and always.

6. I am completely balanced in every aspect of my being, physically, emotionally, spiritually, and soulfully from this moment forward. I am fully energized, healthy, and free.

7. My potential is unlimited and continues expanding moment to moment.

8. All of my current and future relationships are balanced, harmonious, and loving.

9. From this moment forward, I experience freedom, health, harmony, and an endless stream of prosperity. I no longer have any needs because I am taken care of across all areas of my life beyond my most

favorable expectations. I am free to give at the very highest level of service, and this expression of love flowing from me creates eternal happiness and peace for me and everyone I touch.

IV. (**Fifteen to twenty seconds**) Focus on your eternity ring (a representation of the lasting commitment you have made to yourself discussed at the beginning of Chapter 10).

In addition to reminding you of your personal promise to continue loving and respecting yourself, this ring can also symbolize the constant prayer field that is always available to protect, guide, and sustain you. Envision the Light of God surrounding and strengthening you moment to moment as you focus on this image of eternity enveloping your finger. Let it remind you of the magnitude of strength that is constantly supporting your growth and expansion. Your only job is to activate this Mighty Power by allowing it to penetrate every particle of your being as you acknowledge and give thanks for the unlimited possibilities that It provides. If you forget, just begin again.

Imagine this is as "A Message from Source"

In loving you unconditionally, I am free of expectation or requirement of you. I spend My moments being endlessly entertained by the ongoing stream of adventures I am able to experience—all because you decided to co-create with Me our life together here on planet Earth. Incredible! I am constantly amazed and astonished at your endless creativity on our mutual behalf. Take a moment with Me here to reflect on it all. Can you see why I continue to marvel at your genius in being a "stand in" for Me?

As for your perceived mistakes—please, do find a way to let go of any lingering, needless reminders of those. It is impossible for you to grow while mired in guilt as you brood over your "shameful" past. Since the entire reason you signed up for this earthly mission was to develop at an accelerated pace, don't you sort of want to get on with it? Here are some helpful hints to catapult you forward: 1. let go of guilt (believing you have been a villain) 2. avoid being a victim. Of course, the quickest way to bypass the victim/villain debacle is first and foremost to forgive yourself for any and all things you believe you did wrong. Once you get the knack of releasing your deep dark secrets to Me (of course, we don't really have any secrets from each other), you will find that you are no longer interested in holding others hostage for their "betrayal" of you. Try to remember the big picture here. They showed up to participate in your healing. That is all. That is it.

Let's take your mother for example. There are probably at least a few things you wish she would have done (or would be doing) differently, correct? Well, actually, when you look at where she came from, how ever could she have mastered the art of perfect mothering? And as for your dad—most all of you have got issues with him on some level. Please take a moment with Me here to look at his conditioning and training. Did anyone teach him the importance of self-love?

So here is the point. Try loving yourself so much that you actually can begin to have unlimited compassion for yourself and all that you have accomplished in this life-time—regardless of your "mistakes." Keep releasing every single perceived failure, shortcoming, and regret, to Me. (Remember, I don't judge anything.) Repeat these exercises until you feel less and less burdened by your past "errors." Now then, begin to witness how your tolerance of you will transfer to others, including your parents. And while you're at it, try being grateful for something they did for you— even if it was just bringing you into the world. In the absence of their participation, would we be having this conversation? Realize that when you are able to balance and harmonize your relationships with the ones who brought you into being (with My help of course), you will witness more and more magic and miracles in all of your relationships. Trust Me. It works.

Now then, as you are becoming lighter and lighter from your place of self-acceptance, understand that this "lightness" is what you were meant to experience here. As you continue feeling more buoyant and alive, you will simultaneously lose the desire to change anyone else. You simply won't want to waste your precious energy trying to get others to see the light. Rather, you will only want to concentrate on being that light, yourself. As you continue to glow, your entire planet will benefit. For when the light is shining, there can be no darkness.

It is time for you to rise to a place of exaltation. If you are reading the words on this page, you have been specifically called to a place of leadership by Me. There are only a few requirements necessary for your participation in this role. Just commit yourself to living in a state of love, triumph, liberation, joy, prosperity, peace, health, and well-being—from this moment forward. Whether you believe it or not, you have chosen to be a "way shower." Even though you may not realize it, you have already been showing the way for quite a while now, so it is high time to live your life from inspiration—lose the drama and dance (I may have stolen that line from our author). That means no more having to learn things the hard way through pain and suffering—ever again.

And oh, do consciously bring in that column of light (mentioned earlier) as often as possible. Your visualization of this beacon surrounding you at all times notifies me that you are a willing receiver. You see, I am constantly beaming this light. Though in order for it to be effective, it must be grounded somewhere by an enthusiastic recipient. Since things have gotten more than a little scrambled there on planet Earth, in order to unravel the "crossed wires" and blown-out circuits that have interrupted the "light flow," it will take quite a few of you to focus. Think light, light, light and then more light. And of course, everyone is destined to become "enlightened," anyway. It's just a matter of time. Though wouldn't you rather be on the cutting edge of it all? Ya, that's what I'm talkin' about.

One of the quickest ways to download this light (aside from visualizing the bright golden column literally coming into your head) is through genuine gratitude for anything (regardless of what it is). If you find yourself challenged on what to be grateful for, I suppose you could start out by being glad you weren't born a woman in Afghanistan—unless, of course you were born a woman in Afghanistan, in which case you are probably quite accelerated in your ability to experience appreciation. More than likely, your circumstances have seemed quite dire, even though it was you, who chose this situation for your growth and expansion. Well done—really well done. Hard stuff. (Again, I remind you, no need to suffer any more in order to grow—we are finished with that paradigm.)

Regardless of your circumstances, however difficult they may seem (Afghanistan or not) please try to avoid taking the world too seriously. Recognize the grand cosmic potential for a love story here (I believe the author launched this material alluding to such). You were destined to love and be loved. As your poet Robert Frost once said, "Earth's the right place for love: I don't know where it's likely to go better." (Who do you think inspired him with those words)?

Before signing off here, I should mention the whole "living in the present" thing, currently popular among some of you on the spiritual journey. Look, I know it seems challenging, but give it a try. If you do, I think you will find yourself with a lot more time for day-dreaming your joys—and then manifesting those day dreams. And as you do, take note of all of the synchronicities being coordinated on your behalf (compliments of Me). I should mention that there are just a couple of minor details, which differ among those who seem to be challenged in manifesting their dreams and the ones who bring them into form—like Jack Canfield (author of Chicken Soup for the Soul). He is a marvelous example of bringing the light through, while creating unending opportunities for himself and everyone he touches.

Every messenger (including Jack Canfield) who has ever inspired you started on the same page as you—with a dream and a vision. As they got more clarity on what they wanted to create, they visualized the outcome (frequently), while allowing Me to coordinate all of the people, places, circumstances and events (details) that would most accelerate their progress. They surrendered the "how" of it all to me. As they let go, they were effortlessly advised on when to take an action, and when to sit back, allowing My grace to weave the magic and miracles.

Rest easy. If you are reading this message, you are well on your way to manifesting your dreams. And while you're at it … remember, I am with you forever, always, and beyond. I love you more than is comprehensible to you now—though someday you'll get it. Until then, know that I am really laid back. (I do have eternity, you know.) Oh yes, one more thing. You can't get it wrong no matter what—I got your back."

Love, *The Source*
P. S. We can talk anytime you want. All you have to do is ask.

RECAP, REFLECTIONS, AND REMINDERS

Chapter 1: If you continue to believe that the longing in your soul will be satisfied by something or someone outside of yourself, this will perpetuate your misery and suffering. Once you decide to *become* all of the things that you are seeking from somewhere else, your suffering will begin to cease. And you will be a magnet that attracts others who are bringing forward their own version of *Magnificence*—without you doing a thing. No stewing, fretting, waiting, or wondering—anymore—*ever again.*

Chapter 2: Be a Queen. Don't even *think* Princess.

Chapter 3: Lose the slave-girl identity. Notice even the subtlest of ways in which you give away your power. You are not helping anyone (least of all yourself) by playing small. Stand tall. Pay attention to what is true for you and then share this truth clearly, avoiding the temptation to be right. Be willing to negotiate without compromise. (Compromising is when you give in. In negotiation, the two sides communicate on how to combine their viewpoints for the benefit of the whole).

Chapter 4: As Queen, you *must* trust your internal wisdom. Avoid any temptation to keep looking for the answers outside. Seek wise counsel when necessary while using discernment, realizing that the buck stops with you. Assimilate what you have learned while remembering who is in charge. Then realize that *true* masters have no need to prove anything.

Chapter 5: Hold your power. Don't be attached (or addicted) to a "love" object. Remember, attachment is "anti-love" and has its roots in dependency and need. All relationships continue to morph and change, regardless of how long they last. So, to the extent that you can, direct your focus on personal growth while making your contributions (*even if he evaporates*)—and know that you always have something solid in your life (your own developing sense of self). The more you focus on what is true for you, the happier you will be, right now. Of course, you cannot control what is true for him or any other. You have merged your paths so that you can grow in a direction that would otherwise be unavailable to you. You do not cause each other's happiness. Rather, you expand the possibility for a greater joy from your already-happy states as you journey together.

Chapter 6: When challenges arise, *do not project your pain*. If he falls from grace, remember that you are not exempt from the same fate. Avoid the temptation to pontificate in righteousness as you focus on his wrongdoing. Instead, move as quickly as possible back to growth. Remember, every situation in your life can be seen as an opportunity for your learning. It is up to you to determine the most honest and expedient way to get the lesson. Take responsibility for your part. Notice what triggered you about his behavior and be willing to share without a need to blame him. Instead of whining or complaining, dig deep and find out what is really going on here. You may have a breakthrough. And breakthrough or not, you must continue to really see what is true for you in the situation. Consult your open heart for the answers. You will know. You do know. Remember the Indiana Jones *leap of faith*. Be courageous in taking that first step, destined to support you in crossing the crevice of doubt.

Chapter 7: Don't be attached to *any* outcome, any person, or anything in general. Do not wait for the phone to ring—*ever again*. If you do find yourself pondering when you will get the call, *phone home to yourself.* Give back to your life *now* all of the moments you wasted in yearning for him (or anyone else for that matter) to dial you up.

Chapter 8: Keep identifying your passions. The key to your life's purpose lies in the inspirations that continue to stir and stimulate your soul. The longing that has persistently tugged at your heart for as long as you can remember has nothing to do with what someone or something can do for *you.*

Your perceived emptiness can only be resolved by an internal exploration. You must continue digging if you are going to uncover the exquisite jewels that are uniquely yours to expose. As you focus more and more on your passions and inspirations, you will be effortlessly guided to your own glorious treasure chest. Any straining or striving to find happiness (as in the right boyfriend, husband, or job) will no longer be an issue because you will have re-directed your focus, relaxing more fully—moment to moment—into who you *really* are (*Queen*). As you recognize your own *Magnificence*, you will realize that there is nowhere to go and nothing to find. And then, guess who shows up to join you?

Chapter 9: In making a decision to live like a Queen every day, you will follow your insight and intuition (the voice of the soul) instead of your instincts (the voice of fear). In doing so, you will continue to recognize real love, both your own and that of another. Of course, you will never be tempted to settle for anything less again.

Chapter 10: In opening fully to your Queenly nature, you will become more and more practiced in developing the art of joining others who are living out their own version of *Magnificence*. In being true to yourself, you are allowing your beautiful heart to flower—and as it does, other blossoming hearts will show up to join you.

Chapter 11: It is your responsibility to create a legacy of royalty for your daughters and sons. They are watching you. If you act like a "slave-girl," that behavior is what they may replicate (as in your daughters behaving like a slave, and your sons being in the "master-mode"). If you conduct yourself like a Queen, you are bequeathing to them their true and rightful heritage. Isn't that what they deserve? Do not let them down. And, don't be too hard on yourself if you believe you have fallen short. Just begin again. *Right now ...*

Chapter 12: Keep practicing. Stay alert. You are a living demonstration for every soul you touch, regardless of how brief your encounter. Continue being keenly aware of what is resonate for you and follow that. The world will keep doing what it does. Your responsibility is to be true to your own ideals on this sacred pilgrimage to freedom and happiness. And, you might as well focus on each moment. Don't get caught up in the whole *getting to the destination* thing. At some point, we will all probably have to realize that as long as we are drawing breath (and more than likely beyond that breath), we're never going to be finished. Kind of a relief, isn't it?

EPILOGUE

As mentioned in the beginning of chapter twelve, you will occasionally find yourself wondering if this "stuff" really works. It may seem at times that you are not making much progress—if any progress at all. You still freak out; you still wish he would call—or you wish *anyone* would call; and you still want someone or something to save you. Have patience with yourself. Remember, unwinding from a mind influenced by conditioning, which started a few billion years ago, requires a lot of faith and fortitude. Have heart. You have already jumpstarted yourself beyond what you ever thought possible even a few weeks ago. It wasn't really *that* hard, was it? *You can do it.* Don't forget. You have immeasurable support. Now, take out your magic mirror and look to see how utterly *Magnificent* you are. Don't you deserve to be happy right now? Be the Queen and change your life forever. Love yourself, love the world. It is time. You are the one. Begin.

New Stories New Enchantments

The Call

I am a star in the Universe

I live in a sea of infinite light

I am the illumination that extinguishes darkness.

I am the white point ... the convergence of all color,

The origin of Truth

The emergence of Presence.

All that ever was and ever will be,

Is the life-breath in very cell of my being.

There have been no others before me.

And so shall there be no others after me.

I am the one.

It is here, now that I bring forth the essence of who I am.

I vibrate with the cosmos in my own creative dance.

My essence is still, constant and ever-present.

I share the manifestation that is my highest good

Toward the benefit of all.

In my truest state: LOVE

I am the happiest most powerful being in the Universe

I melt into all that is, was and ever will be.

I am answering the call.

—Luann Robinson Hull

Do you realize everything that had to coordinate and synchronize just so you could be here, right now, exhaling and inhaling? The sheer fact of your very existence is a statistical improbability. And so, YOU are a miracle. Now, start (or continue) living from your miraculous state. Oh, and remember Casanova's advice: *""Be the flame, not the moth."*

Peace, love, joy, and happiness be with you ... *right now.*

Luann Robinson Hull

But you do not see, nor do you hear, and it is well. The veil that clouds your eyes shall be lifted by the hands that wove it, and the clay that fills your ears shall be pierced by those fingers that kneaded it. And you shall see. And you shall hear. Yet you shall not deplore having known blindness, nor regret having been deaf. For in that day you shall know the hidden purpose in all things, and you shall bless darkness as you would bless light.

—*Kahlil Gibran*

ADDENDUM

Dear Readers,

The book you now hold in your hands was first published nine years ago, sourced from a paper I had written called "The Myth of Prince Charming"—which I eventually adapted for my dissertation. The thesis was for Matthew Fox's Doctor of Ministry program created for Masters level professionals wanting to "re-invent" their work from a philosophical, spiritual lens. I had dissolved a ten-year partnership just before starting that program, began seeing someone else, left him midstream, then resumed that relationship four years after completing my Doctorate. Within another four years I would win two awards for this book, formally acknowledging my desire to share the lessons I'd learned and create a 'new love story' on Planet Earth.

But somehow those lessons failed to penetrate the innermost cores of my own heart and soul. Once again, I was treading water in a distorted relationship, painful in its own right but also a catalyst to dig in and continue my work. Fox and other mentors inspired me to broaden my scope—giving me hope that there was a way to transcend my conditioned propensities and help others to do the same. What instinctive tendencies etched into our subconscious minds drive us to behave in ways that cause us pain and suffering? How can we transcend those tendencies? Why do educated women (myself included) repeatedly revert to outdated patterns of relating to men—even as ancient patriarchal systems (and the fairy tales perpetuating them) are clearly crumbling?

I wanted answers, not only to understand myself but also to help other women facing obstacles in their relationships and life-paths in pursuit of personal expansion, transformation, and optimal destiny. As a result, I have been engaged in an ongoing quest to delve into wide-ranging explorations of body, mind, and spirit—discovering along the way that many theories, practices, and neuroscience itself have been evolving in fascinating ways since I finished *Happily*. The energies of their constant interplay offer us the clues that will ultimately resolve the riddles of minds that shackle us in limitation. This book has served as a primer for unleashing those clues. It has also birthed a sequel, *Self Belonging: Embrace the Wisdom of Soul and Science and Live Your Best Life*, to be published in 2021. It is my sincere hope that both books will help liberate you from the places where you are stuck, freeing you to flourish in your own life and in the life you share with others.

With gratitude for our mutual dedication to consciousness,

Luann Robinson Hull

ACKNOWLEDGEMENTS

First, I would like to thank God, who continued to bless me with the passion, momentum, enthusiasm, and inspiration to bring this material forward regardless of any perceived challenges. And then I offer my heartfelt appreciation to all of the people who have continued to support me with their insights, love, compassion, and most of all, a belief in me and this project. They have each been expressions in form of that 'Godly blessing.' Included among them are the late Winnie Shows and Josephine Schallen, editors of early drafts of the material; and Wendy Sherman, literary agent of Wendy Sherman Associates, who came on board when the book was in its beginning stages—agreeing to take me on because, she said, "The material lifted my spirits."

I am immensely grateful for Teri Rider, publisher of Top Reads Publishing, who enthusiastically agreed to publish the second edition of this material, and to Fauzia Burke, of FSB and Associates, for connecting us. Without the faithful support of my masterful editor and friend, Karen Connington, who took painstaking effort in going over every minute detail of the material, the book you now hold in your hands would not have been possible. I also want to acknowledge Rachelle Sparks, copy editor, whose curiosity and interest in the material was palpable, and Chelsea Robinson for her meticulous line editing.

Birgitta Strobel, a master at creating beautifully inspirational art on canvas, designed our cover, a lovely rendition of her painting, "My Father's Garden." This piece, that deeply touches me, was inspired in the garden nurtured by Birgitta's father in the days prior to his untimely death. To me, the painting sets the tone for all of us to consider tending our own gardens, and the beauty inside and outside ourselves. It also reminds us to take great care in deciding how we want to spend our precious lives and with whom—for we cannot know when we too, will be 'called to the Heavens.'

This book has its foundation in the wisdom of a multitude of gifted and wise teachers. Among them is Matthew Fox, founder of the University of Creation Spirituality program, where I earned my doctorate in Ministry and discovered the core inspiration for Happily. Mel Bricker, Ana Perez-Chisti, and Margaret Wheatley were beloved professors in that program. Cynthia Bourgeault, Father Thomas Keating, Neale Donald Walsch, Gary Zukav, Emmet Fox, Eckhart Tolle, Joseph Campbell, Deepak Chopra, Gandhi, Kahlil Gibran, Anandagiri, Pema Chodron, Adyashanti, Masaru Emoto, Greg Braden, His Holiness the Dalai Lama, Geshe Lobsang Tanzen Negi, Matthieu Riccard, Richard J. Davidson, David Hawkins, Ernest Holmes, Carl Jung, Osho, Pia Melody, Candice Pert, James Redfield, Henri Nouwen, Don Miguel Ruiz, Scott Peck, Mariana Bozesan, David Whyte, Marianne Williamson, and Ken Wilbur—have also been profoundly influential. I am deeply grateful to all mentioned here and a multitude of others, who have brought their knowledge and heart to this work.

Finally, for my beloved family, I am most grateful of all: for my late parents, Catherine and Lewis; for my loving and loyal brother, Steve; for my beloved sons, Nes, and Stephen; for my lovely daughter-in-law, Laura; for my precious grandchildren, Vivien and Theo, and for my former husband, Nestor, who gifted me with our glorious sons.

In service to consciousness, I am faithfully yours,

Luann Robinson Hull
July 2, 2020

BIBLIOGRAPHY

Adyashanti. *The Impact of Awakening*. Open Gate Publishing, 2000.

Andrews, Andy. *The Traveler's Gift*. Thomas Nelson Publishing, 2002.

Ardagh, Arjuna. *Awakening to Oneness*. Sounds True, 2007.

---. *The Translucent Revolution*. New World Library, 2005.

Auel, Jean M. *Clan of the Cave Bear*. Crown, 1980.

Austen, Jane. *Pride and Prejudice*. Modern Library, 2000.

Baer, Greg. *Real Love*. Avery, 2004.

Barks, Coleman. *The Essential Rumi*. Harper Collins, 1995.

Baum, Frank L. *The Wizard of Oz*. Tom Doherty Associates, LLC,1993.

The Bible. King James Version, Frank J. Thompson Publishing, 1929.

Bogle, April L. "Testing Faith." *Emory Magazine*, Winter 2010.

Bolen, Jean Shinoda. *Goddesses in Older Women*. Harper Collin, 2001.

Braden, Gregg. *The God Code*. Hay House Publishing, 2005.

---. *The Mystery of 2012, Predictions, Prophecies, and Possibilities*. Sounds True, 2007.

Casanova. Directed by Lasse Hallström. Touchstone Pictures, 2006.

Chodron, Pema. *The Wisdom of No Escape*. Shambhala Publications, 1991.

---. *Start Where You Are*. Shambhala Publications, 1994.

---. *When Things Fall Apart*. Shambhala Publications. 1997.

---. *The Places That Scare You*. Shambhala Publications, 2001.

---. *Comfortable with Uncertainty*. Shambhala Publications, 2002.

Chopra, Deepak. *How to Know God*. Crown Publishing Group, 2000.

---. *Peace is the Way*. Harmony, 2005.

Crowley, Chris, and Henry Lodge. *Younger Next Year*. Workman Publishing, 2005.

Cutler, Howard, and Dalai Lama XIV. *The Art of Happiness*. Penguin Putnam, 1998.

Darwish, Nonie. *Cruel and Unusual Punishment*. Thomas Nelson Publishing, 2009.

De Mille, Agnes. *The Life and Work of Martha Graham*. Random House, 1997.

Easwaran, Eknath. *The Bhagavad Gita for Daily Living*. The Blue Mountain Center of Meditation, 1975.

Emoto, Masaru. *The True Power of Water*. Beyond Words Publishing, 2005.

Feild, Reshad. *The Last Barrier*. Element Books, 1976.

Fischer, Louis. *Gandhi: His Life and Message for the World*. Penguin, 1982.

Foundation for Inner Peace. *A Course in Miracles*, 1985.

Fox, Emmet. *The Ten Commandments*. Harper Collins, 1953.

---. *The Sermon on the Mount*. Harper Collins, 1966.

Fox, Matthew. *Meditations with Meister Eckhart*. Bear & Company, 1983.

---. *Original Blessing*. Bear & Company, 1983.

Gladwell, Malcolm. *The Tipping Point: How Little Things Can Make a Big Difference*. Back Bay Books, 2002.

Haley, Alex. *Roots: The Saga of an American Family*. Doubleday & Co., Inc., 1976.

Hartmann, Thom. *The Last Hours of Ancient Sunlight*. Three Rivers Press, 2004.

"It May Take Years." *Science of Mind*, vol. 74, no. 7, 2001, pp. 18-21.

Jung, Carl G. et al. *Man and His Symbols*. Aldus Books, 1964.

Kasl, Charlotte. *If the Buddha Dated*. Penguin, 1999.

Keen, Sam. *To Love and be Loved*. Bantam, 1997.

Kempton, Sally. "Change for Good." *The Yoga Journal*, March/April 2005, pp 55-61.

Khan, Hazrat Inayat. *The Awakening of the Human Spirit*. Omega, 1982.

Kopp, Sheldon P. *If you Meet the Buddha on the Road, Kill Him: The Pilgrimage Of Psychotherapy Patients*. Bantam,1982.

Kornfield, Jack. "How Compassion and Forgiveness Can Sing Us Into Unity." *Science of Mind*, vol. 74, no. 7, 2001, pp.15-17.

Krohn, Katherine E. *Oprah Winfrey*. Lerner Publishing Group, 2004.

Lemonick, Michael D. "The Biology of Joy." Time Magazine, 9 Jan. 2005, pp 12-17.

Lennon, John, and Paul McCartney. "All You Need Is Love." Capitol Records Ltd, 1967.

---. "Magical Mystery Tour." Capitol Records Ltd, 1967.

March of the Penguins. Directed by Luc Jacquet. Bonne Pioche and the National Geographic Society, 2005.

Martel, Yann. *The Life of Pi*. Random House, 2001.

Maslow, Abraham. *Religions, Value and Peak Experience*. Penguin,1976.

Mellody, Pia. *Facing Love Addiction*. Harper Collins,1992.

Nelson, Mary Carroll, and Miguel Ruiz. *Beyond Fear: A Toltec Guide to Freedom and Joy, The Teachings of Don Miguel Ruiz*. Council Oak Books, 1997.

Nouwen, Henri J.M. *The Inner Voice of Love*. Random House, 1999.

Oddenino, Kathy. *Love, Truth and Perception*. Joy Publications, 1993.

Opie, Iona, and Peter Opie. *The Classic Fairy Tales*. Oxford University Press, 1974.

Osho. *Your Answers Questioned: Explorations for Open Minds*. St. Martin's Press, 2003.

Palmer, Harry. "The Path to Happiness." *The Avatar Journal*, vol. 4, 2005, pp 2-3.

Pearson, Carol S. *Awakening the Heroes Within: Twelve Archetypes to Help Us Find Ourselves and Transform Our World*. HarperOne, 1991.

Peck, M. Scott. *The Road Less Traveled*. Touchstone, 1978.

Pert, Candace. *Molecules of Emotion: The Science Behind Mind-Body Medicine*. Scribner, 1997.

Pinchbeck, Daniel. *2012: The Return of Quetzalcoatl*. Tarcher, 2006.

Pipe, Watty. *The Little Engine That Could*. Platt and Munk, 2003.

Queen Noor. *Leap of Faith: Memoirs of an Unexpected Life*. Miramax Books, 2003.

Rasha. *Oneness*. Jodere Group, 2003.

Redfield, James. *The Secret of Shambhala*. Warner Books, 1990.

Rilke, Rainer Maria. *Letters to a Young Poet*. Translated by Stephen Mitchell, Vintage, 1984.

Rinpoche, Sogyal. *Tibetan Book of Living and Dying*. HarperOne, 1992.

Ruiz, Miguel. *The Four Agreements: A Practical Guide to Personal Freedom*. Amber-Allen Publishing, 1997.

---. *The Voice of Knowledge*. Amber-Allen Publishing, 2004.

Sheldrake, Rupert. *New Science of Life: The Hypothesis of Morphic Resonance*. Park Street Press, 1995.

Skinner, John. *Revelation of Love*. New York: Image, 1997.

Stevens, Anthony. *Archetypes: A Natural History of the Self*. Routledge, 1990.

Taliaferro, Charles. *Love, Love, Love: And Other Essays*. Cowley Publications, 2006.

The New Merriam-Webster Dictionary, Merriam-**Webster**, 1989.

Thurman, Robert. *Inner Revolution*. Riverhead Books, 1999.

"Visionary, Statesman, Master Teacher: His Holiness the Dalai Lama." *Science of Mind*, vol. 78, no. 1, 2005, pp. 15-21.

United States Constitution. Bill of Rights of the United States of America.

Tolle, Eckhart. *The Power of Now*. Namaste, 1999.

---. *A New Earth*. Penguin, 2005.

Twist, Lynne. *The Soul of Money: Transforming Your Relationship with Money and Life*. W. W. Norton and Co. Publishing, 2003.

U2. "Pride (In the Name of Love)." Island Records, 1984.

Walsch, Neale Donald. *Conversations with God: An Uncommon Dialogue, Book 1.* G.P. Putnam's Sons, 1996,

---. *Conversations with God: An Uncommon Dialogue, Book III.* Hampton Roads Publishing Company, 2003.

Weiss, B. *Only Love is Real: A Story of Soulmates Reunited.* Grand Central Publishing,1997.

Welwood, John. *Perfect Love Imperfect Relationships.* Trumpeter Books, 2006.

What the Bleep Do We Know. Directed by William Arntz. Roadside Attractions, Samuel Goldwyn Films, 2004.

Whyte, David. *The Heart Aroused: Poetry and the Preservation of the Soul in Corporate America.* Crown Business,1996.

---. *Crossing the Unknown Sea: Work as a Pilgrimage of Identity.* Riverhead Books, 2002.

Wilber, Ken. *The Eye of Spirit: An Integral Vision for a World Gone Slightly Mad.* Shambhala, 2001.

Williamson, Marianne. *Return to Love: Reflections on the Principles of "A Course in Miracles."* Harper Collins Publishers, 1992.

---. *A Woman's Worth.* Random House, 1993.

Williamson, Marianne. "A Radically New Life." *Science of Mind*, vol. 78, no. 7, 2005, pp.15-22.

Yogananda, Paramahansa. *Autobiography of a Yogi.* Self-Realization Fellowship Publishers, 1994.

Vanzant, Iyanla. *Yesterday, I Cried.* Simon and Schuster, 1999.

Zukav, Gary. *The Seat of the Soul.* Fireside, 1989.

www.centerhealthyminds.org/about/founder-richard-davidson

www.cnn.com/2006/HEALTH/03/21/profile.rezai/index.html

www.compassion.emory.edu/cbct-compassion-training/index.html

www.newbrainnewworld.com/

www.sheldrake.org

Thank you for reading!

Dear Reader,

I hope you enjoyed **Happily Ever After ... Right Now: Stop Searching for Mr. Right and Start Celebrating YOU**.

As an author, I appreciate getting feedback. I would enjoy hearing your thoughts and your own stories of your experiences after you read my book. You can write me at the addresses below.

Like all authors, I rely on online reviews to encourage future sales. You, the reader, have the power to influence other readers to share your journey with a book you've read. In fact, most readers pick their next book because of a review or on the advice of a friend. So, your opinion is invaluable. Would you take a few moments now to share your assessment of my book on Amazon, Goodreads or any other book review website you prefer? Your opinion will help the book marketplace become more transparent and useful to all.

And if you liked **Happily Ever After ... Right Now,** be sure to check out my next book, **Self Belonging: Embrace the Wisdom of Soul and Science and Live Your Best Life**, which takes the concepts and ideas in **Happily** further and in more depth.

Thank you so much for reading **Happily Ever After ... Right Now,** and please visit my online pages below to learn more about how you, too, can live your best life.

Luann Robinson Hull
luannjlt@aol.com
luannrobinsonhull.com
Instagram: LuannRHull
facebook: @LuannRobinsonHull

About the Author

Luann Robinson Hull is a trailblazing leader in the field of human development. With a Masters in Clinical Social Work, and a Doctorate in Ministry, she brings a powerfully diverse background to the world of personal growth and well-being. Her 25-year career, which includes researching both neuroscience and spiritual practices that help to transcend maladaptive patterns of behavior, allows her to be a reliable and definitive expert on how to unravel the ravages of the mind.

Luann is a motivational speaker and professional group facilitator. She resides in the mountains of Colorado where she hikes year-round, often in a state of curiosity inspired by Thoreau's idea that we "spend one day as deliberately as Nature, and not be thrown off the track by every nutshell and mosquito's wing that falls on the rails."

CPSIA information can be obtained
at www.ICGtesting.com
Printed in the USA
BVHW032209271121
622688BV00006B/175

9 781970 107142